CHRISTIANITY IN CEYLON;

Frontispiece.

The Jayatawanarama.—Ruins of Pollanarua.

page 33.

CHRISTIANITY IN CEYLON

ITS INTRODUCTION AND PROGRESS UNDER THE PORTUGUESE, THE DUTCH, THE BRITISH, AND AMERICAN MISSIONS:

WITH AN HISTORICAL SKETCH OF THE

BRAHMANICAL AND BUDDHIST SUPERSTITIONS.

BY

SIR JAMES EMERSON TENNENT

K.C.S., J.J. D., &C.,

WITH ILLUSTRATIONS

GYAN

Published by

GYAN

Gyan Publishing House
5, Ansari Road
Daryaganj, New Delhi-110002
Phone: 011-47034999, 9811692060
E-mail: books@gyanbooks.com

Distribution Network
gyanbooks.com
India, USA, Canada, UK, Australia, France

ISBN : 978-81-212-3245-6 (PB)
First Published, 1850

2nd Impression 2020

Printed at: Gyan Press, Delhi.

Christianity in Ceylon
Author: Sir James Emerson Tennent

CHRISTIANITY IN CEYLON;

ITS INTRODUCTION AND PROGRESS UNDER THE PORTUGUESE, THE DUTCH, THE BRITISH, AND AMERICAN MISSIONS:

WITH AN HISTORICAL SKETCH OF THE

BRAHMANICAL AND BUDDHIST SUPERSTITIONS.

BY

SIR JAMES EMERSON TENNENT,

K.C.S., LL.D., &c., &c.

With Illustrations.

LONDON:

JOHN MURRAY, ALBEMARLE STREET.

1850.

CHRISTIANITY IN CEYLON.

Entrance to the Great Temple of Dambool.

page 32

BY SIR JAMES EMERSON TENNENT.

TO

THE RIGHT REV. ROBERT KNOX, D.D.,

LORD BISHOP OF DOWN AND CONNOR, AND DROMORE,

This Narrative,

ILLUSTRATIVE OF THE INFLUENCE

OF

EDUCATION IN THE DIFFUSION OF CHRISTIANITY,

IS DEDICATED,

WITH ESTEEM AND REGARD,

BY

THE AUTHOR.

CONTENTS.

CHAPTER I.

THE MIDDLE AGES AND THE PORTUGUESE PERIOD.

CHAPTER II.

THE DUTCH PERIOD.

CHAPTER III.

THE BRITISH PERIOD.

CHAPTER IV.

THE BRAHMANICAL SYSTEM.

CHAPTER V.

BUDDHISM AND DEMON WORSHIP.

CHAPTER VI.

MORAL AND SOCIAL CHARACTER OF THE SINGHALESE.

BUDDHU.
From the Gal Wihare, Ruins of Pollanarua.—(p. 34.)

INTRODUCTION.

For some years past I have been engaged in the preparation of a work on Ceylon, its history, its topography, its capabilities, its productions, its government, its present condition, and its future prospects as a colony of the Crown.

It will account for much that might otherwise seem abrupt or obscure in the following chapters, to state that they were originally commenced as portions of the plan which I had thus sketched for myself, and in which the religion of the people and the progress of Christianity necessarily occupied a prominent place. But as the inquiry proceeded, I found it so far exceeded in interest what I had at first anticipated, that the materials I had collected became at once too important to be omitted, and too extended to form a subsidiary portion of a more comprehensive work. Hence their appearance in the present form.

The sketch of the Buddhist superstition will be found to differ in many essential particulars from its aspect as described in other countries of the East, but my object has been to present the features of Buddhism as it exists in Ceylon; and for this purpose I have availed myself largely of the observation and experience of those Christian missionaries who have made the religion of the natives, and the sacred books in which it is embodied, an object of patient and profound investigation. I believe that the account which I have given will be found to be not only more copious, but more correct, than any similar notice which has hitherto been published of the popular superstitions of the Singhalese.

The same observations apply to the chapter which treats of the Brahmanical system as cultivated by the Tamils of Ceylon; though in its details it presents but few variations from the tenets and practice of Hindooism generally on the continent of India.

The narrative which I have compiled from

authentic sources as to the state and prospects of Christianity will, I trust, be read with interest by all who look on missionary labour not merely in its loftier capacity as the disseminator of immortal truth, but who regard it in its incidental influence as the great pioneer of civilization and the most powerful agent for the diffusion of intellectual and moral enlightenment.

Nor can I lay down my pen without an humble yet confident hope that this exposition of facts which have fallen under my own immediate notice as to the success of missionary toil, and the inroad which has been made, through its instrumentality, upon the ancestral and national idolatries of Ceylon, will operate as an encouragement to those by whom these exertions have been supported, as an assurance that their labours hitherto have not been in vain, and a demonstration of the fallacy which falsely proclaims that the religions of India are inaccessible to Gospel truth, and unassailable by its influences.

The Alu Wihare, Matelle. p. 31.

CHAPTER I.

THE MIDDLE AGES AND THE PORTUGUESE PERIOD.

Nestorian Christians in Ceylon in the Sixth Century—Disappearance of Christianity between the Sixth and the Sixteenth Centuries — Accounts of Early Travellers—Portuguese Conquest, A.D. 1505 — Their singular Expedients for converting the Singhalese—St. Francis Xavier, "the Apostle of India" — Conversion of the Hindoos — Conversion of the Buddhists — State of Christianity on the Arrival of the Dutch, A.D. 1638.

CHRISTIANITY IN CEYLON.

CHAPTER I.

THE MIDDLE AGES AND THE PORTUGUESE PERIOD.

THE earliest notice of the existence of Christianity in Ceylon is that of Cosmas Indopleustes, an Egyptian merchant, and afterwards a monk, who published his 'Christian Topography' in the reign of Justinian, in order to vindicate the cosmography of the Old Testament from what he believed to be the heresies of "the Ptolemaic system."[1] Cosmas, who was

[1] The Χριστιανικὴ Τοπογραφία of Cosmas Indopleustes, or Indicopleustes, has been edited by Montfaucon, and will be found in his Collectio Nova Patrum, vol. ii., Par. 1706. The portion relative to Ceylon and the plants and animals of India was printed by Thevenot, with a French translation, in his *Relations de divers Voyages curieux*, vol. i. There are some legends to the effect that Christianity had been preached in Ceylon by St. Thomas and St. Bartholomew; but there is no reasonable ground for believing that India was ever visited by an apostle, although the tradition is supported by St. Jerome and Chrysostom, by Athanasius and Eusebius, and it was so firmly believed in the early ages of the Church that Alfred the Great sent Swithelm or Sighelm, the Bishop of Sherburn, on an embassy to India to visit the shrine of St. Thomas. (Palgrave's Anglo-Saxons, p. 185; Sharon Turner's History of the Anglo-Saxons,

himself a Nestorian, tells that in Taprobane[1] there existed a community of believers, with an episcopal form of discipline, priests, deacons, and a liturgy. This slender statement has afforded material for enlarged speculation as to the doctrines, the extent, and duration of an early Church in Ceylon. It has been assumed as proof of the conversion of the Singhalese prior to the fifth and sixth centuries; and the author of the 'History of Christianity in India' propounds it as more than probable that the Church so implanted survived till the arrival of the Portuguese in 1505, when "their buildings no doubt shared the fate of the temples of Buddhu, which they (the Portuguese) pulled down, and with the materials erected churches of their own religion on all parts of the coast."[2]

But a reference to the original authority disposes at once of these eager conjectures.[3] Cosmas ex-

vol. ii. p. 148.) There is a still more curious tradition to the effect that Ceylon had been visited, and the Christian faith introduced, by the Eunuch of Candace, whose conversion by Philip is recorded in the Acts of the Apostles. (Hough's History of Christianity in India, vol. i. pp. 30, 32, 42; Baldæus, p. 280.)

[1] The ancient Greek name of Ceylon.

[2] Hough's History of Christianity in India, vol. iii. b. vii., ch. 2, p. 74. The assertion is given on the authority of Cordiner (Description of Ceylon, vol. i. p. 154), but it is entirely conjectural, and at variance with the testimony of every traveller in Ceylon during the middle ages.

[3] *Δύο δὲ βασιλεῖς εἰσὶν ἐν τῇ νήσῳ, ἐνάντιοι ἀλλήλων. ὁ εἷς ἔχων τὸν ὑάκινθον, καὶ ὁ ἕτερος τὸ μέρος τὸ ἄλλο, ἐν ᾧ ἐστι τὸ ἐμπόριον καὶ ὁ λιμην . . ἔχει δὲ ἡ αὐτὴ νῆσος καὶ ἐκκλησίαν*

pressly declares that the members of the church in Ceylon were *Persians*, and merely sojourners—a portion, no doubt, of that concourse of merchants and travellers who then resorted to the northern parts of the island as the great depôt and emporium of Eastern trade[1]—but that the natives and their kings were of a different religion. As to doctrine, the probability is that they were of the same faith and form of ecclesiastical government as the Syrian churches in the southern promontory of India, which were founded in the third or fourth century by Christians from the Persian Gulf, whose successors to the present time have preserved a form of Christianity, however corrupted, and maintained an uninterrupted connexion with the original Church; first through the See of Seleucia, and since through the Patriarch of Antioch. But with the decline of Oriental commerce, and the diminished resort of merchants from Arabia and Persia, the travellers and adventurers who formed the members of the first Christian body in Ceylon ceased to frequent the shores of Manaar; and Christianity,

τῶν ἐπιδημούντων Περσῶν Χριστιανῶν· καὶ πρεσβύτερον ἀπὸ Περσίδος χείροτονοίμενον καὶ διάκονον καὶ πᾶσαν τὴν ἐκκλησιαστίκην λειτουργίαν.—οἱ δὲ ἐγχώριοι καὶ οἱ βασιλεῖς ἀλλόφυλοί εἰσιν.—*Cosmas Indopleustes: Thevenot, Relations*, &c. &c., vol. i.; *Ibid.*, l. xi.; *Montfaucon, Coll. Patr.*, v. ii. p. 336.

[1] ἐξ ὅλης δὲ τῆς Ινδικῆς καὶ Περσίδος καὶ Αἰθιοπίας δέχεται ἡ νῆσος πλοῖα πολλὰ, μέση τις οὖσα, ὅμοιως καὶ εκπέμπει.—*Cosmas Ind.*, l. xi.; *Montf.*, vol. ii. p. 337.

never firmly rooted, gradually decayed and disappeared.

Between the sixth century and the arrival of the Portuguese in the sixteenth, we have but few accounts of the internal condition of the island, and no mention whatsoever of a Christian community.

The "two Mahomedans," Ibn Vahab and Abou Zeyd, whose narratives have been translated by Renaudot,[1] and more recently and completely by Reinaud, describe Ceylon in the ninth century,[2] and record the division of the island between two kings, as mentioned by Cosmas, one of whom was, of course, the Rajah of Jaffna. The authors are altogether silent as to the existence of any form of Christianity, although Abou Zeyd states that "the king who then reigned permitted the free exercise of every religion; and the island contained a multitude of Jews as well as of many other sects, even Tanouis or Manichees." As to the faith of the sovereign and the mass of the people, they say that "the king makes laws which are the fundamentals of the religion and government of the country; and here are doctors and assemblies of learned men, like those of the Hadithis of Arabia. The Indians repair to these assemblies, and write

[1] See note A, at the end of the chapter.

[2] See Pinkerton's Collection of Voyages, vol. vii.: The Travels of Two Mahomedans through India and China in the Ninth Century. Translated from the Arabic by the Abbé Renaudot: p. 183, 217.

down what they hear of the lives of their prophets and the various expositions of their laws."[1]

Four centuries later, Marco Polo, the Venetian traveller, made his way to Ceylon about the year 1290 A.D.; he declares that "the inhabitants were idolaters;"[2] and it is scarcely credible, had a

[1] "Le royaume de Serendyb a une loi et des docteurs, qui s'assemblent de temps en temps, comme se réunissent chez nous les personnes qui recueillent les traditions du Prophète. Les Indiens se rendent auprès des docteurs, et écrivent, sous leur dictée, la vie de leurs prophètes et les préceptes de leur loi. . . . . On trouve dans l'île de Serendyb une communauté de Juifs qui est nombreuse. Il y a également des personnes des autres religions, notamment des Dualistes (les Manichéens). Le roi de Serendyb laisse chaque communauté professer son culte."—Transl. par Reinaud, vol. i. p. 128. (See Note B, end of this chapter.)

[2] Travels of Marco Polo, a Venetian, in the Thirteenth Century. Translated by W. Marsden. 4to. London, 1818. Like other travellers of that period, Marco Polo dwells on the wealth and fertility of Ceylon, its rice and sesamum; its milk, flesh, and wine from the trees (toddy). "There is here the best sappan wood that can anywhere be met with. The island produces rubies more beautiful and valuable than are found in any other part of the world; and likewise sapphires, topazes, amethysts, garnets, and many other precious and costly stones. The King is reputed to have the grandest ruby that was ever seen, a span in length, the thickness of a man's arm, brilliant beyond description, and without a single flaw. It has the appearance of a glowing fire, and its worth cannot be estimated in money. The Grand Khan Kublai sent ambassadors to this monarch to offer for it the value of a city, but he would not part with it for all the treasures of the world, as it was a jewel handed down by his ancestors on the throne." The people of Ceylon, he adds, "are by no means of a military habit, but abject and timid, and when there is occasion to employ soldiers they procure them

Christian Church—however small—been then in existence, that he, a Christian himself, would have omitted all mention of so interesting a fact.

Ibn Batuta, the adventurous Moor who traversed almost all the countries of Asia in the fourteenth century, and visited Ceylon about 1324 A.D.,[1] is equally silent in relation to Christianity; although he is particular in describing the Emperor as an infidel, and records the proceedings of the Brahmans and Buddhists, and the pilgrimage to the sacred footmark on the summit of Adam's Peak.

Thus, notwithstanding the remarkable preservation of Christianity in India throughout this gloomy period amongst the Syrian churches on the Coromandel coast, and its permanent adoption by the Tamils and other tribes of the peninsula, its light appears to have been but transiently kindled and to have speedily become extinguished on the opposite coast of Ceylon. If it ever included in its communion any of the native inhabitants of the islands, they must have relapsed into idolatry shortly after the departure of its original founders. The Tamil sovereigns of Ceylon, however tolerant the dynasty may have been in the fifth and ninth centuries, ex-

from other countries in the vicinity of the Mahomedans." The stone referred to by Marco, if it existed at all, was most probably a carbuncle.

[1] The Travels of Ibn Batuta. Translated by Professor Lee. Published by the Oriental Translation Committee. Lond. 1829.

hibited themselves at a later period as persecutors of Christianity; but the more immediate cause of its disappearance from Ceylon was in all probability the rising influence of Mahometanism, and the arrival of its followers from Persia and Arabia,[1] whose descendants to the present day abound on the sea-bord of the island, and are known by the popular designation of "Moors."[2] On the arrival of the Portuguese, A.D. 1505, and their conquest of the maritime provinces, the doctrines of Brahma and Buddhu were the prevailing religions respectively of the Tamils to the north and of the Singhalese throughout the rest of the island.

Information is scanty as to the nature of the means adopted by the Portuguese for the introduction and establishment of the Roman Catholic religion in Ceylon.[3] There is no proof that compul-

[1] According to Hamza of Ispahan, the Persians under Cosroes Nouschirevan, one of the Sassanide dynasty, made the conquest of Ceylon in the early part of the sixth century: "inter maximas victorias a Kesra Anuschirvano reportatas sunt expugnationes urbium *Serandib*, Constantinopoleos et provinciarum Arabiæ felicis." (*Hamzæ Ispahan. Annalium*, lib. i. chap. iv. vol. ii. p. 43. Leipzic, 1848.) And Reinaud has published in the 'Journal Asiatique' for February, 1845, p. 156, a passage from Beladori, in which he alludes to the establishment of a Mussulman colony in Ceylon towards the end of the seventh century.

[2] For an account of the Moormen of Ceylon, see note C, end of the chapter.

[3] The records of their government have entirely disappeared; they were taken to Goa on the conquest of the island by the

sion was resorted to by them for the extension of their own faith, or violence employed for the extinction of the national superstitions; and the probability is that the priests and missionaries of the Portuguese were contented to pursue in Ceylon the same line of policy and adopt the same expedients for conversion which had already been found successful by their fellow-labourers on the opposite continent of India.

Their possessions in either place were detached, their tenure uncertain, and in danger at all times, from the jealousy or hostilities of the neighbouring princes; and from the analogy of the two cases, the presumption is warranted that the Portuguese in Ceylon, under the pressure of similar circumstances, followed the example and instructions of the Viceroy and Archbishop of Goa, and that the amount of assistance from the civil power, on which the Roman Catholic clergy could rely, did not ordinarily extend beyond the personal influence of the Captains-General at Colombo and the favours and partiality exhibited by successive governors to all who were willing to conform to their religion.[1]

Dutch, whence they were removed to Lisbon, and afterwards transferred to Brazil. In their absence there is little or no historical evidence of the system of proselytism pursued by their clergy, or the amount of its success, beyond the imperfect notices of the Dutch historians, and the still existing traditions of the Singhalese themselves.

[1] Hough's History of Christianity in India, vol. ii. b. 3, c. 2, p. 349. See Letter of John III. to the Viceroy of Goa in

Those acquainted with the national character of the Singhalese, with their obsequiousness to power, and the pliancy with which they can accommodate themselves to the wishes and opinions of those whom it may be their interest to conciliate, will have no difficulty in comprehending the ease with which the Roman Catholic clergy, under such auspices and with such facilities, succeeded in an incredibly short space of time in effecting multitudinous conversions; and although the peculiar religion of the Hindoos in the northern province necessarily presented obstacles more formidable than those opposed by the genius of Buddhism in the south, the missionaries engaged in the task were not devoid of expedients by which to overcome both. In the instance of the Singhalese the miracle was accomplished with ease; the mountain submissively came over to Mahomet; and in the other and more obstinate one of the Tamils, Mahomet was equally prepared to succeed by making his own approach to the mountain.

In point of time the conversion of the Singhalese

1546, A.D.; Baldæus, c. xxii. p. 646. His Majesty lays down the principle that "Pagans may be brought over to our religion not only by the hopes of eternal salvation, but also by temporal interest and preferment"—and he therefore directs that on professing Christianity they were to be provided with places in the Customs, to be exempted from impressment for the navy, and sustained by the distribution of rice out of the public revenue. Baldæus, Descrip. Malabar, Coromandel, and Ceylon; Churchill's Collection of Voyages, vol. iii.

Buddhists to Christianity preceded by several years the earliest attempt to reclaim the Tamils in Ceylon from the superstition of Brahma. The Portuguese got possession of Colombo in 1505, but it was not till 1548 that they obtained such a footing in the northern province as to enable their missionaries to commence their labours with security amongst the natives of Jaffna. Immediately after constructing the fort of Colombo the adjoining districts were erected into a bishopric,[1] and under the directions of the new prelate Christianity was speedily proclaimed throughout the Singhalese districts, but it was not till A.D. 1544 that it was first preached to the Tamils of the north by "the Apostle of India," St. Francis Xavier. He was invited from Madura by the Parawas or Fisher caste, who had established themselves around the pearl fishery of Manaar, of whom he baptized from *six to seven hundred*;[2] but almost immediately after

[1] The tomb of Don Juan de Monterio, the first Christian prelate in Ceylon, was discovered in 1836, in effecting the repairs of the Battenburg Bastion.

[2] Hough's History of Christianity in India, b. ii. c. 3, p. 188. Letters of the Abbé Du Bois, p. 3. There is something remarkable in the circumstance of the Fisher caste being everywhere the earliest and most eager converts to Christianity in India; so much so as to render it questionable whether it be only an accidental coincidence, or the result of some permanent and predisposing cause. The *Parawas* or fishermen of Cape Comorin were the earliest proselytes of St. Francis Xavier, and they have still a pride in alluding to the fact that they were the first, as they have since been the most faithful and abiding of his

they were cut to pieces by the Rajah of Jaffna, who was incensed at their apostacy. His efforts to extirpate Christianity from his dominions were, however, utterly futile: the influence of the Portuguese and their priests was too powerful to be long resisted, his own sons and relations became converts, and flying from Ceylon they placed themselves under the protection of the Viceroy of Goa.

converts. It was by the fishermen of Manaar that he was invited to Ceylon in 1544, and notwithstanding the martyrdom inflicted by the Rajah of Jaffna, and the persecution with which they were visited by the Dutch, that district and the adjacent boundary of the Wanny has to the present day been one of the strongholds of the Roman Catholics in Ceylon. Again, it is amongst the *Parawas* or Fisher caste of the Singhalese that the Roman Catholics have at all times been most successful in their efforts to christianize. Their chapels and churches occur at all points along the sea-coast, on the western side of Ceylon; and the fishermen as far south as Barberyn are, to a great extent, Roman Catholics. When the British Government in 1840 abandoned the tax upon fish, by which the fishermen contributed annually about 6000*l.* to the revenue, so strong was the influence of the Roman Catholic priests, that this apparently onerous impost was at once transferred by the fishers to the Roman Catholic church, by whom it has ever since been collected, or farmed for collection, in the same manner as when it was paid to the Government. Is it that there is an habitual tendency to devotion and veneration for the Supreme Power amongst those who go down to sea in ships and see the power of God in the great deep? Is it that, being a low caste themselves, the fishermen of India and Ceylon acquire a higher status by espousing Christianity? Or is there any sympathy with a religion whose first apostles and teachers were the fishermen of Galilee?

John III., King of Portugal, in commenting on this auspicious event, directed De Castro, the Viceroy of India, as "the conversion of this royal youth was of great moment," to be careful of his person, and to provide for his education and maintenance; but above all to take "a slow and secure but a severe revenge on the tyrant of Ceylon."[1] The opportunity of gratifying this desire for retribution was not long delayed. The power of the Portuguese in Ceylon was gradually but irresistibly extended in the direction of Jaffna, and within three years the Rajah, alarmed for his own security, made overtures to Xavier, avowed his readiness to embrace Christianity, and through St. Francis' intervention he was admitted to alliance with Portugal and received a subsidy of 100 soldiers to garrison his capital. The first employment of this friendly force was the erection of a fortress at Jaffnapatam, and eventually his dangerous allies relieved the Rajah altogether of the cares of royalty, expelled him from the island, and incorporated his kingdom with the dominion of Portugal.

Thus masters of the whole sea coast of Ceylon, the Portuguese felt more at liberty to pursue their schemes of ecclesiastical supremacy; but still a striking difference was observable in the nature of the several localities, and consequently in the character of their operations in the south as compared with those in the northern provinces of the island. In

[1] Baldæus, p. 647.

the former, amongst the Singhalese and Buddhists, they were still compelled to proceed with a becoming degree of cautious circumspection from their vicinity to the native princes of Cotta, whose dominions extended from Chilaw to Colombo; and still more from apprehension of their more hostile neighbour the King of Kandy, whose frontier was less than forty miles from their outposts. In Jaffna, on the contrary, remote from any Hindoo potentate, and separated from the Singhalese by vast forests and inhospitable deserts of sand, the physical and almost insular position of their new conquest gave it the compactness and security of a fortified district, within which, with the complete command of the sea, they were effectually protected from intrusion or control. The whole extent of the peninsula was thus brought by them under the authority of the Church; it was divided into parishes, each of which was provided with a chapel and schoolhouse, and, where required, a glebe for the residence of the Franciscan priest who was to officiate; and the ruins of these ecclesiastical edifices even at the present day attest the care and expenditure which must have been applied to their construction. In Jaffna itself they had a church and a College of Jesuits at the west end of the town, a church and convent of St. Dominic on the east, besides a convent of St. Francis; and when the Dutch made themselves masters of the fortress in 1658, there marched out, according to Baldæus, from forty to fifty ecclesiastics, Jesuits, Franciscans, and Dominicans.[1] In short, there is sufficient evidence extant connected with this province of Ceylon to justify the assertion that within a very few years from its occupation by the Portuguese, almost the entire population of the Jaffna peninsula, including even the Brahmans themselves, had abjured their idolatry and submitted to the ceremony of baptism.[2]

Here the question naturally arises, by what agency and expedients were these multitudinous conversions accomplished in defiance of the notorious antagonism of the Brahmanical system? and the inquiry becomes the more interesting, from the fact that the success of the Roman Catholic clergy at this period appears to have been more extended and complete amongst the apparently impracticable Hindoos of the North than it afterwards proved amongst the pliant and apathetic adherents of Buddhu in the Southern and purely Singhalese portions of the island. Amongst the latter a commencement was effected, in the first instance, by the influence of authority and the prospect of gain; and however unsound and discreditable may have been their earlier incentives to nominal conversion, there is palpable evidence to establish the fact, that once enrolled as Roman Catholics, the imagination

[1] Baldæus, c. xlv. p. 798.

[2] A tract privately printed at Colombo, in 1848, by a native gentleman, on 'the Rise and Progress of the Catholic Church in Ceylon.' By S. Casie Chitty, district judge of Chilaw.

of the Singhalese became excited, and their tastes permanently captivated, by the same striking ceremonial and pompous pageantry by which the Roman Catholic religion recommended itself at a later period to the Tamils and Hindoos.

When Christianity was first preached to the natives of India by Xavier, it was proclaimed by him with much of the simplicity and apostolical zeal which have since characterised the ministrations of his Protestant successors. But notwithstanding the multitude of his converts, St. Francis has recorded in his letters to St. Ignatius Loyola his own disappointment at discovering the inward unsoundness of all he had outwardly achieved;[1] and the open apostacy which afterwards manifested itself among his converts, suggested to those who succeeded him in his task the necessity of adopting a more effectual machinery for arousing the attention of the Hindoos, and overcoming their repugnance to the reception of Christianity. The Jesuits, who resorted in prodigious numbers to Hindostan during the period which followed the death of Xavier, persuaded themselves, by the partial failure of his system, that no access was to be gained, and no footing established in the confidence of the natives, without an external conformity to their customs and habits, and a careful avoidance of any shock

[1] Letters on the State of Christianity in India, in which the conversion of the Hindoos is considered as impracticable. By the Abbé Dubois, Missionary in Mysore. London, 1823. P. 3.

to their prejudices, religious and social. Under the cover of such a policy, it was conceived that a silent approach might be effected, and the edifice of their ancient superstition undermined, almost before its defenders could discover that its assailants were opponents. In pursuance of this plan of assault, Christianity in the hands of those by whom it was next offered to the heathen assumed an aspect so extraordinary, that the detail would exceed belief, were it not attested by the evidence of those actually engaged in the execution of the scheme. The Jesuits who now addressed themselves to the conversion of Hindostan, adopted the determination to become all things to all men for the accomplishment of their object; withholding till some more favourable time the inculcation of Christian simplicity, and adopting in the interim, almost without qualification, the practices of heathenism. To such an extent did they carry this policy, that in the charges which were eventually lodged against them before the Holy See by the other religious orders in India, it was alleged to be doubtful whether the Jesuits, by affecting idolatry and tolerating it amongst their proselytes, had not themselves become converts to Hindooism rather than made the Hindoos converts to the Christian religion.[1]

[1] Letters of the Abbé Dubois, p. 8. A striking account of these almost incredible proceedings of the Jesuits, extracted from the authority of contemporary Roman Catholic writers, is contained in the Calcutta Review for October, 1844, vol. ii.

They assumed the character of Brahmans of a superior caste from the Western World; they took the Hindoo names, and conformed to the heathen customs of this haughty and exclusive race, producing, in support of their pretensions, a deed forged in ancient characters, to show that the Brahmans of Rome were of much older date than the Brahmans of India, and descended in an equally direct line from Brahma himself.

They composed a pretended Veda, in which they sought to insinuate the doctrines of Christianity in the language and phraseology of the sacred books of the Hindoos.[1] They wore the *cavy*, or orange robe peculiar to the Saniassees, the fourth, and one of the most venerated, sections of the Brahmanical caste. They hung a tiger's skin from their shoulders, in imitation of Shiva; they abstained from animal food, from wine, and certain prohibited vegetables; they performed the ablutions required by the Shasters; they carried on their foreheads the sacred spot of sandalwood powder, which is the distinctive emblem of the Hindoos;[2] and in order to sustain their assumed character to the utmost, they affected to spurn the Pariahs and lower castes who lay no claim to the same divine origin with the Brahmans.[3]

[1] See Asiatic Researches, vol. xiv., for an account of the spurious or *Ezour Vedam*.

[2] "*Their spot is not the spot of his children*: a perverse and crooked generation."—Deut. xxxii. 5.

[3] Letters on the State of Christianity in India. By the Abbé

In carrying out this system, the Jesuits not only contended that they were justified in the employment of such means by the sanctity of the object they were to accomplish, but they derived encouragement and facility from the many points of resemblance presented by the religion of their own church, as compared with the practices of the idolatry which they came to overthrow. "If," says the Abbé Dubois, himself a Roman Catholic missionary in India, "any one of the several modes of Christian worship be calculated more than another to make an impression and gain ground in India, it is no doubt the Catholic form, which Protestants consider idolatry. Its external pomp and show are well suited to the genius and disposition of the natives. It has a *pooja*, or sacrifice, processions, images, and statues; *tirtan*, or holy water; feasts, fasts, and prayers for the dead; invocation of saints and other practices which bear more or less resemblance to that of the Hindoos. Of these facilities and coincidences the Jesuits availed themselves to the utmost; they conducted the images of the Virgin and the Saviour on triumphal cars, imitated from the orgies of Jaggernath;[1] they introduced

Dubois. P. 5, 69, 70, 130.—Hough's Reply to the Abbé Dubois, p. 62.—History of Christianity in India. By the Rev. J. Hough. Vol. iii. b. v. c. 3, p. 216, 250.

[1] "A car approaches, covered with awnings of silk, and decked with garlands of flowers. It is surmounted by a female statue, and dragged slowly by a tumultuous crowd. She bears the *timbashi* on her head, a ring through her nose, and the sacred

the dancers of the Brahmanical rites into the ceremonial of the Church; and, in fine, by a system of mingled deception and conformity, and a life of indescribable privation, they succeeded in superseding the authority and the influence of the Franciscans throughout Southern India, and in enlisting multitudes of nominal converts to the Church.[1] At length, scandalized by their proceedings, the attention of the see of Rome was directed to the conduct of the Jesuit fathers, who did not conceal in their defence that, "from motives of prudence, and not to risk the revolt of their converts, they had been under the unpleasant necessity of overlooking many reprehensible practices, waiting for fitter opportunities for their gradual suppression. At the same time they exposed

nuptial-collar round her neck. On each side are parasol bearers —one who waves a napkin to brush away the mosquitoes. The car is preceded by dancers, half naked, and streaked with sandal-wood powder and vermilion. Wild shouts ring through the air, and the ear is stunned by the din of trumpets, drums, and barbaric music. It is night; but, amidst a general illumination and the blazing of torches innumerable, rockets, fireworks ascend in every direction. The crowd is all Hindoos, and all bear on their foreheads the accustomed mark of idolaters. The car is the gift of a heathen prince; the dancers and music are borrowed from the nearest pagoda; the spectators are heathens; *but the woman represents the Virgin Mary, and the actors in this scandalous scene are the Christians of Madura.*"—Calcutta Review, vol. ii. p. 96, on the authority of the Mémoires Historiques présentés en 1744 au Souverain Pontife Benoît XIV. Par Le R. P. Nobert.

[1] Abbé Dubois, p. 18, 23.

the danger which they apprehended if the feelings of the Hindoos were hurt, and if the practices so justly complained of were openly reprobated and opposed before the Christian religion should have gained a more solid footing in the country.[1] These arguments were, however, held to be insufficient; the idolatrous practices of the Jesuits were denounced, but without effect, by Pope Gregory XV. and his successors, till, on the strong representations of the Cardinal de Tournon, the apostolic legate at Pondicherry, in 1704, Pope Benedict XIV. issued a rigorous bull, by which he prohibited utterly the superstitious customs (of which a list was enumerated in the decree[2]) which had theretofore been practised by the Jesuits and their missionaries. The Abbé Dubois declares that the result which had been predicted was realized on the promulgation of the edict. The Jesuits complied, but with reluctance, and after reiterated remonstrances and delays; but the number of converts declined, multitudes of proselytes relapsed into idolatry; and nothing but a partial return to the interdicted expedients for conversion has since prevented the extinction of the Roman Catholic form of Christianity in Hindostan.[3]

[1] Abbé Dubois' Letters, &c., p. 8.

[2] Extracts from the List will be found in the Calcutta Review, vol. ii. p. 103 *et seq.*

[3] Letters of the Abbé Dubois, p. 9, 10. Hough's Reply to the Abbé Dubois, p. 62.

As these proceedings were in progress in India during the period when similar exertions were simultaneously made in Ceylon by the priesthood of the same Church, trained in the same seminaries for the work of the ministry, and acting under the orders of the same spiritual superiors, there would be sufficient grounds, even in the absence of evidence more direct, for presuming that the same expedients which had been found to be effectual, if not presumed to be indispensable, for the conversion of Hindoos in India, would be equally resorted to for the same purpose amongst the Tamils and Buddhists of Ceylon. And in aid of such an inference there is abundance of circumstantial proofs that such, to some extent at least, was the fact. Baldæus, who repaired to Jaffna in A.D. 1658, immediately on the retirement of the Roman Catholic priests, describes their churches as fitted up with theatres and stages for the exhibition of mysteries and theatrical representations of the great historical events of Christianity.[1]

[1] "Segnius irritant animos demissa per aurem
Quam quæ sunt oculis subjecta fidelibus, et quæ
Ipse sibi tradit spectator."—*Horace.*

Mendelslo, who travelled in India in 1639, in his narrative of an entertainment given by the Jesuits, at which the Archbishop of Goa was present, after describing various devices and automata representing the Saviour and the Virgin Mary, says:—"There came in also one man, alone, covered with birds' nests, and clothed and masked according to the Spanish mode, who began the farce of this comedy by ridiculous and fantastical postures; and the ball was concluded with the coming in of twelve

The archives of the Dutch Government contain records of the punishment of Roman Catholics, who, in defiance of their prohibition, attempted public processions within their territories;[1] and to the present day, the Roman Catholics in the north of the island continue to celebrate their worship with fireworks and drums, and encompass their chapels with processions, conducting decorated cars bearing idols and garlands which differ only in name from similar observances and processions of the Hindoos.

If, during the government of the Portuguese, such displays were less frequent amongst the Buddhists in the southern portions of the island, it was ascribable to the circumstance that there their authority was less firmly established, and the proceedings of their priesthood were regarded with a more jealous and watchful eye by the priesthood, who had a powerful ally in the Sovereign of Kandy. In Jaffna, on the contrary, its remote and almost insular position secured them from interference; besides which, the Kandyan kings, however interested for the maintenance of Buddhism, were comparatively indifferent to the fate of the Hindoo religion: and the Roman

boys dressed like apes, which they imitated in their cries and postures. As we took our leave of our entertainers, they told us that they made use of these divertisements to reduce the Pagans and Mahomedans of those parts to the embracing of the Christian religion by that kind of modern devotion."—Mendelslo's Travels into the Indies, b. ii. London, 1669.

[1] Records of the Consistory of Colombo, A.D. 1753.

Catholic priests, thus relieved from all apprehension of control, found themselves in a condition to conduct their affairs in the peninsula with a high hand and an outstretched arm. But amongst the Singhalese of the south, their position was in many respects different, and their proceedings appear to have been characterized by greater caution, and conducted on a much more limited scale. In the maritime provinces at the present day there exist no ruins, as in the Tamil districts of the north, of churches or other ecclesiastical buildings of the Portuguese; and beyond the walls of the several forts it is doubtful whether the government had ever encouraged their erection.[1]

Amongst the converts from Buddhism at this

[1] In the fort of Colombo, according to Ribeyro, there were two parishes, of Our Lady and St. Laurence, four religious houses of the Cordeliers, the Dominicans, the Augustines, and the Capuchins, and a Jesuits' College, in which were taught the classics and philosophy. Outside the fort he says that there were seven parishes; but, with the exception of those lying immediately under the walls, it is questionable whether they were provided with separate buildings. Galle contained a convent of St. Francis and a house of Mercy; Caltura had a chapel for the small garrison in the fort; Malwana and Negombo were similarly provided; whilst, to make the contrast more striking between those stations in the south and similar outposts in the northern province, Manaar, Mantotte, and the surrounding district of the Wanny, had no less than fourteen churches for the accommodation of the native Roman Catholics."—History of Ceylon, presented by Captain John Ribeyro to the King of Portugal in 1685. Translated from the Portuguese by the Abbé de Grand, and into English by George Lee, Esq. Colombo, 1847. C. xii. p. 46, 47.

period, whom the Portuguese annalists are naturally the most gratified to record, were successively the Kings of Kandy and Cotta, who embraced Christianity and received baptism at the hands of the clergy of Colombo and Manaar. But it must be observed, that their conversion did not take place till after the expulsion of the former from his dominions by an usurper,[1] and till the other had been driven, by the hostile combinations of his own subjects, to seek the assistance of the Portuguese for the maintenance of his throne. "On the occasion of the latter, the Emperor of Cotta being baptized," says the *Rajavali*, one of the sacred historical books of Ceylon, "many of the nobles of Cotta were baptized likewise; and from this day forward the women of the principal people, and also the women of the low castes—the barbers, the fishers, the hinnawas (mat-makers) and challias, *for the sake of the Portuguese gold*, began to turn Christians and live with the Portuguese; and the priests of Buddhu, who, till now, had remained in Cotta, retired into the interior, to Situak and to Kandy."[2] This statement is confirmatory of the opinion already expressed, that beyond the discountenance of Buddhism within the precincts of their forts, the Portuguese Government were not disposed to adopt any other system for encouraging proselytism than that recommended by the pithy

[1] Baldæus, c. xxiii. p. 717. Ibid., c. v. p. 20.
[2] Upham's Sacred Books of Ceylon, vol. ii. p. 291.

aphorism of King John—that, as an incentive to the conversion of Pagans, the prospect of gain was more likely to prove effectual than the hope of salvation.[1] Nor does it appear that any actual compulsion was employed for the discountenancing of Buddhism throughout the breadth of the Portuguese settlements. The retirement of the priests, alluded to in the *Rajavali*, must have been their voluntary act; and notwithstanding the ascertained repugnance of the government, the great temples of Kalani and others within a short distance of Colombo were still served by the priesthood of Buddhu, and frequented as usual by pilgrims from all parts of the island.

On the death of the Emperor of Cotta in 1597 A.D., the sovereignty of his territory was bequeathed by his will to Don Henry, King of Portugal; and the native chiefs upon this occasion exhibited a spirited, but respectful independence; which, whilst it showed that they were desirous of protecting their own religion from any forcible interference, exhibited at the same time their consciousness of the anxiety of the Portuguese for the substitution of Christianity. On being called on by the Captain-General of Colombo to take the oath of allegiance to their new Sovereign, they asked for time to deliberate and prepare their reply; when they stated with firmness that, as Singhalese, and brought up in principles to which they were firmly attached, it would be difficult

[1] Baldæus, p. 646.

if not dangerous to force them to abandon them, in order to adopt others to which they were strangers. That such changes were generally followed by revolutions fatal alike to the ancient state of things and the new; but that they were willing to serve the King of Portugal as faithfully as they had their own Monarch, provided he and his Ministers were equally disposed to respect the rights and usages under which they had been born. The terms were accepted by the Portuguese, and the Singhalese Deputies signed a submission of their country to the crown of Portugal; with an additional clause, however, inserted by the Captain-General of Colombo on the subject of religion, to the effect that the clergy and religious orders were to be at liberty to preach openly the doctrines of Christianity; that no obstructions should be opposed by the Singhalese to their acceptance by any; that parents should not coerce the consciences of their children; that offences against religion should be cognizable by the constituted authorities;[1] that personal violence should be prohibited in respect of religious belief, and that every one should be at liberty to embrace and hold openly the opinions and the truths with which it might please God to enlighten him.[2]

[1] From this expression it would appear that a branch of the Inquisition had been established in Ceylon; but I have found no more direct testimony to the fact.

[2] Ribeyro, Histoire de l'Ile de Ceylon. Paris, 1701. P. 17, 18.

It was only towards the close of their rule in Ceylon, that the Portuguese turned their attention to the extension of Christianity beyond their own frontier, and attempted to introduce it into the interior of the island. By this time, however, a formidable rival had already grown up to oppose the growth of their influence in the East. The Dutch had obtained a footing at the court of the Kandyan King, and by their advice his Majesty, in 1614, gave a positive refusal to the application of the Portuguese Envoy for the free exercise of the Roman Catholic religion in his dominions, and permission to build a church and a convent at Kandy, with accommodation for 200 or 300 ecclesiastics and laymen.[1] The Dutch had still strong in their remembrance their own struggles for the freedom of the Low Countries from the abhorred dominion of the Roman Catholic government of Spain; they had already discovered, in their settlements in the East, that there was no political security for them, where the Roman Catholic clergy were admitted to any influence; and at a later period on political, not less than on religious considerations, they insisted on the retirement of all European ecclesiastics of the Romish Church from the places which they conquered in India, on the ground that the interests of Holland had everywhere suffered injury from their intrigues.[2] In consistency with

[1] Baldæus, c. xvii. p. 698.

[2] Hough's History of Christianity in India, vol. ii. b. vi. c. 2, p. 373.

the same policy, they prevailed on the Kandyan king, Rajah Singha, in the treaty which he concluded with the Dutch in 1638, to insert a clause by which he bound himself "to suffer no priest, friar, or Roman Catholic clergy, to dwell in his dominions, but to oblige them to depart as the authors of all rebellions, and the ruin of all governments."[1] Thus limited to exertion within the bounds of their own territory, the Portuguese clergy appear to have proceeded sedulously in their work of conversion; and no relic of their rule exhibits more clearly the extent to which their influence had pervaded all ranks and classes, than the fact that to this day the most distinguished families among the Singhalese chiefs bear, in addition to their own names, those of the Portuguese officers, which were conferred on their ancestors at their baptism by the Roman Catholic clergy three centuries ago.[2] The adhesion of these men, however, and of the great mass of the Singhalese, was the result of political conformity, not of religious conviction; and there is no reason to doubt, that along with the profession of the new faith, the ma-

[1] Baldæus, c. xx. p. 714.

[2] *Ernest de Saram* Wijeyesekere Karoonaratne, Maha Modliar of the Governor's Gate; *Johan Louis Perera* Abeysekere Goonewardene; *Don Andries de Alwis* Ameresiriwardene Goonetilleke; *Don David de Silva* Welaratne Jayetilleke; *Don William Adrian Dias* Banderanayeke; *Gregory de Soyza* Wijeyegooneratne Siriwardene, &c. &c. The first are the baptismal or Portuguese, the second the patronymic Singhalese names of the respective chiefs.

jority of them, like the Singhalese of the present time, cherished with still closer attachment the superstitions of Buddhism.[1] It is difficult, on any other ground, to account satisfactorily for the readiness with which so many thousands of the Singhalese consented, almost without solicitation, and altogether without conviction or enlightenment, to adopt a religion which was so utterly new, and whose tenets must have been so entirely unknown to them. It was, in fact, an adoption without a surrender of opinion; and if any scruples were seriously felt respecting the change, they must have been speedily overcome by the prospect of personal advancement, and by the attractions of a religion which, in point of pomp and magnificence, surpassed, without materially differing from the pageantry and processions with which they were accustomed to celebrate the festivals of their own national faith.

[1] "Il avoit fait semblant de se convertir *comme font tous les Chingulais*, et étoit demeuré idolâtre."—Note of the French Editor of Ribeyro. Paris, 1701. Liv. ii. c. i. p. 200.

NOTES TO CHAPTER I.

(A.)

TRAVELS OF THE "TWO MAHOMEDANS."

THE MS. in the Bibliothèque Royale of Paris, which contains the Arabic text of this remarkable book, belonged originally to the library of the illustrious Colbert, whence it passed into the Royal collection. *It is unique,* no second copy being known; and the Abbé Renaudot, who published its contents in 1718 A.D., was long suspected to have been the inventor of what he affected to translate.

The original was written in the year 237 of the Hejira (A.D. 851), at the period when the commercial intercourse with India under the kaliffs of Bagdad was in the height of its activity. It professes to describe the route taken by the traders of Bassora, Bagdad, and Syraf, after issuing from the Persian Gulf, in order to reach the Malabar coast, Ceylon, Java, and India.

The title adopted by Renaudot is however incorrect, as it alludes to the Voyage of *Two Travellers,* whereas in reality the work itself contains the recital of but one, a merchant named Soleyman, who had made the passage to China, which is followed by a critical narrative compiled by a geographer named Abou Zeyd Hassan, from such information as he could collect amongst the mariners of Bassora and Syraf, including, amongst others, a navigator, Ibn Vahab, who, like Soleyman, had himself visited Ceylon and the eastern coasts of China.

This curious book is eloquent in its account of the concourse of merchants to Ceylon at this period, and of its extraordinary riches—the great idol in the temple, of the finest gold—the prodigious sums consumed in the burning of incense—the profusion of precious stones "forced out of caverns and other recesses by the rains," but the search for which was carefully guarded as a royalty of the crown; and in concluding his description of Ceylon, one of the "Mahomedans" says it contains "Valleys of great length which extend to the sea, and here travellers repair for two months or more; in one which is called Gobb Serandib, allured by the beauty of the scenery, chequered with groves and plains, water and meadows, and blessed by a balmy air. This valley opens to the sea, and is transcendantly pleasant." The "two Mahomedans" notice, in terms which are as applicable to-day as they were ten centuries ago, the prevailing vices of the Singhalese, and especially their inordinate love of gambling, of which they say that it is "the usual diversion of the inhabitants of Serandib. They play at draughts, and their principal diversion is fighting of cocks, which are very large in this country, and better provided with spurs than cocks ordinarily are, and besides this they arm them with blades of iron like canjiars. Upon these combats they bet gold, silver, lands, and farms; and they venture also great sums on the game of draughts, which they play with such fury, that those who have not wherewithal often play away the ends of their fingers."—Pinkerton, vol. vii. p. 218. Such is still the passion for gambling in Ceylon, that it was recently found necessary to restrain it by a special law, and the Ordinance No. 3, of 1840, was passed with that view.

(B.)

THE ALU WIHARE.

THE statement of Abou Zeyd in the text, as to the assemblies of learned men by whom the precepts of Buddhism were compiled, is consistent with a tradition still current in Ceylon, that some of the sacred books of their religion were first reduced to writing about the commencement of the Christian era, in a remarkable temple called the *Alu Wihare*, which still exists within two or three miles of Matelle, on the great road leading eastward from Kandy to Trincomalie.

Here some huge masses of gneiss rock, precipitated at a remote period from the craggy summit of an overhanging mountain, have been taken advantage of, and beneath their projecting sides the natural cavities have been converted into chambers by merely enclosing the hollow spaces with front walls pierced with doors and windows. These form, some of them *panselas*, or dwellings of the priests, and others the *wihare* and recesses in which repose the statues and emblems of Buddhu.

The passages between the adjacent rocks are hewn into steps and pathways, and their summits are adapted to the reception of offerings, and rendered sacred by the ruins of *dagobas*, which formerly enclosed relics of the great founder of the national religion.

The scene is peculiarly wild and impressive; and its interest is heightened by the desolation into which the greater portion of the buildings have fallen. It is still the residence of a few priests; but its sanctity and the renown of its antiquity and association with this important event in the annals of Singhalese Buddhism constitute the leading attraction for the devout, who make long pilgrimages to visit it from distant parts of the island. A drawing of it by Mr. Nicholl, A.R.H.A., will be found on the title-page to this chapter.

ENTRANCE TO THE TEMPLE OF DAMBOOL.

In the construction of their temples, generally, the Singhalese appear from the earliest period to have had a remarkable aptitude for converting the recesses under boulders and insulated rocks into sites for their temples and colleges. These supply, without labour or excavation, the place of the innumerable cave-temples which abound on the continent of India, and which have been formed with incredible toil by the Buddhists at a period when their religion was the predominant faith of Hindostan. In the Kandyan country especially these Rock-temples are of frequent occurrence, and the most renowned temple in the island, that of Dambool, built a century before the birth of Christ, has been formed out of the hollow under an overhanging gigantic fragment of gneiss, nearly 500 feet high, the lower side of which serves as the roof of the chamber, and is profusely decorated with paintings and highly-coloured devices.

Opposite p. 32.

The entrance to this singular edifice forms the title-page to the present volume, and ample details of the building will be included in the more enlarged work on Ceylon which I have now in course of completion.

RUINED TEMPLES OF TOPARÉ.

As specimens of the architectural skill of the ancient Singhalese, however, there are no relics in the island to compare with the ruins of sacred buildings which still exist at Toparé, in the eastern province, the site of Pollanarua, the capital of the Kandyan monarchs from the seventh till the fourteenth century. By the side of an artificial tank, so vast as to form a considerable lake, the forest for many miles abounds with prodigious remains of temples, lofty dagobas, and other ecclesiastical edifices, erected chiefly between the tenth and twelfth centuries, and which display a beauty of design and an excellence of execution far surpassing anything, either of a remoter or more recent origin, to be seen in other parts of the island.

Two drawings of one of these vast edifices will be found, the one as a frontispiece, the other opposite p. 32 of the present volume. They represent a side and end view of the ruins of the Jayatawanarama; and in the latter, between the two octagonal towers which form the main entrance, there is seen a statue of Buddhu, 58 feet in height, which occupies the opposite extremity of the building. It is formed of the same materials with the rest of the edifice, brick-work covered with a coating of polished chunam. The decorations of this remarkable structure are evidence of successfully cultivated talent, far excelling anything of a similar description that I have met with elsewhere in Ceylon.

ROCK TEMPLE AND STATUES.

About a mile from the Jayatawanarama, at the extremity of a long street passing between the remains of lofty brick mounds, so vast that they are now covered with timber trees; and bordered on either side by the ruins of numerous buildings, religious or palatial; we come suddenly on a singular rock temple, called by the natives the *Gal-wihare*. The perpendicular face of a sloping cliff has been sculptured into colossal statues of Buddhu, one upwards of 45 feet in length, in a reclining position; one half as high, erect; a third, 16 feet high, in the ordinary posture in which Buddhu is most frequently represented—seated, with his feet folded beneath him; and a fourth in the same attitude placed on an altar within a small temple, hollowed out of the face of the rock, and elaborately ornamented with designs in excellent taste.

A view of this very beautiful specimen of Eastern art forms the vignette prefixed to the Introductory Chapter of the present work. A full account of the ruins of Toparé, which present on many points a striking similarity to the ancient buildings discovered in Mexico and Central America, will be found in my general work on Ceylon and its antiquities.

(C.)

THE MOORMEN OF CEYLON.

THIS active and enterprising race are to be found in every province of Ceylon; residing wherever the locality presents a favourable opening for trade, or traversing the remote and secluded districts to barter manufactured commodities for the produce of the interior. In the eastern province and at Trincomalie they are engaged in the felling and exports of the ebony, satin-wood, and other cabinet woods with which the forests abound; at Batticaloa they are weavers and owners of coasters and small craft which ply to the continent of India; in the southern province they are the principal retailers of the goods imported from Europe and China; and in Colombo and the west they conduct the lucrative trade which has grown up since the introduction of coffee planting and the opening of estates throughout the hills of the interior.

Strange to say, this energetic and intelligent community possess no record of their own origin, nor even any tradition of the period or the country whence they arrived in Ceylon. They have no points of identity with the Singhalese: their religion is Mahomedan, and their language that of the Tamils in the southern peninsula of India. They are conscious of a foreign origin; and the Singhalese, who are equally ignorant of their history, occasionally distinguish them by the name of Marakulemiar, or "Mariners."

Their residence in Ceylon has been of a duration sufficiently remote to countenance the belief that they may be a remnant of the Persians, by whom the island was frequented in the fourth and fifth centuries; or perhaps of that expedition who, under Cosroes Nouschirevan, conquered the cities of Ceylon in the beginning of the sixth.—Hamza Ispahanensis, Annal., lib. i. c. iv. p. 43, vol. ii. Leip., 1848.

From the sixth to the sixteenth century the Arabs and Persians monopolised exclusively the trade between India and the Red Sea:—"On les a vus établis dans l'île de Socotra; ils étaient probablement aussi sur la côte de Sofala, aux environs du golfe de Cambaye, *et dans l'île de Ceylan*. Tout porte à croire que, *mêlés aux Persans*, ils exerçaient dès lors dans ces parages le même ascendant qu'au XVe siècle, lorsque les Portugais, faisant le tour de l'Afrique, répandirent pour toujours le nom Européen dans les mers de l'Orient. L'influence des Persans et des Arabes dût s'accroître à mesure que la puissance Romaine perdit son ancien prestige."—Reinaud, Relation, &c., Discours Préliminaire, p. xxxix. Paris, 1845.

The ordinary belief of the Europeans is that the Moormen are Arabs by descent; and the establishment of a Mussulman colony before the close of the seventh century is alluded to by Beladori or Ahmed in a chronicle of the Arab conquests in Europe and Asia.—Journal Asiatique, Févr. et Mars, 1845.—Fragmens Arabes et Persans relatifs à l'Inde, Fragm. v., p. 156.

But there are peculiarities in the habits of the Singhalese Moors which lead to the conclusion that they are of Persian rather than Arabic origin.

As Mahomedans they belong to the sect of the Shahis, who prevail in Persia and India; whilst those of Arabia the West are Sonees.[1] And the conjecture is strengthened by the circum-

[1] The principal difference between the two divisions of Mahomedans lies in the alleged rejection by each of certain holy men and companions of the Prophet who are held in high veneration by the opposite sect.

D 2

stance that their lebbes or priests, who are elected by them from those most deeply versed in the Koran, officiate in the mosques and deliver their discourses in Persian.

The Singhalese and Tamils are jealous of their substantial prosperity, and suspicious of their shrewdness and ability as dealers, but they are unable to supersede or dispense with them: they are still dependent on the Moormen for every agency and service by which profit is to be realized and money made. As Mussulmans, the Moors of Ceylon exhibit less devotion and earnestness than I have observed amongst the followers of the Prophet in any other country where his faith prevails. They seem on no occasion to allow their religious ceremonies to interfere with their secular pursuits; nor have I ever seen a Mahomedan of Ceylon, like a Turk or an Arab, pause in the midst of his occupation, when the *azan* or hour of prayer arrives, to make his prostration and perform his *rakat*. They have mosques in every village, but neither minarets nor muezzims to call the faithful to their devotions; and all their energies and efforts seem to be reserved for their festivals, which combine merriment with religion, and afford an opportunity for amusement and display. Their weddings are celebrated with much noisy and costly ceremonial; but the Christian population of the island is seldom reminded of the presence of these followers of Mahomet, except on the occasion of their Mohurrum and their annual processions to commemorate the martyrdom of Hussun and Hossein. Their funerals, too, are conducted with peculiar rites. The corpse, after being washed and anointed by the lebbe and sprinkled with powder of sandal-wood, is borne in a coffin without a bottom (its place being supplied by plaited tapes), and carried on a bier decorated with flowers, which are afterwards planted on the grave. The procession is accompanied by mourners, who chant the funeral cry of the Mahomedans; and every believer, as he hears it approach, ceases his occupation, and comes out to accompany the funeral to the burial-ground.

Colossal Statue of Buddhu at the Aukane Wihare. p. 76.

CHAPTER II.

THE DUTCH PERIOD.

Breach of faith with the King of Kandy — Dutch Persecution of the Roman Catholics — Present Condition of the Portuguese Descendants in Ceylon — Establishment of the Reformed Religion — Extraordinary Conformity of the Natives — Expedients to convert the Buddhists — Educational System of the Dutch — their Ecclesiastical System in Ceylon — Active Measures against Buddhism — Decline of Christianity — Increasing Influence of the Roman Catholics — Failure of the Dutch to extend the Reformed Religion in Ceylon; and its Causes.

CHAPTER II.

THE DUTCH PERIOD.

THE Dutch commenced their career in Ceylon under auspices and circumstances calculated, in the highest degree, to enhance their moral as well as their political influence. They had already attained reputation in the East by the vigour with which they had established themselves in the Indian Archipelago, and the address with which they had laid the foundation of future prosperity in Java, Formosa,[1] Amboyna, Sumatra, and the Moluccas; and simultaneously with the rise and expansion of their power, was the gradual degradation of the Portuguese, and the decline of their authority on the continent of India. As rulers, the policy of the Portuguese in Hindostan had been characterized by perfidy and encroachment; as merchants, they were pre-eminent for rapacity and deceit: and in their demeanour towards the natives of all ranks and religions, they had excited an

[1] The Dutch were not expelled from Formosa till 1661 A.D., when the island was surprised by the Chinese pirates under Koxinga, who, amongst other victims, dispatched or made prisoners upwards of thirty ministers of the Dutch Church. Baldæus, c. xix. p. 634.

unusual feeling of disgust and impatience by their personal insolence and tyrannical assumption.

In Ceylon, their political career towards its close had been equally faithless and aggressive, and in 1636 the King of Kandy, Raja Singha, impressed by the superior character and bearing of the Dutch, addressed a letter to the Governor of Palliacatta on the Coromandel Coast, in which, after reciting the dishonourable and the violent conduct of the Portuguese, he invited the Dutch to an alliance for their expulsion from Ceylon.[1] He informed the ambassadors, who were subsequently sent to him from Batavia, that he could have no confidence in the Portuguese; that no union with them was safe; that in defiance of engagements and treaties, they violated his frontiers, plundered his country, and set fire to his villages and towns; and so long as they had an inch of land in the island, there would be no protection from their tyranny, and no security from their insults.[2] The result of this negotiation was, an agreement by

[1] See the Letter in Baldæus, c. xix. p. 703. The King, adopting the European titles, which he had learned in his intercourse with the Portuguese, styles himself *Emperor* of Ceylon; *King* of Kandy, Kotta, and Jaffnapatam; *Prince* of Ouva, Matura, and the Four Korles; *Grand Duke* of the Seven Korles and Matelle; *Earl* of Trincomalie and Cottiar; *Marquis* of Oudenuwere; and *Lord of the Sea-ports* of Colombo, Madampe, Calpentyn, and Manaar, and of the Fishery of Pearls and precious Gems, and Lord of the Golden Sun.

[2] Ribeyro, b. ii. c. v.

which the Dutch were to be permitted to erect fortresses on the eastern coast, to facilitate their operations against the Portuguese on the west; that the King of Kandy was to bear all the expenses of the war, and the Dutch were to hand over to him instantly all the fortresses and territories which should be wrested from the enemy.

At the very outset of their career, however, the Dutch were betrayed into an act of perfidy not less flagrant than those which had led to the degradation and expulsion of their predecessors. In open violation of the express terms of their engagement, they retained possession of their conquests, and precipitated a fresh war with their ally, to whose assistance they had been invited. They established themselves firmly at Galle, Colombo, and Jaffna;[1] and having driven the Portuguese in succession from every fortress on the coast, they succeeded by right of conquest to the whole of their territorial possessions in Ceylon.

In consistency with their uniform practice elsewhere, the reformed church of Holland was formally established as the religion of the colony, and the first Presbyterian clergyman commenced his ministrations on the 6th October, 1642. Still burning with resentment, however, against their European rivals, the first efforts of their newly acquired power were directed against the Roman Catholic clergy. Those who were found in Colombo on its surrender, and

[1] Galle, 1640. Colombo, 1656. Jaffna, 1658.

those who marched out with the troops on the subsequent capture of Jaffna, were summarily transported to the continent of India; and an unfortunate Jesuit, whom sickness had prevented from accompanying his colleagues, on the surrender of the latter fortress, was beheaded by the Dutch because he had failed to disclose the existence of a plot, to which he had been made privy in the solemn confidence of the Confessional, but was utterly unconnected with the designs of the conspirators.[1] The insults offered by the Dutch to the images on the altars of the Roman Catholic chapels during the war were equally exasperating to the Portuguese, and the discomfited captain-general of Colombo, in narrating the events of the siege for the information of his government, says, "his pen wants words to describe the affronts put on their holy things by the heretics, who took the statue of the Apostle St. Thomas, and after they had cut off the nose, knocked it full of great nails, and shot it out of a mortar, November the 16th, into our ditch."[2]

The same fury against the Church of Rome continued at all times to inspire the policy of the Dutch

[1] Baldæus, c. xli. pp. 780, 798, 799.

[2] A True Account of the Siege of Colombo, carried on by Raja Singha, King of Candy, and the Hollanders, till the surrender of that Fortress. By Antonia de Souza Coutinho, Captain-General of Ceylon.—Churchill's Collection of Voyages, vol. iii. p. 761.

in Ceylon; and their resistance to its priesthood was even more distinct and emphatic than their condemnation of the Buddhists and Brahmans. In 1658, a proclamation was issued, forbidding, on pain of death, the harbouring or concealing of a Roman Catholic priest;[1] but such a threat was too iniquitous to be carried into execution; and the priests continued their ministrations in defiance of the law. In 1715, a proclamation was issued, prohibiting public assemblies, or private conventicles of the Roman Catholics, under heavy fines for the first and second offence, and chastisement, at the discretion of the magistrate, for the third.[2] In the same year, by a plakaat, which was afterwards renewed from time to time, it was forbidden for a Catholic clergyman to administer baptism under any circumstances;[3] and in 1733, the proclamation of 1658 was republished against entertaining or giving lodging to a priest,[4] but with no better success; for twelve years later, the same sanguinary order had to be repeated[5] by a fresh plakaat of

[1] Dutch Records. Colombo. Proclamation, dated 19th September, 1658. Renewed by Proclamation, 10th August, 1743.

[2] Ibid. Proclamation, 11th January, 1715. Renewed 1751, by Proclamation of 31st July, "for prohibiting the intrusion of Roman Catholic priests, and holding private or public meetings, under pain of severe punishment."

[3] Ibid. Proclamation, 8th August, 1715. Renewed 25th February, 1745.

[4] Ibid. Proclamation, 25th March, 1733.

[5] Ibid. Proclamation, 25th February, 1745.

the governor. In 1748, it was forbidden to educate a Roman Catholic for the ministry;[1] but within three years it was found necessary to repeat the same prohibition, as well as to renew the proclamation for putting down the celebration of the mass.[2] Notwithstanding every persecution, however, the Roman Catholic religion retained its influence, and held good its position in Ceylon. It was openly professed by the immediate descendants of the Portuguese,[3] who had remained in the island after its conquest by the Dutch; and in private it was equally adhered to by large bodies of the natives, both Singhalese and Tamils, whom neither corruption nor coercion could induce to abjure it.

These measures of the Dutch, so much more stringent than any similar proceedings of their predecessors, in regard to religion,[4] had naturally the effect, more or less, of driving the Roman Catholics and their clergy from the maritime provinces; and Rajah

[1] Dutch Records. Proclamation, 10th August, 1748.

[2] Ibid. Proclamation, 31st July, 1751.

[3] See note A, end of this chapter.

[4] The only writer who has ventured to do any justice to the conduct of the Portuguese in regard to religion as compared with that of the Dutch in the same particular, is the Rev. Mr. Bissett, who, under the name of Philalethes, published in 1815 an account of Ceylon, in which he guardedly observes that "the Portuguese were more tolerant in religion than the Dutch, and the Dutch were *less tolerant than they ought*."—A History of Ceylon from the Earliest Period to the year MDCCCXV., p. 277.

Singha, enraged at the deceit which had been practised upon him by the Hollanders, in retaining possession of the forts on the coast, readily offered them an asylum in his dominions around Kandy.[1] Upwards of 700 Portuguese families are said to have established themselves in Ruanwelle, at the foot of the Kandyan hills; a colony of Mookwa Christians, from the coast, were encouraged to settle at Galgammoa; and to the present day there exists in the village of Wahacotta, amongst the mountains of Matelle, a community of Roman Catholics, speaking the language, and in other respects undistinguished from Kandyans, but who are known to be the descendants of the Portuguese who had there sought concealment from the persecution of the Dutch in the low country.[2]

In the mean time the latter proceeded steadily and systematically with the work of Protestant conversion. In the peninsula of Jaffna they took possession of the Roman Catholic churches. They established one school at least in connexion with each; and Baldæus, one of their earliest missionaries, has related, with much minuteness, the small amount of religious instruction which he found it expedient to insist on preparatory to admission into membership with the Reformed Church of Holland.[3]

[1] Records of the Dutch Consistory at Colombo, A.D. 1689.

[2] See note B, end of this chapter.

[3] Baldæus, c. xliv. p. 793.

A seminary was opened at Jaffna, for the instruction of teachers and catechists; and he records that in 1663, within five years from the arrival of the Dutch, 12,387 children had been baptized, 18,000 pupils were under instruction in the schools, and 65,000 converts had become "Christian men and women in the kingdom of Jaffnapatam."[1] Besides these, in 1655, there were upwards of 8000 converts in Manaar and the Wanny; and in 1688, the number of Christians throughout the province of Jaffna was represented as exceeding 180,000.[2] How imperfectly even the smallest of these numbers must have been looked after, both in regard to elementary teaching and spiritual instruction, may be inferred from the circumstance deplored by Baldæus, that for the care of all his churches and schools he had, in 1663, but two or three clergymen of the reformed religion, where the Portuguese had formerly employed upwards of forty Roman Catholic ecclesiastics.[3] And, as if in anticipation of a doubt as to the sincerity of the outward profession made by his converts, he candidly states, that "though Christians in name, and qualified to discourse rationally of the ten commandments, and other doctrinal points, they still retained many of the superstitions of paganism."

[1] Baldæus, c. xlvi. p. 810.

[2] Hough, Hist. Christ. in India, vol. iii. b. vii. c. ii. p. 491. —See note C, at the end of the chapter.

[3] Baldæus, c. clvi. p. 811.

Whilst matters were proceeding thus triumphantly amongst the Hindoos in the north of the island, the progress of the Dutch ministers was not quite so rapid or remarkable in the Buddhist districts of the South. The Singhalese exhibited by no means the same alacrity as the Tamils in accepting in succession the conflicting doctrines of the Church of Rome at the hands of the Portuguese, and those of the Church of Holland from their successors; and it was soon found expedient to exert, if not open coercion, at least some gentle violence to quicken their apprehension. With this view proclamation was publicly made that no native could aspire to the rank of modliar, or be even permitted to farm land or hold office under the government, who had not first undergone the ceremony of baptism, become a member of the Protestant church, and subscribed to the doctrines contained in the Helvetic confession of faith.

The operation of this announcement was such as may be readily anticipated. Many of the lowland chiefs who had been recently baptized by the Portuguese, and who still bore the family names which had been conferred upon them by their Catholic sponsors, came forward to abjure the errors of Rome. The landowners, and those who aspired to be petty headmen, and police vidahns of their villages, were equally prompt to exhibit themselves possessed of the necessary qualifications for office; and even Brahmans of Jaffna and Manaar, unwilling to forego the prospects of dignity and emolument, which were attainable upon such easy conditions, made a ready profession of Christianity, although they forbore to lay aside the beads and other symbols of heathenism.[1]

Education, in the proceedings of the Dutch clergy, was in almost every instance made available for pioneering the way for the preaching of Christianity. The school-house in each village became the nucleus of a future congregation;[2] and here, whilst the children received elementary instruction, they and the adults were initiated in the first principles of Christianity. Baptism was administered and marriages solemnized in the village school-houses, and, in order to confer every possible importance on these rural institutions, the schoolmasters appointed by the scholarchal commission had charge of the thombos or registers of the district in which these events were recorded, and thus became the depositaries of the evidence on which the rights and succession to property were mainly dependent.

The course of education in the village schools was limited and the instruction gratuitous, but the most remarkable feature in the system was that the attendance of the pupils was *compulsory*, and enforced by

[1] Baldæus, c. xlvii. p. 814.

[2] From an Account of the Dutch Church in Ceylon, collected from the Records of the Consistory, preserved in the Wolfendahl Church at Colombo. By the Rev. J. D. Palm. Journal of the Ceylon Asiatic Society, No. 2, p. 134.

the imposition of fines upon the parents. These fines were the cause of continued refractoriness amongst the natives, dishonesty amongst the teachers, and annoyance to the commission; but experience had demonstrated that their rigid enforcement was the only effective expedient for maintaining attendance at the schools.[1]

For nearly thirty years matters wore the appearance of proceeding successfully under this combined system of encouragement and compulsion; but about the year 1670 the records of the Consistory begin to exhibit evidences of uneasiness on the part of the labouring clergy, and contain complaints of the stubborn opposition of idolaters and the hostile interference of the Roman Catholics and their priests. As to education, where religious prejudices did not intervene, the natives in general exhibited a desire to secure it for their boys; but it required many years to overcome the aversion even of nominal Christians to the education of their daughters, and, above all, their unwillingness that females should be taught to write.

In the southern parts of the island, and especially at Matura, which has always been pre-eminent as the stronghold of Buddhism and the residence of its

[1] An Account of the Educational Establishment of the Dutch in Ceylon. By the Rev. J. D. Palm, Colonial Chaplain of the Dutch Church in Colombo. Journal of the Ceylon Asiatic Society, No. 2, p. 107.

most learned professors, the hostility of the people was more intense than around Colombo; their opposition to education was more openly and forcibly avowed, and the evil was aggravated by an edict of the Dutch to prohibit the marriages of those professing Christianity with the unconverted worshippers of Buddhu. But notwithstanding these discouragements the success of the educational system exceeded what might have been reasonably expected; the gross number of pupils in the Singhalese districts varied from 30,000 to 40,000, and, at the close of the Dutch government in Ceylon, the number of children under instruction in all parts of the island was little short of 85,000.

For ecclesiastical purposes, as for educational, the Dutch divided Ceylon into the three divisions of Colombo, Jaffna, and Galle. There were congregations of Europeans amongst the military and civilians at the forts, and upwards of one hundred native churches throughout the coast and interior. But notwithstanding the facilities and encouragement thus held out by the Civil Government for the extension of Christianity, the history of its progress was but the history of its struggles with inherent difficulties and opposition, before which the energies of its promoters were gradually exhausted, and the result of the labours eventually disappeared. Foremost amongst these was the resistance offered by the genius and influence of the national idolatry of the

Singhalese. In the southern province, above all, the contest was unequally sustained by the Dutch; and nothing but coercion and pecuniary fines served to keep up a show of pupils in their schools and enforce attendance on their instructions in the principles of Christianity.

According to the Report of the Chaplain of Galle in 1680, "idolatry was then on the increase: so much so as to render him doubtful of the propriety of baptizing the children of natives, lest that which is holy be given unto dogs." Every thing was "*pro forma*, and by constraint;" and though the authority of the Government led the Singhalese to adopt the name of Christianity, they were utterly ignorant of its power, and not only refused to send their children for instruction, but declined themselves to attend the preaching of the Gospel.[1] Their teachers, too, with but three or four exceptions, only laboured from the motive of gain, without the slightest regard either for their own souls or those committed to their care, and some were even reported to the Consistory as being professional devil-dancers.[2] At a still later period[3] the Dutch ministers of Colombo, apparently disheartened by the deceptive results of their labours, and embarrassed by a multitudinous assemblage

[1] Records of the Consistory of Colombo, A.D. 1730.

[2] The Rev. Mr. Palm's Account of the Dutch Church in Ceylon, pp. 16, 17.

[3] A.D. 1684.

of converts in name but idolaters at heart, represented to the Governor in council that the reason why they designated the natives only as "*nominal* or *baptized* Christians" was, because many made a profession only from considerations of personal advantage; and that native Christianity throughout Ceylon was in an unsound and critical condition, notwithstanding the peremptory orders of the Government "for the prevention of devil-worship and other heathen superstitions, as well as against the practices of Popery, to which some are still strongly inclined."[1]

This latter allusion was not without its foundation in fact; for as the influence of the Protestant clergy declined, that of the Roman Catholic priesthood had risen into unexpected importance. Their worship, notwithstanding every discouragement, had maintained its hold on the natives by its gaudy ceremonial; whilst the less attractive teaching and sterner discipline of the Dutch could only be sustained by prospects of personal advantage or enforced by pecuniary fines. At Jaffna, in particular, and amongst the Tamils and Fisher caste along the western coast, its ascendency was neither weakened by persecution nor undermined by corruption.

From Kandy, where they had been alternately invited and proscribed by the kings, the Roman Catholic priests made their way into the low country,

[1] The Rev. Mr. Palm's Account, &c., p. 27.

visiting in secret their scattered flocks, and administering the Sacraments in defiance of the plakaats and prohibitions of the Government.[1] Amongst the most distinguished of these preachers was Joseph Vaz, of the Oratory of St. Philippo Neri, at Goa, whose adventurous journeys and imprisonments, and his extraordinary zeal in the service of his Church, have obtained for his memory amongst the Roman Catholics of Ceylon a veneration little short of that accorded to the name of St. Francis Xavier in India. He prevailed on the King of Kandy, in 1694, to permit him to rebuild the churches of the Roman Catholics in the Bogambra suburb which his predecessor had directed to be destroyed; and having been appointed by the Bishop of Cochin his Vicar-General for Ceylon, he prosecuted his labours with such vigour and success that in an incredibly short space of time he had re-established the Catholic communion in its former strongholds at Jaffna and Manaar, extended its influence in the maritime provinces, and added to the Church upwards of 30,000 converts from the heathen.[2] Father Vaz died at Kandy in 1711, but the impulse which his fervour and toil had communicated to the advance-

[1] Lectures on the Roman Catholic Church. By N. Wiseman, D.D., Bishop of Melipotamus. Sect. vii. p. 231.

[2] The Life of Father Joseph Vaz, founder of the Catholic Mission of St. Philippo Neri in Ceylon. Abridged from Dorego's Work, by S. Casie Chitty, Esq., Ceylon Civil Service. Colombo, 1848, pp. 16, 25.

ment of his religion underwent no apparent diminution after his decease; and at length the Dutch Government, abandoning whatever portion of practical moderation may have characterized the earlier years of their rule, were persuaded by the Protestant ministers to adopt a more active, but, as it eventually proved, an equally ineffectual policy for the forcible suppression of Popery. The Dutch clergy and their consistories appear at all times to have been inclined to religious coercion; [1] but it was only when alarmed by the increasing pressure of the Roman Catholics that the Government yielded to their solicitations, and ventured to enforce the series of measures which have already been enumerated, and which were designed, not merely for the restraint of the priests, but the actual extinction of the Roman Catholic religion in Ceylon. The priests thus proscribed were, however, far from being silenced; they abandoned their open residence in the territories of the Dutch, and retired to villages and towns on the Kandyan frontier, whence they returned, in various disguises, to visit their congregations throughout the maritime districts.[2] The proclamations of the

[1] The Rev. Mr. Palm's Account of the Dutch Church in Ceylon, pp. 35, 50.

[2] Bishop Wiseman, quoting from the *Peregrinacion del Mundo* of Don Pedro Cabrero Sebastian, Predicador Apostolico (Naples, 1682, p. 277), relates in his Lectures some extraordinary exploits of that missionary in administering the sacraments by stealth to the Roman Catholics in all parts of Ceylon.

Government were either too late to be effectual, or too tyrannical to be carried into force; and in 1717, only two years after their renewed promulgation, the Roman Catholics were in possession of upwards of 400 churches in all parts of Ceylon, whilst the Dutch Presbyterians had barely one-fourth the number either of congregations or converts. Other measures equally unwise and abortive followed those of 1715. Roman Catholic marriages were at first heavily taxed,[1] then ordered to be solemnized only by ministers of the Reformed Church, or by the officers of the Court of Justice;[2] and all this proving ineffectual, their celebration by a Roman Catholic priest was at last absolutely prohibited, and their registration declared void.[3] Their burials were forbidden in cemeteries of their own, and extravagant fees were exacted on their interment in those attached to the Protestant churches.[4] Roman Catholics were declared equally with heathens to be ineligible to office; and freedom was conferred upon the children of all slaves born of Protestant parents, whilst those of Roman Catholics were condemned to

Lecture vii. p. 232. Dorego, in his Life of Father Vaz, records similar escapes and persecutions.

[1] Dutch Government Proclamation, 15th Sept., 1758.

[2] Ibid., 24th Dec., 1776.

[3] Ibid., dated 19th Dec., 1776.

[4] Philalethes, p. 182. Lord Valentia's Travels, vol. i., p. 309.

perpetual servitude[1]—a device so short-sighted as to counteract the intentions of its framers by giving every slave-holder an interest in preventing the extension of Protestantism.

Measures of a similar nature were, about the same period, resorted to for the suppression of Buddhism, but with no better ultimate success. In 1682 the Governor Lourensz Van Pyl, yielding to the entreaties of the consistory, issued a *plakaat*, imposing penalties on devil-dances and similar idolatrous ceremonies; in 1688 permission was refused to the King of Kandy to erect a Buddhist Temple within the Dutch territory;[2] and a few years later, application was made by the Protestant clergy to have the Buddhist worship prohibited at the great temple of Kalany, within a few miles of Colombo, and for authority to build a schoolroom on the ruins of a heathen *madua*, or preaching-house, which stood in its immediate vicinity. The Government were reluctant to take so bold a step as the suppression of one of the most ancient Buddhist foundations in Ceylon, apprehensive that they would draw down the vengeance of the King of Kandy, with whom it was then expedient to cultivate peace and alliance. They expressed their willingness, however, to impose a penalty on such nominal Christians as should be

[1] Bertolacci's Account of Ceylon, Introd., pp. 60, 72. Records of the Dutch Consistory of Colombo, A.D. 1751.

[2] Valentyn, c. 17, quoted by Hough, vol. iii. p. 91.

convicted of idolatrous practices;[1] and they gave an authority for the establishing of the Christian school as requested. The experiment was unsuccessful; the school-house was opened, but the resort of pilgrims to the temple became more multitudinous than ever, and the clergy in their extremity appealed from the timid policy of the local authorities to the supreme authority at home, to enforce the plakaat of Van Pyl against the idolaters of Kalany. The Dutch East India Company complied; and in 1692 they declared the Buddhist ceremonies at Kalany to be prohibited, and ordered the priests to withdraw from the temple.

Notwithstanding this and similar measures, the progress of conversion amongst the Buddhists was still unsatisfactory and unsound. The proscription, both of popery and idolatry, was found to be insufficient without the compulsion of converts, and this was resorted to so undisguisedly as to attract the attention and draw down the ecclesiastical censure of the clergy in Holland. In 1700 A.D., the Classis of Amsterdam addressed a remonstrance to the Consistory of Colombo, impelled by their anxieties for the state of the Church in Ceylon. They state that

[1] In 1711 the Dutch Government found it necessary to carry this intention into effect, and by a proclamation issued on the 6th of June in that year a Christian convicted of participating in any of the ceremonies of heathenism was declared liable to be publicly whipped and imprisoned in irons for the space of a year.

it has reached their ears, and on high authority, "that in some places attempts are made by improper and unjustifiable means to coerce the natives to a reception of Christianity, *that is, of baptism*; that they who are not baptized are declared to have forfeited a third of their property, and fines are imposed for the purpose of compelling attendance at the schools and at church.[1] They remind the Consistory that if such things are, they are not of Christ, nor calculated to advance his kingdom; that compulsion can never generate conviction, nor penalties inculcate belief; and that those who are constrained by such inadmissible means, though they may submit to call themselves Christians, must remain the enemies of Christ.

Twenty years later the prospect was equally sad; and in 1730, the Consistory of Galle took occasion to place upon record their own views of the obstacles which prevented the growth of Christianity. These were, in the first instance, the influence of the native chiefs, who, though they had assumed the designation of Christians in compliance with the wishes of the Government, were still "incorrigible Buddhists;" and in their pride of caste, they required separate churches to be erected specially for themselves, to which even their own wives were to be inadmissible. Secondly, the public prevalence of idolatry, and the secret adhesion to it, notwithstanding the pretence of

[1] The Rev. Mr. Palm's Account of the Dutch Church in Ceylon, p. 42.

Christianity. Every action of the lives even of professing Christians was represented to be regulated by the practice and precepts of Buddhism: "when a child is born, they still consult the astrologers; when it is sick, they hang charms round its neck; and even after baptism they discontinue the use of its Christian name, and a heathen name is given it as usual on the first occasion of its eating rice. They will undertake no work without ascertaining a lucky day for commencing; and when sick or in adversity they send for the devil-dancer in preference to their clergy. When they marry, it must be in the propitious hour; and when they die, their graves are decorated with leaves of the tree sacred to Buddhu, and cocoa-nuts and rice are piled around as food for the departed. They make offerings to the idols at Kattragam, they bestow gifts on the mendicant servants of the temple, and, in short, the highest benediction they can pronounce on their friends is, 'May you become a Buddhu!' For the prevalence of this hypocrisy and infidelity the clergy blame the remissness of the Government in not enforcing the penal laws of 1682; and still more the licentious and offensive lives of the Europeans themselves, who encourage the natives in debauchery, and show them an example in the practice of every vice."[1]

Such was the condition of Christianity about the

[1] The Rev. Mr. Palm's Account of the Dutch Church in Ceylon, pp. 52, 53.

time when Baron Imhoff assumed the government of Ceylon in 1736; and in handing over his authority to his successor, in 1740, he left on record his views as to the means of its extension, and the necessity of a greater number of missionaries to preach to the natives in Singhalese, Malabar, and Portuguese; and that these should be desired "to abstain from sending in lists of the converts they had made to Christianity, when they only cause that religion to be ill understood and ridiculously observed. The Romish priests," he continues, "do the Company much injury; they are zealous in their opposition to its interests, and very closely united amongst themselves; and it is my opinion that they never will be put down till we send out more efficient teachers of our own faith."[1]

It would appear that obstacles to the extension of Christianity from the influence of idolatry were even less apprehended than the difficulties now encountered from the rising ascendancy of the Roman Catholics, whose numbers had actually multiplied under persecution. They had churches in every district from Jaffna to Colombo; and in 1734 they extended their operations to the Southern Province, and with such success that the Presbyterian clergy of Galle, distracted by the impracticability or apostacy of the natives, gave way before this accumulation of hostile influences: from 1745

[1] Lee's Edition of Ribeyro's Ceylon, App. 176.

A.D., the district was left for some years altogether without the services of a Protestant minister.[1]

No circumstance is more demonstrative of the relative condition of the two Churches at this period—of the increasing strength of the Romish priesthood—the apprehension of the Dutch clergy—the spirit of the Consistory and the policy of the Government—than their treatment of the Roman Catholic community of Negombo and the surrounding korles, in which their numbers have been at all times more considerable than in any other district in the south of the island. In 1750 the Roman Catholics of this place, about twenty-two miles distant from Colombo, assumed sufficient courage to lay before the Government the grievances and disqualifications under which they laboured, and to entreat a reconsideration of its policy with a view to their relief. They complained, that being sincere believers in the tenets of their own Church, which had been espoused by their forefathers two hundred years before, it was a violence offered to their conscience to be compelled, under penalties, to send their families to be instructed in doctrines which they rejected, and an offence to their feelings to hear them rehearsed by their children on their return home from school. They admitted frankly, that whilst in terror of the law, and to avoid the fines imposed by the Government, they so far conformed as to have their children

[1] Lee's Edition of Ribeyro's Ceylon, pp. 54, 59.

baptized by the ministers of the Reformed Church; they were, nevertheless, in the habit of having the same children baptized a second time by the clergymen of the Church of Rome. They lamented that, being compelled to deny in public doctrines which they cherished in their hearts, this perpetual conflict between their secret convictions and their public profession endangered the salvation of their souls; and they earnestly prayed to be admitted to liberty of conscience and the free exercise of their religion, which no compulsory avowal of Protestantism could ever induce them to abjure.[1]

Their application was referred by the Government for the consideration and opinion of the Consistory of Colombo, who urged strenuously that no relaxation whatsoever might be granted; that the Government regulations, and the fines for non-attendance at schools and at church, should be firmly enforced against Roman Catholics; that baptism by a priest should neither be sanctioned, nor its validity admitted; and that none but Protestant headmen should be invested with authority in the different districts.

The Governor and the Council, whatever might be the strict letter of the law, were by no means prepared to carry matters to such an extreme; they even reminded the Consistory in their reply that it was beyond the province of that body to interfere with penalties or political regulations which were

[1] The Rev. Mr. Palm's Account, &c., p. 60.

properly within the jurisdiction of the civil administration. As to Roman Catholic baptism and its validity, that was a question which they must refer for the instruction of the authorities at Batavia; and as regarded the headmen, and the exclusion from office of all but Protestant candidates, it had been found practically impossible to act uniformly on that principle, as the numbers of such converts had become too scanty to afford a sufficient field for selection.

The prayer of the Roman Catholics was, however, rejected, and the exasperating though ineffectual policy of exclusion and compulsion was still openly pursued. Reaction and retaliation were the natural consequences. Emboldened by a sense of their own numbers and physical strength, the Roman Catholics ventured on a more ostentatious display of their influence over the people; they erected places of worship at Caltura, within a few miles of Colombo, and commenced their public celebration of their festivals with all their accustomed paraphernalia and parade. The governor caused the leader of this movement to be banished to Tutocoreen on the Coromandel coast, where the Dutch had a settlement; serious disturbances followed, and for some years afterwards the districts round Colombo were the scene of continued riots, in which the Protestants were insulted and assaulted by their opponents.

These events seem to have partially opened the eyes of the Government to the inutility of persecution as an instrument of conversion; a reaction immediately followed in favour of a more enlarged toleration, and under the three latest Dutch governors, Falk, Van de Graaf, and Engelbeck, between 1765 and the occupation of Ceylon by the British in 1796, though the penal laws against the Roman Catholics were not formally repealed, they ceased to be rigidly enforced, and their priests were allowed to reside in the Dutch territory, but they were not permitted to wear their sacerdotal vestments or exercise their functions within a certain distance of fortified towns.

There is no record in the proceedings of the Consistory towards the close of the Dutch Government to show that disappointment or discouragement had led to a determination to reduce the ecclesiastical and educational establishments, or to contract operations which had been productive of such unsatisfactory results; but that inference is deducible from the circumstance that such reductions were gradually effected. In 1730 there had been thirteen ministers employed in garrison duty and the superintendence of native instruction, and in 1747 there were but *five* in all Ceylon, and of these but *one* who understood the language of the natives.[1] From this time forward the Dutch sought and received assistance from the Danish mission at Tranquebar, who sup-

[1] Records of the Colombo Consistory, 1730, 1745, 1747. Hough, vol. iii. b. vii. c. ii. p. 103, note.

plied them with types and with printers, educated young men for the ministry in Ceylon, and sent repeatedly clergy from their own establishment to assist in the declining labours of the Dutch. The most remarkable of these visitors was Christian Frederick Schwartz, a name renowned in the annals of Christianity in India, who landed at Jaffna in 1759, and devoted a large portion of the year to preaching and administering the sacrament at every station in the island.[1]

There are unfortunately no accurate data as to the actual number of professing Christians at the close of the Dutch rule in Ceylon and the arrival of the British in 1796; and the records of the Consistory, though they contain returns and statistics down to 1760, are significantly silent after that date. At an earlier period they had been estimated by Valentyn at 420,000,[2] but Hough asserts that before the end of the eighteenth century they had been reduced to 300,000;[3] and it is observable that amongst the mul-

[1] Hough, vol. iii. b. vii. c. 2, p. 27.

[2] In 1722 Valentyn gives the number of

Tamil Christians in Jaffna at	189,388
Singhalese Christians in other places . .	179,845
Christians in the Galle District	55,159
	424,392

Besides 2799 young men and 1493 women, candidates for baptism. Valentyn, c. 17, quoted by Hough, vol. iii. b. vii. c. 2, p. 101.

[3] Ib., p. 104. Philalethes states (p. 191) that in 1801 the

titude of Tamils and Singhalese converts *there is not a single instance on record of a Moorman or Mahomedan who had been induced to embrace Christianity.* It is still less practicable to discriminate what proportion of these large numbers were Christians in heart or merely Christians in name; but the records of the Dutch Government, as well as the casual notices of the historians of the period, leave no room to doubt that in the opinion of their contemporaries the preponderance was considerably on the side of the latter. In fact, had it been otherwise, had these converts been devout and enlightened believers, their prodigious amount would quite warrant the remark of the historian of Christianity in India, that "the progress of conversion in Ceylon under their ministration would have been unparalleled in the history of the Church since the days of the Apostles."[1]

The latest records of the Dutch Consistory, however, contain an expression of their conviction, that even the converts of Jaffna were but Laodiceans in heart,[2] and the Classis of Walchern but a few years before had expressed their fear, from the small number of communicants in proportion to the crowds of

number of native Protestants in Ceylon was 342,000, and that the members of the Roman Catholic Church were still more numerous.

[1] Hough, vol. iii. b. vii. c. 2, p. 93.

[2] Records, 1751.

Singhalese who had been baptized,[1] that their profession was unsound, and the converts themselves "*sine Christo Christiani.*"

Still there is abundant evidence to show that all were not unreal professors. Baldæus and Valentyn have borne their testimony to this fact with impressive moderation; and the latter declares that amongst the native Christians of Jaffna there were many whose conduct and life might put Europeans to the blush. Cordiner, who wrote his account of Ceylon from 1799 to 1804, and, as the first colonial chaplain under the English Government, must have been aware of the state of religion at the time of the British occupation, and personally acquainted with many of the Dutch converts, has stated that although religious knowledge was not perfectly conveyed to the lower orders of the natives, many of the higher ranks became as true believers in its doctrines, and as conscientious performers of the duties of Christianity, as those who adorn the most enlightened regions.[2]

Cordiner, however, must have been but imperfectly informed when he states that the Portuguese

[1] This discrepancy is very prominent in the Ecclesiastical Returns of the Dutch Clergy: for instance, in 1760, of 182,226 natives enrolled as Christians at Jaffna, but 64 were members of the Church; of 9820 at Manaar, only 5 were communicants; and in the same year at Galle and Matura there were 36 members out of 89,000 who had been baptized. The Rev. Mr. Palm, p. 67.

[2] A Description of Ceylon. By the Rev. J. Cordiner, A.M. London, 1807, vol. i. p. 155. Philalethes, p. 191.

compelled the natives of Ceylon to adopt the Roman Catholic religion without consulting their inclination, and that the Dutch, unlike them, had refrained from the employment of open force for the propagation of their religious faith;[1] and Hough, in his important work on Christianity in India, has adopted his assertions without due examination. On both points the historical evidence is at variance with these representations. I have discovered nothing in the proceedings of the Portuguese in Ceylon to justify the imputation of violence and constraint; but unfortunately as regards the Dutch Presbyterians, their own records are conclusive as to the severity of their measures and the ill success by which they were followed. The plakaats and proclamations of the Government, and their orders and regulations at one time for the coercion of the Buddhists, and at another for bribing them to conformity, are sufficient proofs of their system as regarded the heathens; and if any evidence were wanting as to their oppressive and compulsory policy towards the Roman Catholics and their priesthood, it may be found in the legislative acts of the British Government, one of whose earliest measures was to repeal the penal laws enacted by the Dutch, under the operation of which, according to the terms of the preamble of that Act, "the Roman Catholics, a numerous and peaceable body of His

[1] Cordiner, vol. i. pp. 156, 157. Hough, vol. iii. b. vii. c. 2, pp. 74, 75.

Majesty's subjects, were rigorously excluded from many important privileges and capacities."[1] These laws, though they had not been acted upon in all cases, were still found to be a cause of anxiety to those who professed the Catholic religion, and they were accordingly repealed in 1806, when the Roman Catholics were allowed the unmolested exercise of their own religion in every part of Ceylon, relieved from all civil disqualifications, and their marriages declared valid notwithstanding the laws to the contrary which had been enacted by the Dutch.

Whatever may have been the instrumentality resorted to by the Portuguese priesthood, and however objectionable the means adopted by them for the extension of their own form of Christianity, one fact is unquestionable, that the natives became speedily attached to their ceremonies and modes of worship, and have adhered to them with remarkable tenacity for upwards of three hundred years; whilst even in the midst of their own ministrations, the clergy and missionaries of the reformed Church of Holland were overtaken by discouragement; and it is a remarkable fact, that notwithstanding the multitudinous baptisms, and the hundreds of thousands of Singhalese who were enrolled by them as converts, the religion and discipline of the Dutch Presbyterians is now almost extinct amongst the natives of Ceylon. Even in Jaffna, where the reception of these doctrines was

[1] See note D, end of the chapter.

all but unanimous by the Tamils, not a single congregation is now in existence of the many planted by Baldæus, and tended by the labours of Valentyn and Schwartz; and in Colombo and throughout the maritime provinces there are not at this moment fifty native Singhalese, even amongst the aged and infirm, who still profess the form of religion so authoritatively established and so anxiously propounded by the Dutch.[1]

The causes of this failure, however, are neither few nor obscure. Irrespective of the unsubdued influences of idolatry and caste, the doctrines of Christianity were too feebly developed and too superficially inculcated to make any lasting impression on the reluctant or apathetic minds of the natives of Ceylon. The Dutch ministers employed in their dissemination failed to qualify themselves for the task by mastering in the first instance the vernacular tongues of the island;[2] and the Consistory in vain insisted on the

[1] It was a device of the Dutch to circumvent the Roman Catholics by prohibiting the use of the Portuguese language, being that of the priests educated and sent from Goa: the attempt was, however, unsuccessful; and it is somewhat curious that at the present time Portuguese is in almost universal use in all the towns in the maritime provinces, and that Dutch is not only almost extinct, but the descendants of the Dutch have betaken themselves to speak the language of Portugal. See Philalethes, p. 228. Dutch Proclamation, 14th Nov., 1649.

[2] Out of a list of 97 clergymen in Ceylon between 1642 and 1725, as given by Valentyn, only 8 were qualified to preach in the native languages, 4 in Tamul and 4 in Singhalese. Hough, vol. iii. p. 75, 103.

inefficacy of instruction conveyed through the cold and unsatisfactory medium of interpreters.[1] In addition to this, their numbers were too few to render effectual aid to the multitude of their hearers; and in 1722, when the returns showed nearly half a million of nominal Christians, there were but fourteen clergymen in all Ceylon. Notwithstanding the clear perception which the Dutch appear to have had of the salutary influence of elementary and moral instruction in preparing the mind for rejecting the absurdities of heathenism, and embracing the pure precepts of Christianity, the amount of education which they communicated in their schools was infinitesimally small. It seldom went beyond teaching their pupils to read and to write in the language of their district, and even this was discouraged by the supreme authorities at Batavia, who, in communicating with the missionaries of Ceylon, expressed strongly their opinion that "reading and writing are things not so absolutely necessary for the edification of these poor wretches, as teaching them the fundamentals of religion, which are contained in a very few points; and to pretend to propagate Christianity by reading and writing, would be both tedious and chargeable to the Netherlands East India Company."[2] Under a system so superficial and ineffi-

[1] The Rev. Mr. Palm's Account, &c., pp. 5, 8.

[2] Letter of M. Matzuyker, Governor-General of Batavia, to Baldæus, Sept. 18th, 1662. Baldæus, p. 811.

cient, the labour actually bestowed was productive of no permanent fruits; it was but seed sown on stony ground, it was scorched by the sun, and because it had no root it soon withered away.

Again, the system of political bribery adopted by the Dutch to encourage conversion amongst the Singhalese was eminently calculated to create doubts and contempt in the naturally suspicious minds of the natives; whilst they could not fail to conclude that there must be something defective or unreal in a religion which required coercion and persecution to enforce its adoption. Where the former system was apparently successful, it produced in reality but an organized hypocrisy; and when persecution ensued, its recoil and reaction were destructive of the object for the furtherance of which it had been unwisely resorted to. And, lastly, the imprudence with which outward professors were indiscriminately welcomed as genuine converts to Christianity, involved the certainty of future discomfiture. The example of apostacy, under similar circumstances, is more dangerous in proportion than the encouragement wrought by adhesion; and thus the more widely the field was incautiously expanded, the more certain became the danger, and the more frequent the recurrence, of such untoward events. Towards the close of their career, the Dutch clergy had painful experience of this pernicious result, and their lamentations became more frequent over the relapses of their converts, first into the errors of popery, and finally into the darkness of heathenism.[1] At length, in apparent despondency, and in painful anticipation of defeat, instead of altering the system on which they had discovered that they could no longer rely, they merely contracted their missionary operations to the narrowest possible limits; cast upon others the labour in which they were no longer hopeful of success; and, at the final close of their ministrations, the clergy of the Church of Holland left behind a superstructure of Christianity prodigious in its outward dimensions, but so internally unsound as to be distrusted even by those who had been instrumental in its erection, and so unsubstantial that it has long since disappeared almost from the memory of the natives of Ceylon.

[1] Ecclesiastical Report of the Galle District. Records of the Colombo Consistory, 1757.

NOTES TO CHAPTER II.

(A.)

THE PORTUGUESE DESCENDANTS IN CEYLON.

No class of the European descendants who have become naturalized in Ceylon present at the present day so humble an aspect or occupy so low a grade as the posterity of those of the Portuguese whom poverty and other causes compelled to remain in the island after its conquest by Holland. In every particular—in ability, education, and personal bearing—they are inferior to the descendants of the Dutch, who have since been placed in similar circumstances by the arrival of the British. The latter, from their education and capabilities, aspire to offices of rank and responsibility; whilst the Portuguese section of the "burghers" are contented to fill the humbler occupation of tradesmen and artisans. The distinction, thus perpetuated, till it has almost become a characteristic of race, may be traced to the despotic and fanatical policy of the Dutch Government in Ceylon, which, from the commencement of its rule, subjected the Portuguese, on the plea of their being Roman Catholics, to social degradation, excluded them from every office of emolument, and effectually shut them out from every pursuit of industry or path to distinction. They were prohibited, by a proclamation in 1717, from leaving their places of residence without previous information to the authorities and permission obtained, under heavy penalties for the first offence, and "arbitrary punishment" if repeated. So effectually does this course of persecution and oppression appear to have crushed the spirit and benumbed the ambition of those subjected to its influences, that, even at the present day, under a liberal government, and after a lapse of nearly a century and a half, it is rarely that a Portuguese burgher aspires to rise above the position to which his forefathers had been reduced by the penal laws of the Dutch.

(B.)

ROMAN CATHOLIC COLONY IN THE KANDYAN MOUNTAINS.

"IN 1815, when the Kandyan territories submitted to the British Crown, a colony of Roman Catholics, the descendants of those Portuguese who had settled in the interior during the reign of King Raja Singha, were discovered in their mountain fastnesses at Wahacotta, still retaining their attachment to the Christian name and ordinances, although they were hemmed in on all sides by the Buddhists, and had not seen the face of a priest for nearly three-quarters of a century." (Casie Chitty, Sketch of the Roman Catholic Church in Ceylon, p. 21.) Their minister, who was, of course, unordained, was called a *sacristan*. They had one copy of the New Testament in Singhalese, translated by a Roman Catholic priest, but no one of them could read, and the sacristan only knew a few prayers by heart. The community consisted of about two hundred souls, they worshipped the Virgin Mary, prayed before the crucifix, and were married and buried with a form similar to the Roman Catholic Church; but they occasionally visited the temples of Buddhu and made offerings of flowers upon his shrine. (Davy's Ceylon, c. iv. p. 1; Harvard's Account of the Wesleyan Mission in Ceylon and India, Introd. p. lxv., Appendix No. V., p. 333.)

(C.)

DUTCH CONVERTS, A.D. 1684.

FABRICIUS (Jo. Albert), in his Lux Evangelii, gives the following extracts from letters of Hermann Specht, from Colombo, and Adrian de Mey, prefect of the Malabar College at Jaffnapatam, giving an account of the state of Christianity in Ceylon. Specht's letter is dated in 1684, and he says:—"In regno Jaffnapatam sub quo etiam Manaar comprehenditur, sunt, excepto Manaar, secundum supputationem ultimam, et secundum catalogum nobis de illis traditum inventi conversi Christiani centum quadraginta et unum millia, quadringenti et quinquaginta sex (141,456) quorum conversioni præpositi fuerunt quinque pastores; sed ante paucos dies uno pastore mortuo, sunt hoc tempore illis præpositi tantum quatuor pastores." The same authority, writing from Colombo, says:—"Regnum Jaffnapatam habet incolas bis centies mille septuaginta octo millia septingentos et quinquaginta novem (278,759), inter quos incolas sunt Indi Christiani conversi centies mille octuaginta millia trecenti et sexaginta quatuor" (180,364).

Adrian de Mey writes on the 6th November, 1690, and announces his own appointment as prefect of the Malabar seminary for the extension of the Dutch language, as a medium for communicating Christian instruction. But in this and a subsequent communication of the 22nd January, 1692, likewise quoted by Fabricius, he speaks modestly though confidently of the state and prospects of Christianity amongst the Tamils:—"Status ecclesiæ ad huc est talis qualis fuit quando tibi novissime scripsi Malabarici adolescentes in collegio habitantes sunt diligentes egregie proficiunt in lingua Belgica; ita ut spatio unius anni didicerint legere et scribere. Noverunt Christianas orationes et quæstiones ex Borstii libello possunt memoriter recitare, easque ex Belgico sermone in Malabaricum transferre. Cantant etiam Psalmos in nostra ecclesia. Spero Deum deinceps concessurum esse illius gratiam suam et eos impleturum spiritu suo, ut illi adolescentes cum tempore fiant benedicta instrumenta ad propagandum regnum Christi inter hos ethnicos."

(D.)

REGULATION ABOLISHING ROMAN CATHOLIC DISABILITIES.

THE following is the regulation in question, published by the Governor, Sir Thomas Maitland, in 1806:—

REGULATION OF GOVERNMENT.

Present—His Excellency the Governor in Council,

A.D. 1806.

Regulation 4th.—A regulation for taking off the restraints which were imposed upon the Roman Catholics of this island by the late Dutch Government, passed by the Governor in Council on the 27th of May, 1806.

It being His Majesty's most gracious intention that all persons who inhabit the British settlements on this island shall be permitted liberty of conscience and the free exercise of religious worship, provided they can be contented with a quiet and peaceable enjoyment of the same, without giving offence to Government; and it appearing that the Roman Catholics, who are a numerous and peaceable body of His Majesty's subjects, are, by several laws passed under the late Dutch Government, rigorously excluded from many important privileges and capacities; and that, although these laws have not been acted upon in all cases by His Majesty's Government, yet that they are still unrepealed, and a cause of anxiety to those who profess the Catholic religion—

The Governor in Council enacts as follows:—

First.—The Roman Catholics shall be allowed the unmolested profession and exercise of their religion in every part of the British settlements in the island of Ceylon.

Second.—They shall be admitted to all civil privileges and capacities.

Third.—All marriages between Roman Catholics which have taken place within the said settlements since the 26th August, 1795, according to the rites of the Roman Catholic Church, shall be deemed valid in law, although the forms appointed by the late Dutch Government have not been observed.

Fourth.—This regulation shall take effect on the 4th day of June next, that being His Majesty's birth-day.

Fifth.—Every part of any law, proclamation, or order, which contradicts this regulation, is hereby repealed.

By order of the Council,

(Signed) JOHN DEANE,

Secretary to the Council.

Colombo, 27th May, 1806.

(E.)

COLOSSAL STATUE AT THE AUKANE WIHARE.

THE vignette at the head of this chapter represents a remarkable colossal statue of Buddhu, which exists in a secluded portion of the great forest which stretches southward from Dambool in the direction of Kornegalle. A gentleman who had recently traversed it in returning from an elephant hunt came suddenly on this huge relic of antiquity, and at his suggestion I shortly after made a visit to the spot. As usual, a mass of overturned rock has been selected as the site of a temple, which is still occupied by a solitary priest; and close beside his dwelling stands the lonely statue represented in the drawing: it is upwards of 50 feet in height, carved out of the face of the solid stone, and so entirely detached from it, that they are only connected by two small ties of the living stone, which have been left by the artist unhewn, for the purpose of supporting the figure.

The rock is scarped so as to serve as a wall on either side, and there are the remains of hollows at top, which had once sustained the timbers of a roof; but the whole is now open to the sun, and from this circumstance the temple bears the name of the Aukane Wihare. Its construction is of the remotest antiquity, and the priest in charge of it informed us, that solitary and deserted as it seems, it was still visited from time to time by pious strangers, whose sacred books may have made them acquainted with the existence of this gigantic relic in the depths of the forest.

The Banyan Tree—Mount Lavinia.

CHAPTER III.

THE BRITISH PERIOD.

Early Neglect of the Natives — General Relapse into Heathenism — Degraded Character of the "Government Christians"—The Church of England — The Roman Catholic Church and its Progress — The Dutch Reformed Church and its Decline — The Re-establishment of the Protestant Religion amongst the Singhalese — First Arrival of the Missionaries — London Mission, 1804 — Baptists, 1812 — Wesleyan Methodists, 1814 — Church of England Mission, 1818 — The Tamils — The American Missionaries.

CHAPTER III.

THE BRITISH PERIOD.

THERE is something of unusual interest in the period of this inquiry at which we have arrived. Two eras have been reviewed in this brief sketch of the history of Christianity in Ceylon—that of artifice and corrupt inducement practised by the early priesthood of Portugal, and that of alternate bribery and persecution by the clergy of the Church of Holland. We now come to scrutinize the progress made during the third epoch, since the British occupation of the island, when for the first time a legitimate field was offered for the unadorned influence of the Gospel, and a fair and unbiassed trial has been given to the efficacy of truth and simplicity for its inculcation, unaided by the favour and uninfluenced by the frowns of authority.

For some years after the conquest of Ceylon by the British, attention was but sparingly directed to the extension either of Christianity or education amongst the Singhalese and Tamils. Our tenure of the island was uncertain, and our occupation almost provisional, till, by the treaty of Amiens,[1] Ceylon

[1] A.D. 1802.

was definitely attached to the dominions of Great Britain. Four years before, the government of the colony had been confided to the Hon. Mr. North, afterwards Earl of Guilford, who with administrative talents of the highest order combined an enthusiasm in the cause of education, by which at a later period of his life he imperishably associated his name with the regeneration of Greece, as the founder and first Chancellor of the Ionian University.

Mr. North's first efforts as Governor were directed to the promotion of native instruction by reviving and extending the educational system of the Dutch.[1] The tax on the marriages of native Christians was abolished; the Dutch ministers were reinstated in their churches, the use of which, together with the free exercise of their religion, had been carefully stipulated for in the conventions on the capitulation of the various fortresses in Ceylon, and the clergy were invited to itinerate throughout the rural districts at the cost of the Government, for the purpose of keeping alive the knowledge of Christianity amongst the Singhalese. For some years after the British occupation the Presbyterian religion, according to the form of the Church of Holland, was regarded practically as the ecclesiastical establishment of the colony. It was so styled officially by Sir Thomas Maitland in his communications to the Con-

[1] Cordiner's Ceylon, vol. i. p. 160.

sistory of Colombo in 1807;[1] and in 1810 the Earl of Liverpool, then Secretary of State for the Colonies, proposed to reinforce the Dutch clergy by appointments from those ordained by the Church of Scotland, and to receive youths from Ceylon to be educated for the ministry in Edinburgh. It was not till 1816 that the congregations of the Church of England became so numerous that on the suggestion of Sir Robert Brownrigg they were placed under the spiritual superintendence of the see of Calcutta, and an archdeacon appointed to conduct the local administration of the Church in the unavoidable absence of the bishop. But neither this annexation, nor the subsequent erection of Ceylon into a bishopric in 1845, made any fundamental changes in the status and relative rights of the several Christian communities throughout the island, who, both by the statutes and the constitution of the colony, are entitled to equal support and consideration at the hands of the authorities.[2]

The first colonial chaplain of the Church of England was Cordiner (one of the earliest writers on the affairs of Ceylon as a colony of Great Britain), who was appointed in 1797; the number has since been increased to twelve, who, together with the chaplains

[1] Letter of Sir T. Maitland to the Dutch Consistory, 16th January, 1807.

[2] Ordinance of the Ceylon Legislature, No. 1, 1845, to provide for the maintenance of ministers of the Christian religion.

of the churches of Scotland and of Holland, are borne alike on the establishment of the colony. The colonial chaplains, however, have comparatively little practical connexion with the subject now under consideration—the extension of Christianity *amongst the natives*; as the nature of their functions confines them almost exclusively to the towns and forts occupied by Europeans; whilst the more interesting and enterprising duty of carrying education and the Gospel into the Singhalese villages and the seclusion of the jungle has fallen almost exclusively to the lot of the various missionary bodies who have successively settled in the island since 1804.

One of the first acts of Mr. North's government was the revival of the Colombo Academy, a collegiate institution established a century previously by the Dutch, and in which they had trained their native students for the ministry, under the care of their ablest missionaries, Synjen, Kalden, and Wetzelius. Such was the general success of Mr. North's measures that in 1801 the number of schools throughout the colony amounted to 170; and Sir Thomas Maitland, who succeeded him in the Government, exhibited an equal appreciation of the importance of popular instruction, and an equal assiduity in its promotion. He sought the co-operation of the Colombo Consistory for still further restoring the educational institutions and public charities of the Dutch, and he assisted their ministerial labours by the appointment of catechists and proponents. But his operations, like those of his predecessor, were unfortunately circumscribed by the embarrassed state of the colonial finances, from which, by order of the Secretary of State, no larger sum than 1500*l.* per annum was for many years appropriated to the maintenance of native education; a retrenchment the immediate effect of which was to close a multitude of schools which had been opened by Mr. North in all parts of the island.[1]

But we now come to a painful manifestation of the unsubstantial nature of all that had been formerly done by the Dutch in the way of Christian conversion among the natives of Ceylon; evincing at the same time the deep and tenacious attachment of the Singhalese to their own national superstitions. On the arrival of the British, both the Singhalese and Tamils, accustomed as they had been for nearly two centuries to a system of religious compulsion, expected to find on the part of their new masters a continuance of the same rigour which had characterised the ecclesiastical policy of the Dutch. Under this apprehension they prepared themselves to conform implicitly to whatsoever form of Christianity might be prescribed by

[1] In a MS. Autobiography of Christian David, the first Ordained Tamil Minister in Ceylon, deposited in the Diocesan Library in Colombo, he relates that, having been appointed by Mr. North, in 1800, to the superintendence of forty-seven schools in the peninsula of Jaffna, they were all suddenly closed by Sir T. Maitland in 1805, most probably in consequence of the want thus caused of means applicable to their maintenance.

the new Government;[1] and not only did the number of nominal converts exhibit no immediate reduction on the change of rulers, but they were reported in 1801 to have so far exceeded anything ever exhibited by the Dutch, as to amount to no less than 342,000 Protestants, exclusive of a still greater number who professed the Roman Catholic religion. Cordiner, the zealous colonial chaplain, records this agreeable

[1] Buchanan, in his visit to Ceylon in 1806, inquired of the boatman who brought him from Ramisseram, and was one of these "*Government Christians*," what religion the English professed? but he could get no other reply than that "they were neither of the Portuguese nor the Dutch religion."—Christian Researches, p. 184.

The facility with which the Singhalese accommodated themselves in so many instances to the religious predilections of their successive masters, and the anticipations with which they evidently expected a change of the national religion as a necessary sequence of political conquest, is not to be regarded as a manifestation peculiar to the natives of Ceylon, but is more or less a characteristic of Asiatics in general. Territorial conquests in the East have been almost universally followed by the imposition of the religion of the conquerors. There can be little doubt that the establishment of Buddhism itself in Ceylon was the result of a foreign invasion; whilst its extirpation from surrounding localities was equally a consequence of conquest. The records of the Buddhist religion abound with such vicissitudes—with its overthrow by the Brahmanical princes and Mahomedan conquerors of India, and its expulsion from the eastern provinces of Persia, from Affghanistan, Bokhara, and the countries to the north-west —events which led to its extension in the opposite direction, and to its adoption amongst the Tartars and other races to the northward of China, amongst whom it has maintained its ascendancy to the present time.

fact; in the sincerity of his satisfaction over so goodly a retrospect, he looked forward with corresponding confidence to an equally promising future, and declares that the natives of Ceylon were "perfectly free both from bigotry and prejudice: having so long wandered in darkness, they follow gladly the least glimmerings of light; the first openings of religious knowledge are received by them with transport; and they look up with adoration to any one who bestows pains in endeavouring to teach them."[1] This agreeable vision, however, proved as transient as it was unreal; the natives soon came to regard the withdrawal of compulsion to religious conformity only as evidence of religious indifference on the part of their new rulers; and they became still more firmly convinced of the justice of this conclusion on discovering that they were no longer to be *paid* for apostacy, and that a monopoly of offices and public employment was not as theretofore to be jealously preserved for the outward professors of Christianity. Almost with greater rapidity than their numbers had originally increased, they now commenced to decline. In 1802 the nominal Protestant Christians amongst the Tamils of Jaffna were 136,000; in 1806 Buchanan, who then visited Ceylon, described the Protestant religion as *extinct*, the fine old churches in ruins, the clergy who had once ministered in them forgotten, and but one Hindoo catechist in charge of

[1] Cordiner, p. 163, 164.

the province. Vast numbers had openly joined the Roman Catholic communion, to which they had long been secretly attached, and the whole district was handed over to priests from the college of Goa.[1] In the Singhalese districts the decline, though not so instantaneous, was equally deplorable; the 342,000 over whom Cordiner confidingly rejoiced in 1801, had diminished in 1810 to less than half the amount, and numbers of Protestants were every year apostatising to Buddhu.[2]

The rumours of this reaction had not failed to reach England, where they excited anxiety and dissatisfaction; and the Secretary of State, Viscount Castlereagh, so early as 1808, addressed a despatch to Sir Thomas Maitland, to acquaint him with the fact that the measures of his Government had been freely censured for their tendency to discourage the progress of Christianity, and to induce the natives of Ceylon to relapse into paganism.[3] But as the governor had himself represented some time before that the regulation of the Dutch which had rendered

[1] Buchanan's Christian Researches, p. 185. Hough's History of Christianity in India, vol. iv. p. 533.

[2] Hough's History of Christianity in India, vol. iv. pp. 534–538.

[3] In all probability the charges against Sir Thomas Maitland, alluded to in this despatch of Lord Castlereagh, were those which had been published by Buchanan after his visit to Ceylon in 1806, on which occasion he alludes with more than necessary reprehension to what he evidently regarded as the deliberate and culpable neglect of the Government in relation to the religious establishments of the colony.

Christianity an essential qualification for office, had only tended to foster falsehood without diminishing idolatry, Lord Castlereagh afterwards intimated his conviction that the abrogation of the obnoxious rule might have given rise to the current surmises; and he enjoined upon the governor the necessity of devoting every energy to the promotion of education as essential to the extension, if not ultimately identified with the existence, of Christianity itself.

The result of this disheartening demonstration of apostacy throughout Ceylon was not, however, without its uses, and it was, to a certain extent, important in more than one particular. Christian missionaries had already begun to establish themselves in Ceylon; three had arrived in 1804, and at the very outset of their toil they found not only a clear field for their labours, but a striking illustration of the difficulties of their task, and of the hopelessness of attempting anything in mere human strength or in any exclusive reliance upon human devices. The local Government, thus animated by the encouragements of the Secretary of State, and supported by the hearty co-operation of the colonial authorities, addressed itself anxiously to the work of re-establishing Christianity. Proponents were appointed to itinerate the provinces, and baptize the children of the natives; the successive missions of the Wesleyans, the Church of England, and the Baptists were liberally encouraged by the Governor and cordially welcomed by the colonial chaplains and clergy; the Bible Society and the Christian press of India supplied translations of the Scripture and reprints of doctrinal discourses for the use of the Singhalese; education was pressed forward with earnestness and vigour, and such a combination of agencies was speedily brought into action as reason and experience had demonstrated to be most effectual for the diffusion of enlightenment and the inculcation of truth. The success of these renewed efforts was, however, far from satisfactory: the first three missionaries who arrived in 1804 were stationed respectively at Jaffna, Matura, and Galle; but after a patient trial at each place the result was pronounced to be a failure; they succeeded in establishing schools which were but sparingly attended; the Singhalese Christians in the south were represented, after four years' ministration amongst them, to be "worse than the heathen—thousands of them actual worshippers of Buddhu;" and their general estimation of Christianity so low that it was known to the Singhalese only as "*the religion of the East India Company.*" As for the Tamils of the North, after a few years of hopeless exertion, the missionary sent to them was withdrawn; and so universal was their relapse into idolatry, that within a very few years the only Christians who were to be found in the Peninsula were the members of the Church of Rome.[1]

[1] Harvard's History of the Wesleyan Mission in Ceylon,

The causes of this disappointment were, however, to be traced in a great degree to the incautious measures of the Government for arresting this universal degeneracy: measures which, in their practical result, have entailed upon the island an evil which exists to the present time, and one of so much magnitude as still to oppose a serious obstacle to the extension of Christianity.

The proponents appointed by Mr. North and Sir Thomas Maitland proceeded to exercise their functions with a zeal almost untempered by discretion. The administration of baptism was the most prominent, as it appears to have been the most laborious, portion of their duties; and the Singhalese, accustomed for upwards of a century, under the Portuguese and Dutch, to regard baptism as the test and qualification for the enjoyment of numerous civil advantages, still retained the idea that the inheritance of property by their children, as well as other personal privileges, would be contingent on the insertion of their names in the *thombo* or baptismal register of the district. On the periodical visits of the proponent, the *tom-toms* were sounded throughout

Introd., p. lxviii.—Tracy's History of the American Board of Commissioners for Foreign Missions, c. viii. p. 61. One incident of this period, which caused some scandal, was the sale by the Government, in 1805, of the ruined church of Point Pedro, which had been erected by Baldæus. It was bought by a Hindoo, and pulled down to employ the materials in the erection of a Brahmanical temple.

the villages, the children were brought in crowds to be baptized, and the ceremony was performed in many instances by arranging them in rows, the proponent, as he passed along, sprinkling their faces with water, and repeating the formula of the rite. The Singhalese term for this operation was *Christiani-karenewa*, or "Christian making;" but it was far from being regarded as anything solemn or religious. It had been declared *honourable* by the Portuguese to undergo such a ceremony; it had been rendered *profitable* by the Dutch; and, after three hundred years' familiarity with the process, the natives were unable to divest themselves of the belief that submission to the ceremony was enjoined by orders from the Civil Government. Of baptism itself they had no other conception than some civil distinction which it was supposed to confer, and to the present day the Singhalese term for the ceremony bears the literal interpretation of "*admission to rank.*"[1] If two Buddhists quarrel, it is no unusual term of reproach to apply the epithet of an "*unbaptized wretch*;"[2] and when a parent upbraids his child in anger, he sometimes threatens to disinherit him, by saying he will "blot out his baptism from the thombo."

Even to the present day a native child cannot be legally registered without previous baptism by a Christian minister, and the practice of the missionaries (with the exception of the Baptists) serves to

[1] Kula-wadenawa. [2] To-gintu-gua.

perpetuate the evil, as they refuse to solemnize the marriages of individuals unbaptized.[1]

Prodigious numbers of nominal Christians who have been thus enrolled, designate themselves "Christian Buddhists," or "Government Christians," and with scarcely an exception they are either heathens or sceptics.[2] There are large districts in which it would be difficult to discover an unbaptized Singhalese, and yet in the midst of these the religion of Buddhu flourishes, and priests and temples abound. The majority ostensibly profess Christianity, but support all the ceremonies of their own national idolatry, and more or less openly frequent the temples, and make votive offerings to the idol. The rest are alternately Christians or infidels, as occasion may render it expedient to appear; and in point of character and conduct they are notoriously the most abandoned and reckless class of the community. But in speaking of these classes under the designation

[1] "The dexterity of the natives in overcoming difficulties in this respect is amusing. A man in Malwana, being alarmed during an attack of sickness that he should die before his son and heir could be baptized, sent for his brother, who, instead of carrying the child all the way to Colombo, *borrowed an infant in the town*, and had it baptized and registered by a Wesleyan minister in the name of the absent child, who was at home. In this way the same infant has been frequently baptized many times."—MS. Notes by the Rev. J. Davies, Baptist Missionary, Ceylon.

[2] "When we ask the people their religion, the common reply is, We are of the Government religion."—Ibid.

of Christians, a wide line of distinction is to be drawn between them and the missionary converts, whose adhesion to Christianity, however imperfect may be their inward convictions, is at least an act of premeditation, and ensures a certain degree of circumspection in demeanour; whilst no similar obligation is felt to be incumbent upon those whose nominal addiction to Christianity is merely the result of an accident.

It will readily be imagined that the existence of such a body, at once so numerous and so regardless, must be highly prejudicial to the extension of genuine Christianity; and every individual who has had personal experience of its effects has borne his testimony to the fact that nothing has so effectually deterred the Singhalese in their first approaches to the truth as the apprehension of being identified by their conversion with a class whose reputation and whose practice are alike an outrage on the religion in which they were born, and an insult to that which they profess to have adopted.

THE ROMAN CATHOLIC RELIGION, under the British administration, has maintained the same ascendancy, and exhibited the same energy, which it had previously manifested throughout the patronage of the Portuguese and the proscriptions of the Dutch; and, at the present day, its members form by far the most numerous community of Christians in Ceylon. In the maritime provinces they were permitted an unrestricted liberty of worship by the proclamation of 1806; and although the political state of the country, for some years after the acquisition of the Kandyan kingdom, rendered it expedient to impose certain restraints on the visits of their priests to the interior, these were enforced exclusively with a view to their personal safety, and they, as well as every civil disability, were abolished by the Act for the relief of Roman Catholics in 1829. Since that period, the exertions of their clergy have been perseveringly directed to the conversion of the Kandyans; but their success has been much less signal than amongst the low country Singhalese and the Tamils—a circumstance ascribable not only to the stronger influence of Buddhism, cherished as it was by the Kandyan kings, but to the greater ascendancy of caste, and the difficulty of reaching the people except through the instrumentality of their chiefs. The Singhalese of the coast have proved more tractable converts, from the circumstance that their longer association with Europeans has, to a great extent, broken down this brrier of caste; but in the Kandyan mountains the system flourishes in ranker luxuriance, under the conjoint influence of the Buddhist priest and the headman.

Caste in Ceylon is a conventional discrimination of rank,[1] not a religious separation of race, such

[1] Caste, as it exists at the present day amongst the Buddhists of Ceylon, is purely a social distinction, and entirely disconnected with any sanction or pretensions derivable from their system of

as exists amongst the Hindoos on the continent of India; and the enforcement of these distinctions is essential for supporting the pretensions and dignity

religion. Nor is evidence wanting that even at a comparatively modern period such was equally its aspect amongst the natives throughout the continent of India, by whom caste was regarded not as a sacred, but a secular discrimination of ranks. The earliest notices of India by the Greek historians and geographers enumerate the division of the people into Brahmans, Kshatryas, Vaisyas, and Sudras; but this was a classification which applied equally to the followers of Buddhu and of Brahma; nor were the members of either section held ineligible for the offices of the priesthood. Arrian, when he names the class of Brahmans at all, refers to them not as an order of priests, but as the bearers of arms and defenders of fortresses against the assaults of Alexander; and his description is more applicable to caste as it exists under Buddhism than to its development at the present day in the Brahmanical system. Strabo describes the Brahmans as eating indiscriminately with other castes, and Fa Hian recounts their conduct as merchants and seamen—practices and pursuits utterly at variance with the sacred character which they now arrogate, and reconcilable only on the conclusion that caste, even so lately as the fifth century of our era, was a secular arrangement, the exclusive claim to which has been subsequently arrogated by the Hindoo priesthood; in proof of which it may be cited that Fa Hian and the other Chinese travellers of the fifth and seventh centuries commemorate their intercourse with Hindoos of every caste, including *Brahmans who were Buddhists*:—"D'après le récit de Shakya, le peuple Indien était divisé en cinq castes. La première comprenait les guerriers; la seconde, les suppresseurs des crimes, ou les Brahmanes; la troisième, les ouvriers et les commerçants; la quatrième, les chasseurs et les bergers; *la cinquième, les prêtres* et les *ascètes*. Il n'est point ici question des Brahmanes comme caste religieuse—tout au contraire: *la cinquième caste, loin d'être exclusive, était composée d'individus sortis des quatres autres castes.*"—Maupied, Essai sur l'Origine des Principaux Peuples Anciens, c. viii. p. 193. For

of the hill chiefs. Hence, although the authority of the priesthood could at any time be exerted to discourage it, as opposed to the principles of their faith, the alliance between them and the chiefs, in relation to this question, has at all times been maintained for mutual advantage; the priests upholding the social ascendancy of the headmen, and the headmen, in return, protecting the Buddhist religion from the encroachments of Christianity. Were Buddhism and its worship to decline, the priests would have reason to apprehend the reversion to the Crown of the lands formerly granted for the maintenance of the temples, to the possession of which their personal influence is, in a great degree to be ascribed; whilst the chiefs, on the other hand, deprived of the support and co-operation of the priesthood, might equally despair to re-establish their feudal supremacy over the Kandyan people. A Kandyan, upwards of seventy years old, when recently pressed by a Roman Catholic clergyman to declare openly his conviction of the truth of Christianity, which he had already privately avowed, declined resolutely to do so. "I admire your religion," said he, "and believe in its reality; but before I embrace openly its doctrines, *you must first effect the conversion of the chief*: and I promise that not only I, but

an account of the changes in the system of caste in India, and the supersession of the inferior ranks by the encroachments of the Brahmans, see Mountstuart Elphinstone, Hist. India, vol. i. b. ii. c. 1.

my household and followers, will then adopt your belief, so soon as you are prepared to assure us of his previous sanction and example."[1]

Apart from the authority thus assumed by the headmen and priests, and which, it will be perceived, is entirely a feudal and not a religious obligation, the Roman Catholic clergy profess to have encountered little real opposition from the actual influence of heathenism, and still less from Buddhism than from the more enslaving superstitions of Brahma. In common with the ministers of almost all Protestant churches, they complain that the obstacle they have had to encounter arises from *apathy* on the part of the Singhalese, which no excitement can arouse, and a listlessness and indifference which no apprehension can excite; and however reluctant to avow their obligations to the efficacy of processions and ceremonial display, the experience of the Roman Catholic clergy has demonstrated that it is only by the influence of such expedients that they have been enabled to arrest the attention of the natives, and acquire the first accession of converts to their church.

In furtherance of this policy, every facility has been afforded by the genius and coincidences of Buddhism itself; not only in the familiarity of its votaries with the accustomed range of devices common to all communities, whether Christian or

[1] MS. Statement from the Roman Catholic Bishop of Usula, Vicar Apostolic of Ceylon.

heathen, which address themselves to the imagination through the avenue of the senses, but likewise in the similarity of the tenets, which are characteristic of the respective observances of each. Buddhism, like the ceremonial of the Church of Rome, has to some extent its pageantry and decorations, its festivals and its fireworks, its processions, its perfumes, its images, its exhibition of relics, its sacred vestments, and its treasures of "barbaric pearl and gold." It has its holy places and its pilgrimages in prosperity and health, and its votive offerings in calamity and disease. The priests of both are devoted to celibacy and poverty, to mortification and privation. Each worship has its prostrations and genuflexions, its repetitions and invocations, in an ancient, and to the multitude an unintelligible tongue; and the purgatory of the one has its counterpart in the transmigrations of the other. Both have their legends and their miracles; their confidence in charms, and in the assistance of guardian saints and protectors: and in the general aspect of their outward observances, not less than in the concurrence of many of their leading beliefs, it is with the least conceivable violence to established customs, and the slightest apparent disturbance of preconceived ideas, that the Buddhist finds himself at liberty to venture on the transition from his own faith to that of his new advisers.

One remarkable circumstance, too, is observable in their converts, however meagre may be their acquaintance with Christianity—that the number of nominal Christians who still adhere in secret to the rites and tenets of Buddhism, is infinitely smaller amongst the Roman Catholics than amongst the professors of any other church in Ceylon; an incident which has been ascribed to the overruling influence of the Confessional, and the unintermitted control which it exerts over the feelings as well as the actions of its votaries. In fact, if any evidence were wanting to substantiate the real ascendancy thus acquired and maintained by the Church of Rome, it would be found in the munificence with which the natives contribute habitually for its support, and the liberality which they have manifested in the erection of costly chapels and highly decorated altars for its worship.[1] It is due, likewise, to its priesthood to declare, that whatever may be their individual feelings towards Protestantism and its agents, they have carried on their operations in Ceylon with an absence of active jealousy, and an abstinence from any direct interference with the ministrations of the clergy of other denominations, who have chosen the same sphere of labour with themselves. They acquiesced, at an early period, in the free circulation of the Scriptures amongst their disciples;[2] they mani-

[1] For the present condition of the Roman Catholic religion in Ceylon, as regards its schools and congregations, see Note A at the end of this chapter.

[2] Hough's History of Christianity in India, vol. iv. b. xii. c. iv. p. 546.

fested no opposition to the religious instruction communicated to the native pupils in other schools; and Harvard, himself a Protestant missionary, has borne his willing testimony to the sincerity and demeanour of the Roman Catholic converts; whom he describes "as more detached from the customs of paganism, more regular in their attendance on the religious services of Christianity, and in their general conduct more consistent with the moral precepts of the Gospel, than any other religious body of any magnitude in Ceylon."[1] However merited may have been this testimony of Mr. Harvard, or however truthful as regarded the comparative claims of the several Christian communities at the time when it was written, the thirty years which have since elapsed have so far altered their relative aspects, that the converts of the Roman Catholic church may fairly rest their moral reputation on their own merits, without being indebted to a comparison invidiously instituted with those of others, who, in point of conduct and Christian bearing, exhibit no evidences of inferiority. It is true that the use of the Bible is not openly prohibited to their flocks; but as yet no effort has been made by the Roman Catholics to supply the Singhalese with a version in the language of the island; and I have learned, with some regret, that within a very recent period the disposition to

[1] Harvard's Narrative of the Wesleyan Mission in Ceylon, Introd., p. lxvii.

non-interference so highly commended on the part of their priesthood, has not been altogether without exceptions. It is just to them to state, at the same time, that the instances which have reached me of a contrary indication, bear less the character of opposition to the measures of others, than of vigilance to protect their own converts from intrusion; nor should it be a matter of surprise, if, in places where the Roman Catholics have established schools for the education of their flocks, they should exert every legitimate influence to induce the attendance of their children at their own, in preference to resorting to similar institutions maintained by Protestant clergy.

Unhappily the field for exertion in Ceylon, a vast expanse of which is yet untouched and unbroken, is sufficiently wide to enable each Church to choose an area for its own toils, without interfering with the labours or the success of others; and the familiarizing of the heathen, however imperfectly, with the name and aspect of Christianity, even in its least purified form, cannot be otherwise regarded than as an advance into the hitherto undisputed dominion of idolatry, and a lodgment preparatory to its eventual conquest.[1] Even as an agent of social progress its importance is self-apparent; and however superficial may be their religious convictions

[1] MS. Notes on the Church of England Missions among the Cingalese. By the Rev. A. D. Gordon.

on the part of the great mass of the population, there are to be found, amongst the Roman Catholic Singhalese, men whose morality is as undoubted as their attachment to the forms of the adopted religion is sincere, and whose conduct and demeanour as Christians are as consistent and becoming as those of any other sect in Ceylon. This is not the less true or important notwithstanding the admitted fact, that the ignorance of the vast majority is still crass and unenlightened; and if so much can be effected even by a perverted form of Christianity, the prospect of ultimate triumph is rendered the more bright and encouraging through the instrumentality of a purer faith operating under circumstances at least equally favourable.[1]

The decline of the DUTCH REFORMED CHURCH, since the British occupation of Ceylon, has been gradual, but uniform. At no time had it attained any ascendancy over the Singhalese: it exhibited externally none of "the poetry of Popery;" and whilst the imagination of the natives was unattracted by the stern simplicity of its exterior, their minds were unprepared to be influenced by the truths and abstract principles of its doctrine.[2]

[1] See Note B, end of this chapter.

[2] It is to the labours of the Dutch missionaries in Ceylon, and the anxiety felt in Europe for their success, that the world is indebted for the treatise of Grotius *De Veritate Religionis Christianæ.* It was undertaken at the solicitation of the clergy

On the retirement of the Dutch authorities to Java after the capitulation of Colombo, many of the clergy, and all those of the opulent classes who were in a condition to emigrate, followed the fortunes of the Government, and along with them, took their departure for Batavia. Those who remained, assembled as usual in the fine old churches, the possession of which had been secured to them by treaty, and the Government for a time took on itself the charge of defraying the salaries and other expenses of the ministry. The subsequent fortunes of the Dutch Church, however, and the adverse influences by which it was surrounded, were unfavourable to the continuance even of its diminished prosperity. It was no longer the exclusive religion of the State; the most influential and wealthy of its community had departed; and in comparative poverty and neglect it had to maintain an unequal struggle with the rising pretensions of the Church of England, whose clergy had been appointed as chaplains to the British authorities and the military, and a still more disastrous contest with the Church of Rome, by whose priesthood the Dutch converts were drawn off in prodigious numbers.[1]

of Holland, and was originally intended as a handbook for heathen missions, and for the use of the seamen embarked in the expeditions to India and the East.

[1] In 1798 the Consistory of Colombo earnestly besought the governor to take effectual measures to secure the congregations

After the landing of the English the officiation of the Dutch clergymen had been altogether withdrawn from the outstations and the natives, and confined almost exclusively to the several congregations within the forts of Colombo, Matura, and Galle. But in a very short period their ministrations were still further contracted even here: Galle and Matura ceased to be provided with resident clergy of their own persuasion; the use of the Dutch churches was liberally granted by the Consistories to the chaplains of the Church of England; and only once or twice in each year the Dutch clergy of Colombo made periodical visitations for the administration of the sacrament. This decline was, however, in no degree to be attributed either to any hostile influence of the Government or any failure to perform its engagements to the Dutch; and the *Classis* of Colombo, in its assembly in 1805, at the very time when serious apprehensions were expressed that the Dutch communion would be speedily extinct in Ceylon, recorded in the archives of Wolfendahl that "everything connected with their religion had, by the favour and protection of the British, stood and continued in the same order as under the Netherlands Government."[1] Their own clergy were, however, old and infirm, and

from the influence of the Roman Catholics; and proponents were appointed and paid by the British Government with this express view, to officiate at Negombo, Chilaw, and Calpentyn.

[1] Records of the Consistory of Colombo, 1805.

no possibility was apparent of procuring others from Holland.

In 1813, so extensive had been the decline of Christianity, not only as regarded the professing members of the Reformed Church of Holland, but amongst those attached to every other Protestant community in Ceylon, that the entire ecclesiastical establishment of the Colony consisted of but three chaplains of the Church of England, two German Presbyterians, of whom one was stationed at Colombo and the other at Galle, and about half a dozen Proponents—a clerical officer peculiar to the Church of Holland, with functions intermediate between those of a catechist or deacon of the Church of England and those of a probationer or licentiate of the Church of Scotland.[1]

[1] On the first occupation of Colombo, and for several years afterwards, the Church of England service for the troops was celebrated in the church of the Dutch Presbyterians at Wolfendahl; and, about the year 1800, so liberal were the views of the Consistory in such matters, that they acquiesced in the appointment of a proponent, under the direction of the Church of England chaplains, to officiate to that portion of the congregation who were already exhibiting an inclination to exchange the Presbyterian for the Episcopalian discipline. This friendly arrangement continued uninterrupted down to 1815, when a large number of the Singhalese and Tamils having openly attached themselves to the English communion, two churches were expressly erected for their accommodation, and the building at Wolfendahl again reverted to the exclusive use of the Dutch Presbyterians. From that period till very recently the most

At the present moment there are but two clergymen of the Church of Holland in Ceylon; and of the many thousands of Singhalese and Tamils who, fifty years ago, formed the strength of the Dutch communion in the island, barely a remnant are now ostensibly attached to its worship. It may be remarked, too, as an illustration of the confused and imperfect idea formed by the Singhalese of the differences in discipline or doctrines between Protestant sects, that numbers of those who consider themselves bound to attend the ministrations of the Episcopal chaplains paid by the Government, cannot yet divest themselves of the idea that they still belong to the "Hollandish Church."[1] The congregations which still attend the ministrations of the Dutch clergy, are the direct descendants of the old Dutch inhabitants; but their dialect has been gradually exchanged for that of the English and Portuguese; and at this moment there are not above fifty individuals in Colombo who can understand the language in which Christianity was preached to their forefathers by Wetzelius and Baldæus, though still

cordial understanding has been maintained between the clergy of the two establishments, and the buildings of the Dutch have on all occasions been lent without hesitation for the officiation of the Episcopal chaplains.

[1] "*Landse Pallya.*" Landse, the term frequently applied by the Singhalese to anything English or European, is a corruption of *Hollandische*, Dutch.

warmly attached to the Presbyterian worship and discipline. It is not altogether improbable that before many more years shall have elapsed the Dutch service will have ceased, and that its Consistory and members may invite their future ministers from the kindred Church of Scotland, between whom and the Church of Holland there exists little other distinction than the difference of a name.

Such an incorporation would present fewer difficulties than any attempt to supersede the Dutch church by another Presbyterian establishment. Its constitution, already well defined by the laws of Holland, has been recognised by the British Government in other colonies besides Ceylon, and here its doctrines and its discipline have been familiar to the people for upwards of two hundred years. Nor is it likely that the several sections of the Presbyterian church at home, however they might stand aloof from each other, would withhold their assistance, or abstain from ordaining ministers for perpetuating the Presbyterian constitution of the church in Ceylon; which might be regarded by them as neutral ground, inasmuch as it presents peculiarities more or less differing from them all.

Such a proposal would likewise recommend itself to the Singhalese congregations upon other considerations. In many particulars the reformed religion of Holland agrees with the other forms of Christianity in the island, both Roman Catholic and Anglican;

for example, in the celebration of festivals, such as Easter and Christmas, which are not observed by the Church of Scotland, but to which the inhabitants of the colony have been so long accustomed that their discontinuance, to those unacquainted with the argument, would wear the appearance of regardlessness and indifference unfavourable to the influence of a church established in a community so circumstanced. Again, the Church of Holland agrees with the Episcopal churches in the use of a prescribed form of liturgy used by the officiating minister on sacramental occasions. The utility of such a handbook of devotion can hardly be called in question, even by the advocates of extempore worship, in a colony circumstanced like Ceylon, where exhaustion must more or less detract from the fervour of exhortation; and its necessity appears to have already occurred to the authorities at home, as the General Assembly of the Church of Scotland is now taking steps for providing an authorized form of prayer for the members of their own communion in the colonies and remote districts of Great Britain.

But in addition to these considerations, arising out of the constitution of the allied churches, there is another which points forcibly to the propriety of maintaining the Dutch establishment. The Dutch, unlike the English in Ceylon, were essentially colonists in the true sense of the term, whilst the British have at all times been mere sojourners in the island.

The result is, that at the present moment the members of the Reformed Church so far outnumber those of the Scotch Presbyterians, that the latter may, perhaps, be 40 or 50 in Colombo, whilst the Dutch descendants and other Burghers who frequent the Wolfendahl Church are little short of 2000. By such an alliance as I have here suggested, the anomaly would be removed of a highly paid Chaplain officiating exclusively for the former, whilst the spiritual wants of the vast majority are now imperfectly tended by one Dutch clergyman on a very inferior income from the colony; and the fusion of the congregations, whilst it would equalize the labours would add to the usefulness and efficiency of the ministers of each.

With this hasty notice of the ecclesiastical establishments of Ceylon, and of those sections of the clergy who administer more especially to the spiritual wants of the European community, I return to the consideration of the *re-establishment of Christianity among the natives*, and the labours and success of the several missions for its extension amongst the Singhalese and Tamil population. So rapid was the decline of the Christian religion throughout the colony during the period immediately subsequent to the retirement of the Dutch, and so extensive its corruption where it had not actually disappeared, that on the first arrival of the several missionaries of the Baptists, the Wesleyans, the Americans, and the Church of England, between the years 1812 and 1818, the Protestant form of Christianity, and certainly its purity and influence, might be considered almost extinct. The work of conversion was literally to be commenced afresh in many districts, and throughout the island generally, wherever this was to be attempted, a new agency and system were to be introduced, differing in every essential and particular from that resorted to by the clergy of Portugal and Holland. The first missionaries who arrived in Ceylon after its occupation by the English were the three Germans, sent out in 1804 by the London Missionary Society, the imperfect success of whose labours has been already alluded to.[1] These were followed in 1812 by a deputation from the eminent establishment of the Baptists at Serampore; and two years later, by the Wesleyans, led by the lamented Dr. Coke, who expired on the voyage, when within a few days' sail of his destination. To these were added, in 1818, four ordained missionaries of the Church of England. All were welcomed and encouraged by the colonial authorities, and by a mutual agreement the various districts of the island were appropriated by each as the future scene of their labours.

In relating the result of their exertions, and the salutary influence which they have since exercised

[1] See ante, p. 84.

over the civilization and moral condition of the Singhalese and Tamils, it will be more convenient to consider separately their respective operations amongst the Hindoos of the Northern Province and amongst the Buddhist population of the rest of the island, in order to exhibit not merely the distinct nature of the superstitions with which they had severally to contend, but the distinct results of their toils for the conversion and amelioration of each district.

In pursuance of this arrangement, it will be expedient to turn, in the first instance, to the peninsula of Jaffna, in which the two ministers of the Wesleyan mission had established themselves in 1814; and whither they were followed two years later by the American missionaries, and in 1818 by a clergyman of the Church of England. From that time to the present the most intimate understanding and the most cordial co-operation have subsisted between these several bodies; and the largest attainable success has been attendant on their conjoint operations. But whilst the means at the disposal both of the Wesleyans and the Church of England have been circumscribed, from the fact of their being but detachments of a body who have still more extensive establishments in the Singhalese districts, the Americans concentrating all their numbers and force at the one point on which they had established themselves, have conducted their proceedings on a system much more striking in its results, but not less sound and effectual in its working than that of their colleagues and fellow-labourers in the same field. In religion the members of the American mission are selected indifferently from the Congregationalists and Presbyterians, associated with laymen as physicians and conductors of the press, and the whole acting under the instructions of one of the most remarkable associations for the dissemination of Christianity that has existed since the time of the Reformation, 'The American Board of Commissioners for Foreign Missions,' which has its head-quarters at Boston, in Massachusetts.

The first successful settlers in the portion of North America now known as the New England States, were essentially a colony of missionaries,[1] who, having fled to Holland to escape the religious coercion of Elizabeth, emigrated thence to North America in the reign of James I.: where in after years their numbers were reinforced by those whom the intolerant policy of the Stuarts had driven to seek liberty of conscience in the New World. The Charter of James to the "*Plymouth Company*" especially recites that one of its principal objects was the extension of Christianity to the Indians. The Charter of Charles to the "adventurers" associated for planting the province of Massachusetts professes that the design of the king and the colonists is the

[1] See Robertson's America, b. x.

conversion of the natives to the true faith; and the seal of the Company bore the device of a North American Indian, the motto being taken from the cry of the Macedonian in the vision of St. Paul, "*come over and help us.*"

These "pilgrim-fathers" were the first pioneers of the Protestant world, and the first heralds of the reformed religion to the heathen of foreign lands. Their mission is more ancient than the Propaganda of Rome, and it preceded by nearly a century any other missionary association in Europe. It was encouraged by Cromwell and incorporated by Charles II.; and Cotton Mather records that it was the example of the New England fathers and their success amongst the Indians that first aroused the energy of the Dutch for the conversion of the natives of Ceylon.

By degrees a great people grew out of the humble New England missionaries; but they do not appear at any time to have lost sight of the grand object to the prosecution of which they were indebted for their origin. Their labour amongst the Indians extended along the vast continent of North America from Georgia to Canada, and, wisely combining the theory and example of social improvement with the preaching of the Christian religion, they introduced everywhere secular learning and instructions in agriculture and the useful arts in connexion with the teaching of Christianity. The result was signally successful.

The Indians of North America have been eminently distinguished for their readiness to perceive and admit the value of Christianity and civilization; and amongst no other heathens of modern times has the Gospel had such early and decided success, and no other savages have so readily thrown aside their barbarism and become civilized men.[1]

Encouraged by this success in the Western hemisphere, the missionaries of New England next turned their attention to the East, and in 1812, under an Act of Incorporation from the commonwealth of Massachusetts, they commenced those missionary operations in the Old World which have since been extended over Turkey and Greece, Syria, Persia, India, Siam, the islands of the Pacific, and the continent of Africa.

Their first missionaries to India in 1812 were ordered by the Governor-General to leave Calcutta by the same vessel in which they had arrived;[2] and one of them on his return having accidentally landed in Ceylon, was so struck with the opening which it presented for missionary enterprise, and so strongly encouraged by the Governor, Sir Robert Brownrigg, to undertake it, that, in consequence of his representations to the American Board, a Company was sent out in 1816, consisting of three clergymen and

[1] Tracy's History of the American Board of Commissioners for Foreign Missions, p. 20.

[2] Hough's History of Christianity, vol. iv. b. xii. c. iii. p. 512.

their wives, who proceeded to take up their residence at Jaffna, which has since been uninterruptedly the scene of their remarkable and useful labours. Four additional colleagues arrived in 1819, six were added in 1834, and notwithstanding absences, deaths, and removal, the strength of the establishment for many years has been from seven* to eleven ordained ministers, with a physician and other lay officers.

The old chapels and ecclesiastical buildings of the Portuguese and Dutch now rose into unexpected importance, and were assigned by the Government to the Americans, as well as to the Wesleyan and Church of England missionaries, for churches and schools.

In 1820 the success of the American mission in these conjoint objects had been already so decided that it became necessary to form a printing establishment for the supply of the books and translations required for the use of their schools; but by some singular misconception on the part of the Governor, Sir Edward Barnes, the mission was uncourteously refused the permission to use their own types; and the printer, who had actually arrived from America, was ordered within three months to take his departure from Ceylon. The printing-presses were handed over to the missionaries of the Church of England, and for several years afterwards the liberty to use them was withheld from the Americans. This unwise decision was ultimately rescinded by Sir R. W. Horton in 1832; a printing establishment was organized by the mission at Manepy, and from that single institution there have since been issued no less than one hundred and thirty million pages of instruction and enlightenment in English and Tamil for the natives of Ceylon.[1]

From the commencement of their labours no difference of opinion appears to have prevailed amongst the three religious bodies in the north of Ceylon, who had thus undertaken the work of elevating the religion of Christ above the superstition

[1] This was unfortunately only a solitary example of the innumerable impediments against which these zealous philanthropists had to contend in the earlier stages of their undertaking. Death made many vacancies in their little band: pecuniary resources from the United States were occasionally so circumscribed as to compel the reduction of their establishments and the abandonment of schools in the plenitude of their usefulness; and, even when funds were available, there was no regular means for their remittance to a place so remote as Jaffna, to which the transport of specie was dangerous and uncertain, and where there were neither bankers nor merchants through whom to negotiate bills. The indefatigable missionaries, however, struggled boldly with every difficulty, and at length established themselves so thoroughly in the good-will of the natives, and so effectually conciliated the confidence of the colonial Government, that for many years past their operations have gone on without interruption; their expenditure in Ceylon alone has been upwards of 110,000*l.*, irrespective of the large sums devoted to other countries throughout the East.—Tracy's History, p. 89. In addition to this, the Mission have expended, on behalf of the American Bible and Tract Societies, nearly 10,000*l.*

of Brahma. And forewarned by the monstrous deceptions which had been so long and so successfully practised on their predecessors, those who now renewed the attempt to convert the Tamils to Christianity prepared to proceed by a sounder agency and on a more certain foundation than that which had proved so delusive to the Dutch. They had before them the illustration, too recent to be disregarded, of the pliant acquiescence with which the Tamils had so lately accommodated themselves to the wishes and doctrines of their teachers, and exhibited a dishonest conformity in the absence of all real conviction. They had the warning derivable from their sudden apostacy that no credence was to be attached to the sincerity of such multitudinous conversions, the result of no mental exercitation, and the origin of no moral improvement. They had in the experience of others the painful but well-ascertained conviction that it must be a sacrifice of no ordinary magnitude for the Hindoo to exchange for the pure and self-denying morals of Christianity the sensualities of a superstition which extends an indulgence to every passion, and not only sanctions but sanctifies licentiousness. Above all, they had daily and hourly before their eyes the dread spectacle of that formidable superstition which they came to overthrow, but which still enchained with a superhuman tenacity the imagination and intellects of its votaries.

NOTES TO CHAPTER III.

(A.)

PRESENT STATE OF THE ROMAN CATHOLIC CHURCH IN CEYLON.

THE present condition of the Roman Catholic Church in Ceylon, as detailed in a communication made to me by the Right Rev. Caetano Antonio, the Roman Catholic Bishop of Colombo, is as follows:—The island is divided into two sees—that of the north, which includes the Tamil districts of Jaffna and Trincomalie, and that of the south, which comprises the Singhalese population of the island. The number of ordained clergy is thirty-three, assisted by upwards of five hundred Catechists and spiritual teachers, chiefly Singhalese and Tamils, with a small proportion of the European descendants. Their system combines secular education with religious instruction, and their schools are to be found in all parts of the island wherever their chapels have been opened. They have upwards of three hundred churches throughout Ceylon, and 116,000 persons are enrolled as members of their several congregations. Of these, the Singhalese proportion is 83,561, the Tamils 31,952; the remaining 1141 are burghers and Europeans, and their ranks are said to be daily increased by the accession of fresh converts from the heathen. From another source I have heard that their schools in the present year (1849) are forty-six in number, and upwards of two thousand pupils are said to be in regular attendance, one-half of whom are Tamils; but I have reason to fear that the quality of the education is much more meagre and imperfect than in the institutions of other churches. This may be a result of operations so extended as to outstrip the means disposable for their effectual superintendence; but so far as my own observation assists, and it is confirmed by that of others, the scholars of the Roman Catholics exhibit much less diversity of information and less proficiency in that professed to be communicated than I have found in the pupils of similar institutions in Ceylon. Their schools are more numerous in proportion in the Tamil districts of the north than amongst the Singhalese population in the southern provinces of the island.

(B.)

THE ROMAN CATHOLIC CLERGY AND THEIR POLICY.

THE view which I have endeavoured to give of the general operations of the Roman Catholics in Ceylon, and of the results by which they are characterized, is deduced not from any individual representation, but as the conclusion derivable from a comparison of testimony drawn from numerous sources, and confirmed by my own experience and observation. At the same time it is right I should state, in alluding to their position in relation to the clergy of other sects, and the extent of opposition exhibited by them, that I have received from one quarter in which the Protestant missionaries appear, more than any other in the island, to have come into direct collision with the Roman Catholics, a much more intense description of the nature of their hostility and of the benighted condition of their flocks, than I have discovered in the representations of others from whom I have equally sought for information on the subject. I allude to the Baptist missionaries who, in their labours throughout the secluded villages in the western province, have come much into contact with the Roman Catholic priesthood and their agents. They describe the Singhalese Roman Catholics as, of all classes of the natives, the most superstitious, and sunk in ignorance even below the heathen who surround them—the use of the Protestant Scriptures virtually excluded, and no effort made to supply the want by any translation of the Roman Catholic version—no books or tracts on Christianity in circulation amongst them—their schools few and inefficient—of the great mass of the adult population a smaller proportion of Roman Catholics able to read than of any other religious community in the island—and, in short, all the public operations of the priesthood apparently directed on the principle that the less religion is understood, the more it is likely to become reverenced and feared. The authority of the priests over their congregations is described as supreme; their denunciation of heretics unqualified, and the constraint placed upon their own flocks to protect them from the contact of the Protestant missionaries so extreme, as to amount to personal violence; and, in the event of conversions to any other form of Christianity, a Catholic who would venture to renounce his religion would draw down on himself a vengeful persecution unknown to any other class, unless perhaps the Hindoos and Brahmans.—MS. Notes of the Rev. J. Davies, Baptist Missionary, Ceylon.

Entrance to a Hindoo Temple—Colombo.

CHAPTER IV.

THE BRAHMANICAL SYSTEM.

Its Vastness, Mystery, and Power — Its Sacred Books — Its Grand Supports, Caste and Science — Hindoo Mythology — Hopeless Ritual — Worship of Shiva — False Physical Philosophy — Effects of Education by the Missionaries — Boarding Schools and Colleges — Female Seminaries — and their singular Success — Social Elevation of the Tamils — General Results.

CHAPTER IV.

THE BRAHMANICAL SYSTEM.

THE BRAHMANICAL SYSTEM, as that against which the powers and energies of Christianity have been marshalled, has something so stupendous in its dim and undiscovered dimensions, so appalling in the boundless profundity of its dismal dominion, that, viewed from a distance, the boldest may halt in apprehension and the most far seeing pause in dismay. It is not alone the influence of the unnumbered myriads who have passed beneath its gloomy sway, during ages the most remote, nor is it the strength of the multitudes who still prostrate themselves, not humbly but proudly, before that awful despotism which leads captive the body through the corruption of the soul—it is not these alone that alarm the bravest and cause the most confident to quail. Whilst its proportions are so vast as to defy all survey, so unascertained that their outline melts away into mystery and darkness, all that is partially visible appears so compactly consolidated, so formidably sustaining and sustained, that the minutest outwork to be invested seems to summon and concentrate to its defence the same awful authority and mysterious power which govern and support the gigantic mass that towers above it. There is no section, no fragment of this prodigious structure that has not an assigned position and identification with the whole—not the most trivial act of its humblest defender and slave that is not preordained and prescribed, performed and recognized under divine and infallible authority, as a portion of that stupendous system which has been reared and supported by its own intimate intertexture, and rendered apparently impregnable by the fitness, the combination, the harmony and impenetrable union of its parts and members.

Such is the outward aspect of the Brahmanical system to those who come from enlightened lands to gaze in painful astonishment on this colossal structure of idolatrous barbarism; and such, strange to say, undiminished in magnitude and power, does it still present itself to the eyes of the millions who from youth to age have bowed before it, and worshipped, as the embodiment of all earthly wisdom and the perfection of all heavenly science.

The difficulty of effectually assailing the Brahmanical system arises from this mysterious immensity, from the vastness and indistinctness of its huge proportions. It is in this that consists at once its real and its artificial strength—real in the prodigious area over which its baleful influence extends, and in the myriads who bend blindly and submissively before its despotic authority; artificial but still overpowering in the infinitude into which it has multiplied all its component parts. Its mythical cosmogony stretches away beyond the bounds of space; its historical annals extend backwards to the birth of time. Its chronology is recorded, not by centuries, but by millions of millions of ages; and the individuals engaged in one single exploit, minutely commemorated in its archives, exceed in number the whole congregation of human beings that have pressed the earth since the creation of man.

Its events have been chronicled in Sanskrit, a language the most expressive and harmonious that has ever been attuned to human utterance; a language whose characters are declared to be a direct revelation from the Deity himself, and its sounds the accents of the celestials. It is professed that in the revolution of ages the use of this melodious tongue has been withdrawn from the lips of ordinary mortals, and its knowledge has been entrusted to the divine race of the Brahmans alone, to whom it has been permitted to cultivate this dialect of the gods.[1]

[1] It is unnecessary to remark that the pretensions of Sanskrit to this mysterious antiquity are without foundation. Its alphabet is said to be a modification of the characters in which was written the ancient language of the Buddhists, the Pali, of which Sanskrit is a comparatively modern derivative—and the name borne by each is sufficiently indicative of their respective ages; *Pali* signifying the "root," or "original," and *Sanskrit* the "finished" or "polished" language which has sprung

The Vedas and the Shastras, the sacred volumes which contain all imaginable knowledge, and embody all that has been communicated by the inspiration of

from it. It is likewise a significant fact that, although India abounds in sculptured rocks and inscriptions bearing reference to events in the reigns of the earliest kings, "not a single Sanskrit inscription has been found approaching to within six or seven hundred years of the date of those in Pali, the earliest dating in the fourth century of our era."—Colonel Sykes's Notes in Asiatic Journal, vol. xii. p. 415. In like manner the legends on the most ancient coins from all parts of India, from Bactria to Cape Comorin, are in Pali or Pracrit, which prevailed to the very confines of Persia; and if, as Colonel Sykes observes, the extension of their religion claimed by the Brahmans from remote antiquity embraced all these countries on the continent of Asia, thus involving the knowledge of Sanskrit for the study of its sacred writings, surely they would have left us some specimens of their dialect upon coins or on rocks, if the people using it had been numerous, or even if Sanskrit itself had been diffused amongst a few. (See also Maupied, Essai sur l'Origine des Principaux Peuples Anciens, p. 205.) Nor is there anything in the literature of Sanskrit to vindicate its title to an origin so ancient. Its style exhibits all the traces of transition from the first efforts of expression to the highest refinements of grace and inflection; but its historical compositions are so utterly imaginary, that "only one has been yet discovered to which the title of history can with propriety be applied, the Raja Taringini, an account of Cashmir, which dates no higher than the 12th century (Prof. Wilson); and the same high authority has pronounced that the Sanskrit records have established but one historical fact which can be relied on as authentic, the identity of Chandragupta with Sandracottus, the contemporary of Alexander the Great.

The weight of probability is in favour of the opinion of Colonel Sykes, that there is still wanting proof of the existence of Sanskrit until six or seven centuries *after* the extant proofs of the existence of Pali. Notes, &c., p. 335.

Omniscience, are written in this venerated language, and are believed to be as ancient as eternity, and to have issued direct from the lips of the Creator.[1]

[1] The antiquity claimed for the sacred books of the Brahmans has been reduced by modern investigations to a comparatively recent standard. "Sir William Jones," says Colonel Sykes, "in his preface to the Institutes of Menu, broaches a speculation, the reasonableness of which we can test by reference to palpable epochs of improvement in our own and other modern European languages. He says that the Sanskrit of the three first Vedas, that of the Menava Dharma Sastra (Menu) and the Puranas, differs in pretty exact proportion to the Latin of Numa, that of Appius, and that of Cicero, or of Lucretius where he has not affected an obsolete style. He therefore assumes that the several changes in Sanskrit took place in times very nearly proportional to the above changes in the Latin; that the Vedas must therefore have been written three hundred years before the Institutes of Menu, and those Institutes three hundred years before the Puranas. By this calculation Sir William Jones dates the Vedas from the fifteenth or sixteenth centuries before Christ. But as Professor Wilson has proved, from internal evidence, that the Puranas were written or compiled between the eighth and fourteenth centuries of the Christian era, it follows, according to Sir William Jones's hypothesis, that the Institutes of Menu date from the fifth century A.D., and the Vedas from the second century. Both the above are indeed great authorities; but in spite of this startling deduction, from applying Sir William Jones's calculations to Professor Wilson's dates, the absence of Sanskrit inscriptions before the fourth century, and the language of the inscriptions of *that period*, give some weight to doubts respecting the antiquity of all the sacred writings of the Brahmans."—Notes, &c., Asiatic Journal, p. 418. See also Essai sur l'Origine des Principaux Peuples Anciens, &c., par F. L. M. Maupied: Paris, 1844, p. 176. "The Vedas were probably written at different periods, but were compiled in their present form in the fourteenth century B.C."—Mountstuart Elphinstone, b. i. c. 4.

From the Vedas proceed the Upangas and Puranas, those versified commentaries and interminable treatises which compose the wisdom of the East, teaching all arts, expounding all sciences, developing all mysteries, explaining all laws and ethics, embracing all that it becomes man to know, and enjoining all that it behoves him to perform.[1] All these form a body of learning so profound as to be infallible, so vast as to be inscrutable, so voluminous that the mere fragments of these giant epics, which are still accessible to mankind, are computed by millions of stanzas, and the whole existence of an ordinary mortal, though prolonged to the uttermost hour, would barely suffice to initiate him into the first rudiments of the ineffable literature of Brahma.

It is this imposing immensity in which consists the ascendancy and duration of the system; its vastness baffles all scrutiny and defies all human comprehension. The mind of the Hindoo is overawed by the sense of inconceivable extension; he feels it impious to explore where he despairs to comprehend; he bows in distance and in humbleness before the sublimity of mystery, and in the very prostration of his intellect—*he believes.*

[1] "The Puranas, which are eighteen in all, are alleged by their followers to be the works of Vyása, the compiler of the Vedas; but in reality they were composed by different authors between the eighth and sixteenth centuries, although in many places from materials of much more ancient date."—Mountstuart Elphinstone, Hist. India, vol. i. b. ii. c. 2.

But in the benevolent dispensation of Omnipotence there have in later times been those who have boldly ventured nearer to this mighty fabric of superstition, who have penetrated its dim recesses, held aloft the torch of truth and science to explore its hidden foundations, and returned to proclaim to its Christian assailants that the colossal superstructure *is not impregnable.* They have entreated its deluded defenders to descend with them into its forbidden passages, to see and to satisfy themselves of its unsoundness and their own impending danger; but as yet the voice of warning and persuasion has been raised almost in vain; few have had the resolution to follow, and fewer still the courage to be convinced. But one paramount and permanent advantage has been secured; an entrance has been laid open to the most intimate secrets of the system; and all that now remains for Christian energy and perseverance to accomplish is to devise the means by which the alarm may be more widely sounded, and the thoughtless millions led to enter and examine for themselves, and once awakened to a sense of their long delusion, to guide them to security and truth.

It must be apparent how hopeless it would be, within the space I have allotted to myself, to attempt anything like a compendium of the doctrines, the discipline, the observances, and the morals of the Brahmanical superstition; but it is desirable to afford to those whose attention may not have been previously turned to the subject, some faint idea of the magnitude of the system and the obstacles which it opposes to the approach or the ascendancy of Christianity, and at the same time to point out those peculiarities in its structure and constituent parts, the inherent weakness and unsoundness of which present a favourable opening for the entrance of enlightenment, and a prospect of success for the well-directed labours of instruction.

The religion of the Hindoos has hitherto rested securely on two grand supports—the scheme of physical science which pervades all the details of their sacred mythology, and their slavish submission to the divine caste of the Brahmans.[1] These latter, the Levites of the East, have been venerated as the vicegerents of spiritual authority upon earth, the depositaries of all human knowledge and expounders of all heavenly wisdom. From *Brahm*, the universal and self-existent intelligence, by whom the universe was willed into existence (but to whom, strange to say, no temples are erected in Hindostan, since his attributes are too sublime and ethereal to be reduced to any intelligible type under which they could be adequately worshipped), proceeded at the same time the Hindoo Triad, Brahma the Creator,

[1] A comprehensive account of the present state of the Hindoo religion, and the changes which it has undergone, will be found in the third and fourth chapters of Mountstuart Elphinstone's History of India, vol. i. b. ii.

Vishnu the Preserver, and Shiva the Destroyer.[1] To Brahma was confided the formation of all the beings that were to people the myriads of worlds which had been produced from the great mundane egg, and direct from his presence proceeded the countless progeny of animated forms that have since moved throughout the universe.[2]

From his head issued first of all the caste of the Brahmans, and simultaneously with their birth flowed from his lips in finished and substantial form the sacred volumes of the Vedas for the instruction of mankind in all needful knowledge. Of these, from the first march of time, the Brahmans were ordained the exclusive guardians, and the sole teachers and interpreters of their transcendant truths.[3] From the arm of Brahma proceeded the military caste of the Kshatryas, from his breast the Vaishyas, or pastoral and mercantile races, with their innume-

" Brahma, though he seems once to have had some degree of preeminence, was never much worshipped, and has now but one temple in India. It is far different with Vishnu and Siva. They and their incarnations now attract almost all the religious veneration of the Hindoos. The relative importance of each is eagerly supported by their numerous votaries; and there are heterodox sects of great extent which maintain the supreme divinity of each to the entire exclusion of his rival."—Mountstuart Elphinstone, Hist. India, vol. i. b. ii. c. 4.

[2] India and Indian Missions, including sketches of the gigantic system of Hinduism, by the Rev. Alexander Duff, D.D., Church of Scotland Mission, Calcutta, p. 121.

[3] Mountstuart Elphinstone's History of India, b. i. c. 1.

rable subdivisions, and from his foot the laborious caste of the Shudras, whose doom is that of toil and of humbleness, of slavery and degradation.

Caste, in all its visible arrangements, is thus not only referred by the Brahmans to a sacred and lofty origin, but in its distribution and subordination its adjustment from the commencement is asserted to have been unaltered, and it is presumed that to the extinction of the universe it must remain the same and immutable.[1] Caste is not a distinction of *degree*, but of *essence*. A member of one recognized caste could by no merit or exaltation be elevated into one higher in the scale; and if, by the violation of the institutes of Brahma, an individual should be overtaken by the awful visitation of an expulsion from caste, he falls, not into a lower receptacle; for whose rites and institutions, its functions and its duties, he would be utterly disqualified,—but *he drops altogether out of the pale of mankind*. He becomes an "*outcaste*," a pariah, for whom humanity has a form, but no recognized place; a name which concentrates all that a Hindoo holds loathsome and abhorred.[2]

[1] In contradiction of this statement as to the origin and immutability of caste, see Note at p. 91, ch. iii.

[2] "The loss of caste is faintly described by saying that it is civil death. A man not only cannot inherit, cannot contract or give evidence, but he is excluded from all the intercourse of private life as well as from the privileges of a citizen. He must not be admitted into his father's house; his nearest relatives

Thus by the very nature of their religion, ambition and all its civilizing impulses and influences are annihilated, and the highest approval and rewards in a future life are reserved by the Deity for him who, with the most contented submission and unflinching endurance, shall have discharged all the duties and performed all the ceremonial observances peculiar to the caste in which it is his fate to have been born. In this scheme the Brahman, divinely pre-eminent in origin, in wisdom and in power, walks the earth, a thing to wonder at and adore. To envy his exaltation or to dispute his supremacy would no more pass across the mind of a devout Hindoo than to aspire to become a planet or to question the brightness of its effulgence. The Brahman is to the rest of the world the oracle of Omniscience, the fountain of all instruction, the teacher of all duties and functions in this world, and the guide to infinite beatitude in the next.[1] It is a crime amounting to sacrilege in a

must not communicate with him; he is deprived of all the consolations of religion in this life, and all the hopes of happiness in the next. Unless, however, caste be lost for an enormous offence, or for long continued breach of rules, it can always be regained by expiation; and the means of recovering it must be very easy, for the effects of the loss of it are now scarcely observable. It occurs, no doubt; and prosecutions are not unfrequent in our courts for unjust exclusion from caste; but in a long residence in India I do not remember ever to have heard of or met with an individual placed in the circumstances I have described."—Mountstuart Elphinstone, Hist. India, b. ii. c. 1.

[1] Mountstuart Elphinstone, quoting from Menu, says: "A

Hindoo of one of the unprivileged castes to pry into that body of knowledge of which the Brahmans are the sacred dispensers; every study and every science which relies on the operations of mind and intelligence form their exclusive domain; and to the rest of mankind it is permitted only to occupy themselves in those arts and humble occupations in which suc-

Bramin is the chief of all created beings; the world and all in it are his; through him, indeed, other mortals enjoy life; by his imprecations he could destroy a king with his troops, elephants, horses, and cars; could frame other worlds and regents of worlds, and could give being to new gods and new mortals. A Bramin is to be treated with more respect than a King; his life and person are protected by the severest laws in this world and the most tremendous denunciations of the next; he is exempt from capital punishment even for the most enormous crimes; his offences against other classes are treated with marked lenity, whilst all offences against him are punished with tenfold severity." —History of India, vol. i. b. 1, c. 2. The condition of the Shudra or servile class, as described by Menu, is no longer to be found in Ceylon; but its specification is illustrative of the exalted pretensions of the Brahmans. According to Mr. Elphinstone, "The duty of a Sudra is to serve the other classes; but his chief duty is to serve the Bramins. A Bramin must not read the Veda, even to himself, in the presence of a Sudra: to teach him the law, or to instruct him in the mode of expiating sin, sinks a Bramin into the hell called Asamwrita. It is even forbidden to give him temporal advice. A Sudra is to be fed by the leavings of his master or by his refuse grain, and clad in his worn-out garments. If a Sudra use abusive language to one of a superior class, his tongue is to be slit; if he sit on the same seat with a Bramin, he is to have a gash made in the part offending; if he advise him about his religious duties, hot oil is to be dropped into his mouth and ears."—History of India, vol. i. b. 1, c. 1.

cess is attainable by dexterity or strength, and which are entirely independent of imagination and thought.[1]

To rivet more firmly this subjection of the rest of mankind, it is from the lips and at the hands of the Brahmans that all other races and castes are to receive the myths of their religion, the code of its belief, and the ritual forms of its worship, which in number and infinity almost weary imagination, as they have already exhausted ingenuity. It is no figure of speech to say that the duties and formalities, enumerated in the ordinary ritual of the Brahmanical code, are as numberless as the stars of heaven, and countless as the sand on the sea shore for multitude.[2] So vast is their multiplicity, that life itself is declared to be insufficient to comprehend, much less to discharge, their obligations; and the highest aspiration of the devout Hindoo is to master, in one stage of existence, such a fragment of this indispensable knowledge, as may entitle him in other births to take in a still further portion of intelligence; and thus, by successive translations, obtain the infinite bliss of absorption into the eternal essence of the Supreme.

Not merely the principles for the general regulation of life, but all the accessories and circumstantials of conduct, are anticipated and prescribed by the Brahmans with a tenfold greater minuteness than Judaism

[1] Mountstuart Elphinstone, b. i. c. 1; b. ii. c. 1.
[2] Duff's India, p. 152.

ever knew. "All the customs, manners, habits, and acts, however varied or minute, ridiculous or frivolous, loathsome or vile, which can characterize the doings of an individual; or the modes of intercourse, public or private, between man and man; all are believed to be solemnly pre-ordained of God. Every imaginable transaction of life, whether important or trivial; nay, every function of animal nature, is enstamped by the prescription of religious observances. There is, in all of them, an eternal ringing of changes on certain motions, utterances, and substances. There are bathings and washings, and sippings and sprinklings, standings and sittings, walkings and turnings, in every conceivable position; touchings and smellings of various auspicious things; rubbings of the teeth and rinsings of the mouth; changings of apparel and anointings with fragrant oil; deckings with strung and unstrung blossoms and garlands, and wreaths of flowers; perfumings with sandalwood and saffron and aloes; gatherings of dust and scatterings of leaves; kindlings of fires and suspendings of lamps; covering and uncovering of vessels of brass and of copper and of earth; compoundings of honey and rice, of herbs, of roots, and of sugar; offerings of grain and of water, of milk and of butter and curd; repetitions and naming of the *threè* worlds and the *seven*; repeatings of the mysterious monosyllable *aum*; recitings of the holiest of texts, the Gayatri; suppressions of the breath and intense inward meditations; adorations of elements and planets and stars; invocations innumerable of the Triad, and assembled gods and philosophers and sages; in fine, of all animated beings in heaven above or on earth beneath; and all these are again varied and modified, expanded, curtailed, divided or multiplied, combined or transposed, in forms so multitudinous as to verge on infinity. It is as if the whole of these primary elements were thrown into one huge kaleidoscope, and kept ever revolving; at every revolution producing the same substantial elements, but under new forms of arrangement, configuration, and grouping; and so onwards through every additional gyration without limit and without end."[1]

Such is a faint approach to a summary of the ritual observances of a Hindoo; yet these are but the formulæ of his daily and *ordinary* duties, and are irrespective of those more essentially belonging to adoration and *worship*, and of the ceremonies to be performed at the more remarkable periods, and on the more memorable occurrences of life; on the occasion of births, marriages, and interment, each of which forms a voluminous system within itself. They are exclusive of the rites observed in purification and diet, the latter a code of cookery as comprehensive as any ordinary treatise on the art; and these, and ten thousand others equally minute and circumstan-

[1] Dr. Duff, p. 164: see also Mountstuart Elphinstone's History of India, vol. i. b. i. c. 4.

tial, are again diversified and re-arranged to suit the worship of the innumerable minor divinities who divide the honours of adoration with Brahma.[1]

To comply absolutely and unfailingly with all the requirements of a system so multifarious and unbounded, is so manifestly beyond the limited powers, either of intellect or endurance, which have been assigned to man by his Creator, that from infancy to eternity the doom of the Hindoo is helpless and hopeless insufficiency, obligations which he feels that he wants the strength to fulfil, demerits which are unavoidable, and penalties and punishments which can only be averted by the aid and mediation of the Brahmans.

Again, out of this religion of impossibilities and despair, springs another which is its natural consequence—the adoration of the avenging deities, to whose tortures the pre-doomed and defaulting devotee is consigned for the expiation of his offences and sins of omission. Hopeless of earning the approbation of the benevolent principle of the divinity, he seeks to deprecate the wrath of the malignant; despairing of a smile from the Ormuzd of his triad, he turns in terror to avert the frown of its Ahriman. Hence come the impulses to devil worship, the licentious orgies of Shiva, the bloody sacrifices of Kali, the funeral piles of the Suttee, the atrocities of Jaggarnath, the self-inflicted tortures of the fakirs, the

[1] Dr. Duff, p. 153, 164, 170, 176.

parricidal murders in the waters of the Ganges, the revolting festivals of the Durga, the horrors of Charakpooja, and the unearthly carnage of the Phansegars and Thugs.[1] Hence the origin of rites to which it is a desecration of language to apply the designation of *worship*; and which, hopeless of conciliating heaven, seem designed only to move the sympathies of hell. In each and in all its developments, the Brahman, in the full ascendancy of his divine investiture, directs, controls, and animates the system; his supremacy undoubted, his authority unquestioned, and his officiation the appointed link of connexion between the Deity and the other members of the human race.

In this arrangement consists the chief strength of the Brahmanical religion, its exclusion, its impenetrability, and its mystery; but the other grand feature of the system, its *material* and *physical*

[1] "Bloody sacrifices are performed to Siva, though discouraged by the Bramins of his sect, and it is in honour of him or of his consort that so many self-inflicted tortures are incurred on certain days in every year. On these occasions some stab their limbs and pierce their tongues with knives, and walk in procession with swords, arrows, and even living serpents thrust through the wounds; while others are raised in the air by a hook fixed in the flesh of their backs, and are whirled round by a moveable lever, at a height which would make their destruction inevitable if the skin were to give way."—Mountstuart Elphinstone, Hist. Ind., vol. i. b. ii. c. 4. The licentious and obscene worship of Devi, the wife of Shiva, is adverted to by the same high authority in the same chapter.

philosophy, whilst it has been equally designed with a view to overawe the minds of its votaries by its involutions and immensity, is so monstrous in its inventions and so extravagant in its delusions, as to involve the inevitable certainty of its eventual exposure and overthrow.

So far as the doctrines of Brahma profess to deal with abstractions, or to rest upon the authority of a divine revelation, ingenuity and fabrication may discover a defence for its theories against the most formidable assailants; but where its pretensions have been incautiously identified with questions of fact, and its tenets made dependent upon natural phenomena, the whole system becomes accessible to the light of ordinary knowledge, and its errors are susceptible of scientific exposure. As the infallibility of Rome underwent an irretrievable discomfiture when, abandoning the dimness of tradition and the subtleties of theosophists, the Holy Office flung its daring defiance at the philosophy of Galileo; so wherever enlightenment can penetrate, and Science lend her aid as the ally of Christianity, the authority and impostures of Brahmanism must of necessity be overthrown in their encounter with demonstrable truth. This is one inappreciable advantage gained in the conflict with the Brahmanical idolatry, not merely illustrative of the invaluable assistance which education is calculated to lend in the struggle, but almost conclusive as to its hopelessness were the alliance to be overlooked or dissevered. For as all the knowledge of the Brahmans professes to be directly communicated by heaven, all their sciences and arts to be dictated by the Creator, it follows unavoidably that the detection of falsehood in the revelation must be utterly destructive of all confidence in the oracle and its priests.

As regards their science, the anomalous alliance of sublimity and absurdity has never been exhibited in such colossal proportions as in the strange combination in which they are presented in the Brahmanical philosophy.[1] Creations which, in their theory of the universe, extend throughout the immensity of space, when described in their details degenerate into oceans of syrup and seas of clarified butter. Their sacred chronology is rolled backwards into the dimmest distance of time, but the movements of monarchs who lived millions of ages ago, are related with all the solemn minuteness of the Court Calendar of yesterday. They have a system of geography, in which the earth is expanded into dimensions that occupy an area whose diameter is equal to the distance between our planet and the sun; and within this the Hindoo world rests upon animated elephants, whose movements are the origin and explanation of earthquakes. They have a code of physics, so re-

[1] For an account of the 'Physical Errors of Hinduism' see an admirable article under that title by a native gentleman, in No. XXII. of the Calcutta Review, June, 1849.

condite as to be held worthy of the divine omniscience, by which it professes to have been communicated, but which yet includes all the dreams of the alchemists, and all the delusions of magic. They have a science of medicine, so profound as not only to cure all diseases, but likewise to foresee their attacks, and to control and pre-arrange the approach and ravages of death. They have a system of mathematics, by which they profess to explain all the phenomena of the natural world, but which is dependent on the powers of its common, its mystic, and its magical numbers. They have a theory of astronomy, which mounts to the sublime in the boldness of its conceptions, but which descends more congenially to the trivialities of astrology and the freaks of divination;[1] and whilst the professors of this exalted study

[1] The practice of astrology at the present day in Ceylon, and the preparation of the ephemeris predicting the weather and other particulars of the forthcoming year, appears to have undergone little or no change since this custom of the inhabitants of India was described by Arrian and Strabo. But in later times the Brahmans and the Buddhists have superadded to that occupation the casting of nativities and the composition of horoscopes for individuals, from which the *Sophistæ* described by Arrian abstained. Εἰσὶ δὲ καὶ μαντικῆς ὄυτοι μοῦνοι Ἰνδῶν δαήμονες, οὐδὲ ἐφεῖται ἄλλῳ μαντεύεσθαι, ὅτι μὴ σοφῷ ἀνδρί. Μαντεύουσι δὲ ὅσα ὑπὲρ των ὡραίων τοῦ ἔτεος, καὶ εἴ τις ἐς τὸ κοινὸν συμφορὴ καταλαμβάνει· τὰ ἴδια δὲ ἑκάστοισιν οὔ σφιν μέλει μαντευεσθαι.—(Arrian.) Strabo's account is in like manner confined to the issue of the annual ephemeris of the year by the astrologers: Ἔφη δ'αυτοὺς καὶ τα περὶ φύσιν πολλὰ εξετάσαι καὶ προσημασίαν ὄμβρων, αὐχμῶν, καὶ

have so far mastered the operations of actual science as to be able to foretell an eclipse, they have no sounder rationale for their calculations, than the belief that the obscuration is occasioned by the struggles of monsters to swallow the moon.

Wild as these imaginings must seem, they are yet the basis and foundation of the religion of Brahma, and are associated with all the exploits of the triad, all the events of their mythology, and all the chronicles of their innumerable deities; and it will be manifestly idle to suppose that the overthrow of that gigantic imposture can be ever effectually achieved till the foundations of the system have been shaken by the exposure of its imaginary science, and the explosion of its false and fanciful philosophy.

An interesting occurrence at Batticotta, the chief station of the American missionaries in the peninsula of Jaffna, which took place a few years after their establishment, was eminently illustrative of this important fact. Batticotta was till lately the residence of Vesuvenathen, the most celebrated of the astronomers of Ceylon, inasmuch as he concentrated in his own person the accumulated science of his ancestors, who for nine generations had been cultivators of the same study. In his 'Tamil Ephemeris' for 1828, Vesuvenathen had predicted an eclipse of the

νόσων. A note upon this subject, with some specimens of the productions of the modern astrologers of Ceylon, will be found at B, end of this chapter.

moon on the 21st March, at twenty-four minutes past six o'clock P.M., which was to obscure five-eighths of the disc. In this calculation the missionaries had discovered an error: only three-eighths of the disc were to be affected; and the eclipse was to begin fifteen minutes sooner and to continue for twenty-four minutes longer than had been foretold by the astronomer. Confident of his own powers, however, Vesuvenathen recast his calculation, and re-asserted its accuracy. The controversy became public, and excited the utmost attention amongst the Tamil population; and as the time drew near, an influential Brahman assembled the people near the seminary, in order to be witnesses of the approaching triumph of their own religion over the errors of the Christians.

Unfortunately a passing cloud was borne athwart the moon at the precise time when the Americans had predicted the first approach of the shadow; for a moment all was doubt and anxiety, but in the next a small spot was discernible on the north-eastern verge of the moon. "*It is the cloud*," cried the Brahman; but in another minute the cloud was gone; the spot had expanded, and the eclipse was incontestably begun! The missionary led the way to his schoolroom, produced his orrery, and delivered a lecture on the phenomenon which was then visible in the sky; and lighting up the sun in the centre, he so directed the shadow to the moon as to demonstrate to the spectators the theory of what was still passing in the heavens.

But the issue of the contest was not yet fully decided: two other tests remained to be tried, the extent of the obscuration, and the ultimate duration of the eclipse. These were watched with extreme anxiety; and in both particulars the triumph of the American philanthropists was complete.

Still, strange to say, no immediate instance of conversion amongst the Tamils was traced to this public exposure of the fallacies of their favourite science. The missionary who modestly records the story has accompanied it with the remark, that "mere astronomical truth cannot suffice to alter the heart;" but the Hindoos were taught by this incident to regard the American seminary with higher respect; their confidence in their own priesthood was shaken; and the preaching of the missionaries had an easier access to the minds of men.

But however indispensable education and scientific instruction may be found to be in relation to conversions from Brahmanism, its importance and efficacy are discernible on a still wider scale in relation to other superstitions, irrespective of the peculiarities in the belief of the Hindoos. The reliance is comparatively uncertain which can be placed on the permanence of impressions, however seriously made, upon individuals untrained to inquiry, and unaccustomed to examine and determine for themselves. Minds so constituted possess no powers for self-conviction, no defence against argument and external assault; and the first impressions, however genuine, soon give way before the displeasure of relatives, the ridicule of companions, and the influence of the heathen priesthood and other accustomed authorities in matters of faith.

Experience has shown that in order permanently to influence the heathen heart, the missionary must commence by awakening the intellect, and by communicating such a portion of secular knowledge as may expose the absurdities, and eventually demonstrate the subtler errors of idolatry, exhibiting at the same time the purer attributes of Christian morality and the civilizing influences of Christian life. With what force soever these considerations may apply to the difficulties of contending with Paganism under any form, the peculiar genius of the Brahmanical system renders it indispensable to attempt the work of spiritual enlightenment by the preliminary approaches of secular instruction; and hence the efforts of the several missions amongst the Tamils of Jaffna have been addressed earnestly, in the first instance, to the establishment of schools and the general diffusion of secular education throughout the province.

On the part of the Americans all these measures were directed by a far-seeing vigilance, and conducted on a well-conceived system, the result of two hundred years of laborious experience amongst heathens of every hue, and in every quarter of the world. It therefore becomes a subject not merely for Christian satisfaction, but for philosophical inquiry, to mark each stage of the process, and to observe the effect of each successive expedient, by which the mind of a Hindoo is stirred, the inert faculties set in motion, and previous habits of thought disturbed, or thought itself directed for the first time to impressions that had all along been received without any effort of reflection; to trace the first approaches of doubt, and the first cautious discernment of deception; to watch the gradual revision of belief, the displacement of unsoundness, the rejection of error, and the early dawnings of desire for the substitution of truth. Nor is it less important, though less inviting, to investigate the phenomena of failure, whether partial or entire, the numbness of apathy, the resistance of habit, the repulsion of pride, the impenetrability of prejudice, and the indomitable supremacy of delusion.

In all essential particulars the process adopted by the three missionary bodies in the province of Jaffna, the Americans, the Church of England, and the Wesleyan Methodists, has been the same, in regard to their operations both as ministers and teachers. For thirty years these good men have assembled periodically in a "*missionary union*," to combine the results of past experience, and decide on measures for the future. By this means their system has been almost one and the same;[1] and they have altogether avoided, in the eyes of the Tamils, the exhibition of controversial rivalry, which to some extent has impeded the success of the missions amongst the Singhalese in the South. With all of them education has been a diurnal occupation; whilst in their purely clerical capacity they have felt the necessity of proceeding with more cautious circumspection, improving rather than creating opportunities; relying less upon formal preaching than on familiar discourses; and trusting more to the intimate exhortation of a few than to the effect of popular addresses to indiscriminate assemblies.

The first embryo of instruction is communicated by them in the free village-schools, scattered everywhere throughout the district, in which the children of the Tamils are taught in their own tongue the simplest elements of knowledge, and the earliest processes of education; to read from translations of the Christian Scriptures, and to write their own language, first by tracing the letters upon the sand, and eventually by inscribing them with an iron style upon the prepared leaves of the Palmyra palm. It will afford an idea of the extent and perseverance with which education has been pursued in these primitive institutions, that, in the free-schools of the Americans alone, 4000 pupils, of whom one-fourth are females, are daily receiving in-

[1] MS. Notes on the Wesleyan Mission to the Tamils. By the Rev. P. Percival.

struction ; and upwards of 90,000 children have been taught in them since their commencement; a propor tion equal to one-half the present population of the peninsula. At the schools of the Church of England nearly 600 are in daily attendance; and upwards of 700 in those of the Wesleyans.[1]

But the establishment of these primary schools was only one stage in the proposed process of the missions. From the first it became an object of paramount importance to separate the scholars from the example and influence of idolatry, by the establishment of boarding-schools for such as could be induced to reside in them. But the attempt was for years unsuccessful, the natives being utterly unable to imagine a motive on the part of strangers for such devotion of time, toil, and money to an object so purely gratuitous. Their apprehensions were, however, gradually removed; and at every central station of the missions there is now maintained an establishment for the residence as well as the education of pupils.

The principal difficulty to be overcome was that opposed by the distinctions of caste; and the reluctance to permit children to reside under the same roof with their Christian teachers arose not so much

[1] This of course is exclusive of the Tamil schools of the Wesleyans in the eastern province of Trincomalie and Batticaloa, which are numerous and successful. In both provinces taken together the number of scholars constantly under instruction by the Methodists is something upwards of 2000.

from apprehensions of proselytism as from repugnance to permit their association with youths of rank inferior to their own. The missionaries overcame the difficulty, not so much by inveighing against the absurdity of such distinctions as by practically ignoring them, except whenever expediency or necessity required their recognition. In all other cases, where the customs and prejudices of the Tamils were harmless in themselves, or productive of no inconvenience to others, they were in no way contravened or prohibited; but as intelligence increased, and the minds of the pupils became expanded, the most distinctive and objectionable of them were voluntarily and almost imperceptibly abandoned.[1]

When the boarders were first admitted to one of

[1] In 1847 a low caste lad, a Roman Catholic of some ability, was admitted to one of the higher classes in the Wesleyan Seminary at Jaffna. The high caste youths immediately refused to permit him to sit with them, and the native teacher declined any satisfactory interference. Fifty of the pupils, headed by a Brahman, who was also a pupil, came in a body to demand his expulsion; but on this being refused they left the school in a body, and opened a rival establishment of their own, elected the young Brahman assistant-master, and to mark their irritation at the Wesleyans they expelled the Bible and all Christian treatises from the school, which they proceeded to keep open on the Sabbath. The experiment was however unsuccessful; the pupils gradually returned to Mr. Percival, the Brahman accepted employment in a public office, and the teacher who succeeded him, though not himself a Christian, declined to enter on the office till the reading of the Scriptures was restored.—MS. Notes of the Wesleyan Mission, by the Rev. P. Percival.

the American schools at Batticotta, a cook-house was obliged to be erected for them on the adjoining premises of a heathen, as they would not eat under the roof of a Christian; but after a twelvemonth's perseverance the inconvenience overcame the objection, and they removed to the refectory of the institution. But here a fresh difficulty was to be encountered: some of the high-caste youths made an objection to use the same wells, which had been common to the whole establishment; and it was agreed to meet their wishes by permitting them to clear out one in particular, to be reserved exclusively for themselves. They worked incessantly for a day; but finding it hopeless to drain it perfectly dry, they resolved to accommodate the difficulty, on the principle, that, having drawn off as much water as the well contained when they began, the remainder must be sufficiently pure for all ordinary uses.

The success of the free Tamil schools and boarding institutions was followed by the further step of establishing schools for tuition in English, and for elementary instruction of a still more advanced character. These were begun by the American mission in 1830; and it is evidence sufficient of the influence which had been already attained by them, and of the appreciation in which their labours were held by the people, that they found themselves in a position not only to enforce the payment of an annual fee from the pupils in their English schools, but to maintain, with a firm hand, but without any discouragement or diminution of their numbers, a discipline which is essentially and avowedly Christian. No profession of Christianity is required as a preliminary to admission; but once enrolled as a scholar, the little Hindoo must show such an outward respect for the religion, to whose charities he is so deeply indebted, as to lay aside for the moment the distinguishing symbols of his own idolatry. He is not permitted to enter with the mark of ashes on his forehead; and every pupil, whether heathen or converted, is obliged not only to attend public worship on the Sabbath, but to join in the daily reading of the Scriptures and the study of the first principles of Christianity.

Strange as it may seem, their parents entertain no apprehensions of this course, and they urge no objection to the rule. And it is a fact suggestive of curious speculation as to the genius and character of this anomalous people, that in a heathen school recently established by Brahmans in the vicinity of Jaffna, the Hindoo community actually compelled those who conducted it to introduce the reading of the Bible as an indispensable portion of the ordinary course of instruction.

The other missions of the Church of England and the Wesleyans have been equally active, in proportion to their means, in establishing schools of this class.[1] Several years were consumed in maturing

[1] The English schools of the Church of England Mission are

and realizing the schemes of education up to this important point; and then arose the grave question of the ability to proceed much further without the active aid and co-operation of the natives themselves.

As schools and stations increased in number, teachers and agents required to be multiplied in equal proportion. But whence were individuals to be procured to whom that agency could be safely intrusted? Heathen schoolmasters were objectionable; although even to the present day their services have not been entirely dispensed with by the Wesleyans and Episcopalians. To look for additional colleagues from Europe was all but hopeless; and equally hopeless would have been the attempt, in such a climate, by any system of itineration or subdivision of labour, so to distribute the attention of those already on the spot as to meet all the demands which were created by the results of their own efficiency and success. Elementary education had already been extensively provided, and was still more extensively required; but mere elementary

six, and the number of pupils under training upwards of 250 daily. If in point of numbers the results of the Church of England Mission may appear small in comparison with those of the others, it must be borne in mind that their establishment at Jaffna is but one of a number of similar branches in various parts of Ceylon; and that till within a very recent period there were but two clergymen at the stations at Nellore and Chundically. The Anglo-Tamil Schools of the Wesleyans contain about 170 pupils, and have been eminently successful.

education, however it may qualify for the duties and functions of humble life, can never elevate the national intellect, much less awaken the national mind to perceive the delusions of idolatry, and discern the reality of Christian truth.

To prepare the way for this, a further advance was yet to be made, not only in the quality of the instruction, but in the mode and spirit of its communication. To omit minor essentials, the importance of reaching the native mind through the medium of the native language required not only a critical familiarity with the dialect of the Tamils, but a knowledge of their customs and habits of thought, which could be but slowly acquired by any European, however persevering and observant, but which already existed in indigenous perfection in the instance of the intelligent youth of the province. It is impossible for one practised only in European dialectics to be prepared for the difficulty of transmitting views correctly through the medium of translation, where terms, apparently equivalent in the language of both parties, yet suggest to the mind of the listener only preconceived ideas and images altogether foreign to the intention of the speaker,[1] or fail entirely to define the subtler argu-

[1] "If *God* be spoken of, they probably understand one of their own deities, who yields to the vilest passions, and allows his worshippers to do so. By *sin* they understand some ceremonial defilement; or an evil committed in a former birth, for which the person is not accountable. *Hell* is nothing more than a

ments and distinctions, on a clear conception of which ultimate conviction may possibly depend.

For all the purposes I have here imperfectly suggested—for carrying the process of Christian instruction beyond the first stages of preparatory training—for raising the schools of the missions into institutions, whence the first assaults were to issue against the physical and scientific errors and the doctrinal delusions of idolatry—and to cause them at the same time to render back the care which had been bestowed upon them, by yielding in return a rich harvest of tutors and preachers—it became essential to found other establishments with higher aims and pretensions, in which native assistants might become qualified and encouraged to combine their own efforts with those of their benefactors for the regeneration of their country.

Impressed with this conviction, each of the missions at Jaffna proceeded to form for themselves something approaching to a collegiate institution, in which the most eager and accomplished scholars, selected from the primary schools, should be admitted to the study of the more advanced sciences of Europe.[1] That of the Church of England was esta-

place of temporary punishment, and *heaven* but absorption or the loss of individuality. These being the habitual ideas of the native mind, almost everything which forms the subject of a Missionary's address to them is perverted."—Selkirk's Recollections of Ceylon, p. 296.

[1] To the extreme value of such institutions and agency Dr.

blished at Nellore, and afterwards removed to Chundically; that of the Wesleyans, in the great square at Jaffna, was commenced in 1834; and that of the Americans, at Batticotta, is in the midst of a cultivated country within sight of the sea, and at a very few miles distant from the fort. It was opened in 1823, with about fifty students chosen from the most successful pupils of all the schools in the province; and the course of education is so comprehensive as to extend over a period of eight years of study. With a special regard to the future usefulness of its alumni in the conflict with the errors of the Brahmanical system, the curriculum embraces all the ordinary branches of historical and classical learning, and all the higher departments of mathematical and physical

Duff has borne his testimony in terms whose earnestness bespeaks the deep conviction of the writer. "Were the friends of missions to inquire how many young men are engaged in a course of study in the higher departments of knowledge;" instead of asking how many children are receiving instruction in the elementary schools; "they would find in the answer to the first inquiry by far the surer test of the present and prospective advancement of the Hindoos. *So strong is my conviction on this head, that I do not hesitate to say that it would augur more for the real welfare of India were* TEN *privileged to receive the higher instruction rather than* A THOUSAND admitted to the elementary schools." And again—"One central seminary of a higher grade, with its attendant retinue of gymnasia, will do more towards vitally impressing the intellect and heart of the people than any number of mere elementary schools, however indefinitely multiplied."—India and Indian Missions, p. 326 and 328.

science, combined with the most intimate familiarization with the great principles and evidences of the Christian religion.

The seminary, like all others founded by the mission, is essentially a Christian institution. The students reside uninterruptedly under the same roof with their instructors; and although no renunciation of idolatry and no formal declaration of Christian belief is insisted on as a preliminary to admission, still each inmate is required, as a matter of discipline, to be present at the morning and evening devotions of the school, and to attend the Christian worship in the chapel of the college. To participate in the religious observances of the Hindoos is regarded in the student as a disciplinal offence; and so far from this regulation being looked upon as a despotic interference with religious freedom, it is regarded by the students only as a well-understood condition of their admission to a Christian institution, and one with which they voluntarily comply, in order to secure a participation in all the advantages of the college.

The number which the building can accommodate is limited for the present to one hundred, who reside within its walls, and take their food in one common hall, sitting to eat after the custom of the natives. For some years the students were boarded and clothed at the expense of the mission; but such is now the eagerness for instruction that there are a multitude of competitors for every casual vacancy;

and the cost of their maintenance during the whole period of pupilage is willingly paid in advance, in order to secure the privilege of admission.[1]

Nearly six hundred students have been under instruction from time to time since the commencement of the American seminary at Batticotta, and of these upwards of four hundred have completed the established course of education. More than one-half have made an open profession of Christianity, and all have been familiarized with its doctrines, and more or less imbued with its spirit. The majority are now filling situations of credit and responsibility throughout the various districts of Ceylon; numbers are employed under the missionaries themselves as teachers and catechists, and as preachers and superintendents of schools; many have migrated in similar capacities to be attached to Christian missions on the continent of India; others have lent their assistance to the missions of the Wesleyans and the Church of England in Ceylon; and amongst those who have attached themselves to secular occupations I can bear testimony to the abilities, the qualifications, and integrity of the many students of Jaffna, who have accepted employment in various offices under the Government of the colony.[2]

[1] The same system has been adopted, and with equal success, by the Wesleyan Mission in the seminary at Jaffna.

[2] From the similar seminaries of the Wesleyans and the Church of England similar results have been secured. One

But the great effort of the missionaries, and that in which their success has been the most remarkable, is the *education of girls.* In the face of the proverbial jealousy of Orientals as to everything that concerns their women, it required more than ordinary foresight and courage to encounter the difficulty, amounting almost to hopelessness, of effecting any successful result from such an unpromising undertaking as the establishment of female schools, and, above all, of boarding-schools, for the complete separation of girls from their family and friends. No incident in the early struggles of the mission occasioned more severe animadversion of the natives, or created a stronger repugnance to their objects, than the spectacle of the European ladies assuming a prominent position in their own household, and being permitted to sit at table with the males of the family; the idea of a woman presuming to eat in the presence

hundred and eighty students, instructed by the latter, are now filling offices of trust and devoting themselves to professional pursuits in various parts of Ceylon. They have distinguished themselves as scholars and teachers; and as Christians, it has been remarked that amongst those educated at Chundically the proportion who have apostatized to Brahmanism is smaller than amongst an equal number educated at any similar institution. The Bishop of Colombo has borne practical testimony to the soundness and value of the education conducted by the Methodists, and several of the ordained clergy now attached to the Church of England were trained for the ministry at the Wesleyan Seminary of Jaffna. (See Journal of the Visitation Tour of the Bishop of Colombo, 1846, p. 22.)

of her husband being something utterly repugnant to all their previous habits and views of propriety.

As a portion of that social policy which thus condemns the women of India to a position of submissive inferiority and domestic toil, there exists an active hostility to the education of females, as tending to disturb their relative position in society, and to destroy their feeling of passive subordination to the other sex. So universally prevailing is this sentiment, that when the Americans first opened their female schools, reading and writing were sciences unknown to the female population of Jaffna; and it is doubtful whether there could have been found in the peninsula a woman of any rank who knew the letters of the Tamil alphabet.[1]

The first pupils of the American Mission at Oodooville were enticed to come by presents of dress—by the prospect of reward at each stage of their progress—and by the promise of a dowry of five or six pounds, in the event of their remaining in the institution till married with the approval of their teachers. Yet, even when allured by these encouragements, so strong was the prejudice against

[1] Strange to say, the exception to this enforcement of ignorance is almost as degrading as the rule itself; the only Hindoo females amongst whom education is permitted being the dancing girls and prostitutes attached to the temples, who are taught to read and write in order to qualify them for transcribing copies of the songs and stories of the gods.

female instruction, that the parents who had yielded and allowed their daughters to attend were visited with reproaches for their folly, and the children themselves evinced a sense of shame and confusion when, for the first time, they engaged in the novelty of learning to read.

But there was an object to be attained in this undertaking of much deeper importance than might at first be apparent. Notwithstanding the intellectual degradation of women, and the badge of social inferiority imposed upon them, the custom of the Hindoos in Jaffna, in relation to marriages and dower, has invested their females with an authority and control over property, which goes far towards restoring them, in practice and reality, to that position and influence from which ignorance and prejudice have displaced them. It is a paramount object of ambition with Tamil parents to secure an eligible alliance for their daughters by the assignment of extravagant marriage portions. These consist either of land, or of money secured upon land; and as the law of Ceylon recognizes the absolute control of the lady over the property thus conveyed to her sole and separate use, the prevalence of the practice has, by degrees, thrown an extraordinary extent of the landed property of the country into the hands of the females, and invested them with a corresponding proportion of authority in its management.

But distinct from this anomaly, although strongly enhanced by it, is the legitimate influence of the female herself as a wife and a mother, which, as regards intellectual and religious improvement, is capable of being most powerfully exerted, whether for evil or good. A child, educated at one of the missionary schools, whatever might be its attainments as a pupil, could scarcely hope to realize all their ultimate advantages, if directed in its domestic habits and pursuits by the advice and example of an idolatrous mother.[1] A student, trained at any one of the collegiate seminaries of the missionaries, ran a formidable risk of having his early impressions effaced, and his inclinations towards civilization thwarted and neutralized, if married to a Hindoo wife, and possibly constrained to bring up his children in the religion of her family; whilst, on the other hand, an educated Christian girl would be almost certain to encourage and confirm the improving tendencies of her husband, and to secure for her children the same advantages of discipline and instruction, the benefits of which she has learned by her own experience to appreciate. It is, perhaps,

[1] "So long as the Tamil woman is uneducated, she will be the slave that she has been for ages. If she is not brought under that influence of training which boarding-schools alone can supply, the current evils of popular idolatry will be cherished by her; and should she ever become Christian, her Christianity will be of a mixed and meagre description."—MS. Account of the Church of England Mission at Jaffna, by the Rev. J. O'Neil.

not an exaggerated estimate that, under such circumstances, the successful education of one intelligent female is of more value than that of five males.

Fully alive to the truth and importance of this fact, the earliest efforts of the missions were directed to the establishment of female schools, but, above all, of *female boarding-schools*, where Hindoo girls might be domesticated in childhood, and kept pure and uncontaminated till married with the approbation of their Christian guardians. This great object has been achieved, and with such signal success that any individual of ordinary feelings, who will visit the missionary establishments of Jaffna and Nellore and the charming little settlement of the Americans at Oodooville, and witness the happiness and intelligence of their inmates, must ever afterwards retain a deeper interest in the well-directed efforts of the genuine missionary, and cherish a grateful and kindly recollection of the good men who have achieved this triumph of benevolence and Christianity in Ceylon.

The hamlet of Oodooville is in the centre of a tract of very rich land, and the buildings occupied by the Americans were originally erected by the Portuguese for a Roman Catholic church and the residence of a friar of the order of St. Francis. It is a beautiful spot, embowered in trees, and all its grounds and gardens are kept in becoming order with the nicest care and attention.

The institution opened in 1824 with about thirty pupils, between the ages of five and eleven; and this, after eight years of previous exertion and entreaty, was the utmost number of female scholars who could be prevailed on to attend from the whole extent of the province. This difficulty has long since been overcome: instead of solicitations and promises to allure scholars, the missionaries have long since been obliged to limit their admissions to one hundred, the utmost that their buildings can accommodate; and now so eager are the natives to secure education for their daughters, that a short time before my visit, on the occasion of filling up some vacancies, upwards of sixty candidates were in anxious attendance, of whom only seventeen could be selected, there being room for no more. The earliest inmates of the institution were of low castes and poor; whereas the pupils and candidates now are many of them of most respectable families, and the daughters of persons of property and influence in the district.

The course of instruction is in all particulars adapted to suit the social circumstances of the community; along with a thorough knowledge of the Scriptures and the principles of the Christian religion, it embraces all the ordinary branches of female education, which are communicated both in Tamil and English; and, combined with this intellectual culture, the girls are carefully trained conformably to the usages of their country in all the discipline and acquirements essential to economy and domestic enjoyments at home. Of two hundred and fifty females who have been thus brought up at Oodooville, more than half have been since married to Christians, and are now communicating to their children the same training and advantages of which they have so strongly felt the benefit themselves.

In addition to this cheering consciousness of their own success at Oodooville, the missionaries had the satisfaction of finding that their exertions had smoothed the way for similar efforts on the part of their fellow-labourers. The task of the Wesleyan Methodists in founding a seminary of the same class at Jaffna was rendered comparatively easy; and when the Church of England missionaries resolved to make the same experiment at Nellore in 1842, they found that, instead of having to court and canvass for pupils, their embarrassment arose from the multitude of candidates, and the difficulty of making selections with the least possible pain to the disappointed. Their institution contains thirty girls, from six to twelve years of age, who receive the same course of instruction and are subjected to the same economical discipline which has so eminently qualified the pupils of Oodooville for all the domestic duties of life.

I have dwelt at this length on the educational proceedings of the Tamil missions from the deep interest which they attract as practical illustrations of the process adopted—not by mere theoretical philanthropists, but by profoundly experienced men—for the successful introduction of Christianity amongst a heathen race; and because I regard them in their political effect as likely to exert the most powerful and permanent influence on the social condition and material prosperity of this portion of Ceylon. During the last thirty years whilst the process has been in operation, its effect has been year by year to add to the number of highly-educated teachers sent out to mingle with the mass of the native population, to impart their own acquirements, and to stimulate others by the exhibition of the augmented power which knowledge confers for the successful prosecution of every secular pursuit. And, in the mean time, throughout the innumerable hamlets and agricultural groups the number of households is rapidly extending in which one or both of the parents have not only been instructed in the principles and precepts of Christianity, and acquired by domestic training a thorough appreciation of the habits and advantages of civilized life, but are now anxiously engaged in inspiring their own tastes and communicating their own information to their children.

One of the more interesting of these educational establishments remains yet to be noticed—the printing-press of the American missionaries at Manepy, within a short distance of the Fort of Jaffna. As at all the other stations, advantage has been taken of the old chapel and buildings of the Portuguese, which have been repaired and enlarged at the expense of the mission; and the most striking object is a graceful spire, lately erected on the church by the voluntary subscriptions of the natives connected with the establishment, and which, as it towers above the trees, recalls many a pleasant remembrance of home and of England.[1]

The earliest want of the missionaries was books, and, to supply their place, their first tracts and lessons were written on Olahs or strips of the Palmyra leaf, and when carried by the missionary for distribution among the natives these were strung around the neck of his horse. Their printing establishment at present and for many years past has given constant employment to upwards of eighty workmen, all of whom are Tamils educated in the mission schools, who have thus in addition been put into possession of a handicraft by which to earn their subsistence. The publications of their press are, of course, exclusively religious and educational; but it is a further evidence of the

[1] One unequivocal proof of the interest taken by the natives in the progress of Christianity is the liberal subscriptions which have voluntarily been made by them for repairing and beautifying the ancient Churches in the vicinity of Jaffna. That of Potoor, which is occupied by the Methodists, is now in process of restoration; and when completed will present a remarkable object in the midst of an Indian landscape, decorated with all the usual ornaments of pointed Gothic architecture. The Hindoo population made large donations in money, materials, and labour, in aid of this interesting work.

stimulus which has been given to the minds of the natives in general, that for the last seven years a newspaper, under the title of the 'Morning Star,' has been in the course of publication by the missionaries, which has upwards of seven hundred subscribers, of whom five-sixths are Tamils.

In all these operations the feature which eminently characterizes the Protestant missions of Jaffna is the absence of all rivalry, and an eager anxiety to swell the magnitude of the results without any narrow-minded jealousy as to the relative prominence of the agents. The Americans themselves are clergymen of two different communities, associated with laymen in the work of their mission. They co-operate most heartily with the other Christian ministers, with whom they have divided the province of Jaffna; their qualified pupils are always readily granted as teachers for the schools of the Wesleyan Methodists; their printing-press is at the service of them and the Church of England; they live on terms of amity with the Roman Catholic priesthood, who have manifested no open hostility to their system; and they have long since silenced the opposition of the Brahmans, who, with whatever secret apprehensions they may regard missionary operations, have been constrained, chiefly by the interference and influence of the females who have been educated by the missionaries, to abstain from any direct resistance to their proceedings.[1]

[1] This is confirmed by the experience of the Wesleyan Mis-

It will be seen from this hasty sketch that in the assault meditated by the missionaries upon the idolatrous system of the Tamils, the first approaches have all been made through the instrumentality of education, though in every stage of the process the inculcation of divine instruction and the development of the truths of Christianity have formed the aim and object of every measure, and been enforced with earnestness and unremitting devotion. To a casual observer it might seem that an undue precedence had been given to secular, to the prejudice of spiritual teaching; but a moment's reflection will dispel the apprehension when it is borne in mind that the genius of the Brahmanical superstition has itself suggested the order of attack by exceeding the ordinary boundary of theological systems, and engrafting on the subtler abstraction of its creed the unwise ambition to disseminate physical science with all the awful authenticity of divine revelation.[1] It has not

sionaries, who declare that "it is not from the priesthood that they have anything to fear, but from the Brahmanical system, coupled with the Oriental aversion to change and the cementing influence of caste."—MS. Notes of the Rev. P. Percival.

[1] "It is a marked and peculiar feature in the character of Hindooism that instead of confining itself within the proper and lawful bounds prescribed to every theological system, it interferes with and treats of every department of secular knowledge which human genius has ever invented: so that grammar and geography, physics, law, medicine, metaphysics, &c., do each prove as essential a part of Hindooism, as any religious topic with which it is concerned."—Calcutta Review, No. xxii. p. 398.

only proclaimed the all-sufficiency of its own sacred treatises in every conceivable department of learning, but has for ever fixed the landmarks of knowledge where the Shastras have placed them long ages ago; denouncing doubts as apostacy, and prohibiting progress or improvement as blasphemy and crime. To meet this state of things there is no expedient so effectual as scientific demonstration: "in every question of *morals* the appeal is to the Word and the Testimony; but when the laws and facts of *nature* are perverted in the construction of a false system of religion, in opposing that system it is right to invoke the assistance of science; and hence, in addition to other considerations, the particular attention which has been bestowed by the missionaries on mathematics, astronomy, and philosophy."[1]

But in their care for education, the duties of preaching and exhortation have been by no means excluded

[1] Report of the American Ceylon Mission, Jaffna, 1847, p. 39. Mr. Malcolm, who was sent by the American Baptist Board of Foreign Missions on a Tour of Observation in South-Eastern Asia, in speaking of the efficacy of education in weakening the influence of Brahmanism, says, "Wherever Christianity goes (in India), a new system of geography and astronomy must be adopted. It cannot be said that the Missionary may pass this by and preach Christ crucified. His hearers will not let him pass it by. The country he has left cannot exist by *their* system, and the Shastras and the Bagavat must fall if *his* be true. He will be attacked upon it. It will be regarded as a part of his religious belief, and he must clear away *their* cosmogony before he can establish his own faith."—Travels in South-Eastern Asia, &c.

by the missionaries. In their seminaries, and to those immediately under their influence, their ministrations are systematic and unremitting; but as regards either their students or the great mass of the native population, the Americans declare that long experience has taught them to attach much less importance to sermons and crowded assemblies than to the constant encouragement of inquiry, the suggestion of a doubt, or the removal of a difficulty from the path of an individual. The cottage and the palm-grove, the wayside and the bazaar, they look on equally as the post of duty with the schoolroom and the church; and in the latter their preaching is directed to the exposition of the simplest truths of Christianity, with a constant abstinence from all speculative controversy, and a cautious avoidance of the subtleties of sectarians on church discipline and government. According to the letter of their instructions the American missionaries are not to regard themselves "as a society for the promotion of civilization, literature, or the arts, but for saving men;" "their object is not to disseminate the peculiar tenets of any sect, but to make such a proclamation of the Gospel as shall be effectual for the salvation of the soul;"[1] and it is justice to them to record that in carrying out these various plans of operation, they have not departed from the spirit of that rule.

One evening, as I returned to Jaffna from a visit

[1] Report of the American Ceylon Mission, pp. 7, 8.

to one of their more distant stations, I passed upon the road homewards one of their ministers, who is now almost the father of the mission,[1] having been already thirty years in Ceylon. A little Malabar boy followed him with a lantern to be lighted after sunset. He was plodding on foot towards the village where he was about to visit or to preach, with an eager step and his eye thoughtfully bent on the ground. He wore no distinguishing dress, but the salutation of the natives as they passed attested their knowledge of his person and their veneration for his character. I was struck with his mild and intelligent aspect, and his earnest and unassuming demeanour; and I thought at the moment that I had never till then seen realized my previous idea of a devoted and genuine missionary of the Gospel.

In addition to the ordinary services of the sabbath, the Wesleyans attach signal importance to their lamp-light meetings after sunset, when the Tamil peasantry, released from agricultural occupations, resort to their school-houses to discuss the doctrines of Christianity and listen to the reading of the Scriptures. The clergy of the Church of England, together with their ordinary officiation for those who as Christians are already attached to their communion, are equally indefatigable in their labours amongst the heathen; but although the section of the peninsula which is occupied by their mission contains a dense

[1] The Rev. L. Spaulding.

population of upwards of 30,000 Tamils, the number who ordinarily attend their ministrations seldom exceeds an average of twenty individuals.

I come now to the inquiry *what has been the practical effect* of this system upon the minds and morals of the Tamil natives of Ceylon? And looking first to the declarations of the American mission as the most extensive in its operations, as well as the most comprehensive in its experience, I am bound to declare that as yet the ostensible result of their labours falls far short of the expectation which might have been formed from their magnitude and zeal. It is true that in all popular transitions the most powerful impulses are not those which appear first upon the surface, but move in silent and resistless currents beneath; and such I believe to be the case as regards the interest awakened by the missionaries in the minds of the Indians amongst whom their lot has been cast. The leaven is as yet working silently and almost unseen, but there is good ground for confidence that it will speedily and effectually leaven the whole lump.

In regard to their own success in converting the heathen to Christianity in Ceylon, the American missionaries speak with humbleness and timidity, but with confidence rather than self-satisfaction. They dwell more strongly on the difficulties of their task than on their own success in overcoming them; and trusting little to the nominal profession of Christianity, they have been careful to keep a record of the after career of their pupils, in order to discover whether its truths may have penetrated to the heart and influenced their conduct and life.

So conscientious are they in this particular, that after thirty years of toil and devotion they have enumerated *not more than* 680 *nominal converts*, who have been at one time or other received into communion with their churches, and the number now in connexion with them is but 357. It is a striking illustration of the inefficacy of sermons and of popular preaching to the Tamils, unaccompanied by the precaution of previously awakening the mind by education, that from first to last only 200 communicants have been received in thirty years, exclusive of those who had been educated in the schools and seminaries of the mission. Of the whole number one-seventh has been eventually excommunicated for their relapse into heathenism, and even of the remainder the missionaries modestly remark that the proportion which are "*real* Christians can only be known to God."[1] When such is the recorded experience of these excellent and indefatigable men, it requires caution to calculate the proportion of "real" Christians included in the multitudinous returns of conversion by the missionaries of other churches.

The Church of England missionaries speak with

[1] From a Manuscript Account of the American Mission at Jaffna.

equal humbleness of their own labours during the past; and frankly admit, in explanation of the limited amount of ostensible success which they have as yet to point to,[1] that "the work done bears a relation rather to the future than the present," and that of those of their converts who have boldly ventured to avow their change of opinion, few have been tempted to return to their former superstition, and numbers in death have borne testimony to their abiding faith in Christianity.

But however scanty may be the outward evidences of actual conviction, there are symptoms perceptible which afford good grounds of hope for the future. It is a remarkable fact, that since the natives have had daily opportunities of witnessing the blameless lives of the missionaries, and the social happiness which has been diffused even by the partial observance of their purer and more benevolent ethics, there has sprung up amongst the Hindoos of Jaffna a new party of Gooroos, who profess to have engrafted on Brahmanism many of the leading morals of Christianity, and claim them as originally emanating from their own system of religion.[2] The native commu-

[1] The number of the Church of England communicants is about 150. Those of the Wesleyans in 1849 were in the Jaffna Peninsula 147, and in the Eastern Province, at Batticaloa and Trincomalie, 179.

[2] Mr. Percival, in some Manuscript Notes with which he has favoured me on the Wesleyan Mission amongst the Tamils, has thus alluded to the probable results of this system of Christian

nity, not unobservant of these matters, and not indifferent to their political influence, are already venturing on the admission, and it is to be hoped the conviction, that *there is truth in Christianity*, and that it is "a good religion," which must eventually prevail in Ceylon. It is no uncommon remark of the old men, in reply to the exhortation of the missionaries, "Do not urge *me* to change. I am now too old, and must follow in the religion of my fathers; but here are my *children*. Christianity will prevail in their day; and if they will, let them become Christians now."[1]

education, even when it failed to produce actual conversion to Christianity:—"A new and middle class will in all probability arise, more or less Hindoo, but midway between that and Christianity, allied much to the Deistic creed, but strongly impressed with a belief in the Bible. As this body becomes stronger, the Church will be called upon to take special cognizance of them, as affected seriously by its exertions, and requiring the greatest care that 'Christ may be formed in them.' Some persons of this class have already formed a Society which meets near the Temple of Shiva to read the New Testament consecutively, the Anglicised portion of the community being provided with commentaries for reference. This has provoked a rival institution of the Brahmans, who, in defence of their own idolatry, have opened an English Seminary, to which only Hindoos are admissible, to whom weekly lectures are delivered at the Temple of Shiva; and amongst the list of these subjects were the comparative merits of Shivaism and Christianity—a Lecture on Sacred Beads—on the Duties of Women—on Stealing the Property of Shiva—on the Unity of the Deity—on Veneration for Cows—on Charity, Gratitude, Credulity," &c. &c.

[1] MS. Account of the American Mission at Jaffna.

Not only may the first grand object be said to have been thus achieved, by *shaking the confidence of the people in their own superstitions*, but a second important point has been gained. The shrewd and observant Tamils have not failed to perceive that there are worldly advantages, as well as spiritual, which distinguish the professors of Christianity, and that even as a social institution *it has the promise of this life*, as well as of that which is to come. As compared with themselves, they see those who have been educated by the Christians become abler men and more successful than their uneducated companions. They see in them a more cultivated demeanour and a superior bearing, which wins confidence and paves the way to advancement. Amongst those whom instruction has reached, there is no longer the same indifference to crime, and the same indulgence for falsehood and licentiousness. Character has come to be of value to its possessor, and shame has contributed its aid to the discouragement of vice.

The Tamils have the acuteness to discern that all these impressions and principles are imbibed from association with those who act in conformity with the precepts of Christianity; and they have before their eyes the hourly evidence that the aspect of society around them is changing, under the influence of this moral and intellectual training.[1] By the same causes,

[1] Within the last fourteen years standard works in English literature to the value of 2000*l.* have been purchased by the Tamils

the pernicious influence of caste has been shaken; and throughout the whole population of Jaffna there is an air of independence which at once strikes a stranger as being very dissimilar to that exhibited by the Tamils on the continent of India. It is not evinced in any disrespect to authority, or any indifference to the conventional distinctions of rank; but in a greater freedom from that slavish subservience to Gooroos and Brahmans which characterizes the Hindoos of the coast—in an inspiriting consciousness of an improved position in the social scale, and a sense of self-respect, which renders its possessors jealous of unreal pretension and usurped superiority. This, of course, applies but to a portion of the population, though a large and increasing one; but the

of Jaffna, and procured for them from England through the Wesleyan Conference Book-room of London. As regards Tamil literature, the Senior Missionary, Mr. Percival, of whom the Bishop of Colombo has stated that he is reputed to be the best English Tamil scholar in Ceylon (Visitation Tour, 1846, p. 23), has been engaged for thirteen years, in connexion with the American Missionaries and those of the Church of England, in a revision of the Tamil Version of the Scriptures, which is now rapidly approaching completion. Mr. Percival has been actively engaged in numerous works for the natives, and independently of religious tracts and catechisms, he has translated and published by the aid of the American press a Wesleyan Liturgy and Hymns, Doddridge's Rise and Progress of Religion, Rodokant's Bengalee Treatise on Idol Worship, Ashwa Gosha's Tract against Caste, and a variety of similar publications. Works on Geography, Arithmetic, Astronomy, and General Sciences, are now multiplying rapidly in the dialect of the Tamils.

spirit which excites it is abroad, and with the sustained exertions of those by whom it has been evoked, and the continued extension of Scriptural education and intelligence through their unremitting instrumentality, there is reason to cherish a well-grounded confidence in the ultimate triumph of Christianity, and the prevalence of that civilization which is its never-failing concomitant.[1]

[1] "Popular prejudice and bigotry have to a great extent been broken down. The links of caste have in many instances been severed during the last few years; and the effects caused by them have to some extent passed away. Friends have withdrawn themselves for a time from individuals who have had the courage to think and to act independently, but they have relented and renewed all the interchanges of friendship. Temples and festivals are not deserted, but their influence has declined. The Brahman is still clung to, but the profound reverence with which he was formerly regarded has ceased to exist; and though the system of Hindooism is still ostensibly maintained, the number of its *rigid* adherents is becoming comparatively few."—MS. Account of the Church of England Mission at Jaffna. By the Rev. J. O'Neil, Nellore.

NOTES TO CHAPTER IV.

(A.)

THE AMERICAN MISSIONARIES IN CEYLON.

IN some memoranda of a personal visit to the Missionary establishments at Jaffna in the spring of 1848, I made the observations which follow, and which convey the impressions suggested at the moment and on the scene of the useful labours of these remarkable men.

My earliest visits after reaching Jaffna were made to the institutions and schools of the several missions, and especially to those of the American Missionaries. On the evening of my arrival, so soon as the decline of the sun rendered it practicable, I drove to the Printing-office at Manepy, a hamlet within 5 miles of the Fort, embowered amidst luxuriant groves, above which rises the graceful spire of the village church. The establishment was in active operation—the presses in motion, the binding rooms full of bustle and business, and the book stores crowded, like a repository in Paternoster-row, with shelves of bound volumes and piles of printed sheets that rose in columns to the ceiling. The contents of these apartments are all destined for the schools of the various missions, and for almost gratuitous circulation amongst the Tamils of Jaffna.

The Female Seminary of Oodooville is but a few miles from Manepy. It happened to be the commencement of the recess, and the pupils had been dispersed for the holydays; their residences were not, however, very far distant; and having heard of our intention to visit the schools, there was a numerous attendance of scholars who had flocked in joyfully in order that we might not be disappointed of our object. They were most interesting creatures, from six to ten and twelve years old, clad in white jackets, but wearing the gold and silver ornaments and bangles with which the Indians are so eager to decorate their children. In their gentle, and at the same time happy, demeanour as well as in the neatness and modesty of their dress, they showed to much advantage as compared with the scarcely delicate costume of the females of Jaffna in general. But what interested me most was that a number of young married women were present who had been educated at Oodooville. There was a joyous expression in their features, as if they felt proud of their association with a place endeared to them by pleasant recollections; and with which they were still identified in the persons of their children, who had already been enrolled as its inmates. They testified the most agreeable interest in all that passed, in the examination of the pupils; waiting for their answers with lively attention, and expressing their satisfaction with a smile when any of their little favourites made a ready reply. At the conclusion of their lessons and exercises the scholars sang a hymn with Tamil words to a plaintive Hindoo air; and I think I never listened to music more touching, or that left a more pleasing impression on my memory than was produced by the sweet and melodious voices of that happy little choir.

A few days after I enjoyed a similar visit to the female seminaries of the Wesleyans on the esplanade of the Fort, and of the Church of England Missionaries at the fine old Church of Nellore, which has lately been beautified and restored at the expense of the Mission. In both institutions the pupils evinced the same joyous intelligence and the same modest and attractive demeanour which is so charming at Oodooville; and which, more than all other symptoms of improvement, suggests a well grounded confidence in the ultimate success of the judicious system now in progress for the civilization of Ceylon.

The other stations of the Americans lie in a circle within a very few miles of each other; I visited nearly all of them, and found in them the same remarkable character; the fine old ruins of the Roman Catholic buildings restored and re-animated; sometimes the vast aisles of their lofty churches partitioned into separate schools and dwellings for the superintending Missionaries, all surrounded with trim and orderly gardens, and crowds of merry little urchins, like bronze statuettes, amongst the shade of the foliage. Baldæus, in his grave old volume,[1] has given quaint cuts of these stately churches; but it would be difficult, either in the altered aspect of those which are restored, or the venerable ruins of those that still remain, to discover the originals of his very primitive engravings.

Batticotta, the head quarters of the Mission, stands about 6 miles westward of Jaffna, in the midst of well-cultivated rice farms and groves of Palmyra and Cocoa-nut Palm. The whole establishment is full of interest, and forms an impressive and a memorable scene—the familiar objects and arrangements of a college being combined with the remarkable appearance and unwonted costumes of the students; and the domestic buildings presenting all the peculiar characteristics of Oriental life and habits. The sleeping apartments, the dining hall, and the cooking-room are in purely Indian taste, but all accurately clean; and, stepping out of these, the contrast was striking between them, and the accustomed features of the lecture-room with its astronomical clock, its orrery, and transit instrument; the laboratory with its chemical materials, retorts, and electro-magnetic apparatus, and the Museum with its arranged collection of minerals and corallines to illustrate the geology of Ceylon. But the theatre was the centre of attraction, with its benches of white robed students, and lines of turbaned heads, with upturned eager countenances, "God's image carved in ebony." The examination which took place in our presence was on History, Natural Philosophy, Optics, Astronomy, and Algebra. The knowledge exhibited by the pupils was astonishing; and it is no exaggerated encomium to say that, in the extent of the course of instruction, and in the success of the system for communicating it, the Collegiate Institution of Batticotta is entitled to rank with many an European University.

I was present a few days after at a similar examination of the kindred Seminary of the Wesleyan Methodists at Jaffna, conducted by Mr. Percival, one of the most profound Tamil scholars now in India; the course of study was nearly the same,

[1] Folio, Amsterdam, 1672.

the students taken from the same rank of the natives, and the display of classical learning and scientific attainment which I witnessed was in no degree inferior to that with which I had been so much charmed at the American Seminary.

Both at Batticotta and at Oodooville it is a part of the system to apply the annual contribution of some one friend of the Mission, if it amount to the stipulated sum,[1] to the exclusive education of one individual who, on admission, assumes in addition to his own name that of the distant benefactor to whom he is indebted for his presentation. Thus at Oodooville the Tamil girls each bear the Christian and surname of an American lady; and at Batticotta one of the native students was presented by a name somewhat familiar to me as *Mr. William Tennent.*

In addition to the many students who have entered into professional and other employments, numbers educated in the Institution are now residing in their own villages in the immediate vicinity of Batticotta, engaged in agricultural pursuits; and it is a striking illustration of the civilizing effects of such an establishment, in aiding the exertions of the civil power for the improvement of the district, that whereas fifteen years ago there was not a single wheelcart in the district of Batticotta, there are now 150 in the immediate neighbourhood of the village; within the same period ten wells have been dug for one that previously existed; one-third has been added to the extent of reclaimed and cultivated land, and in all directions the country has been opened up by bye-roads and lanes to communicate with the leading highways to Jaffna.

It is not to be presumed that these are the results exclusively of the instruction and intelligence communicated by the Missionaries; but contrasted with the comparatively backward aspect of the districts to which their labours have not yet extended, there can be no question of their title to a large proportion of praise for the support which the Missionary establishments have yielded to the efforts of the Government agent of the district, Mr. Dyke, and the impulse thus comunicated to the progress of improvement and civilization. It is painful to

[1] £4. 3s. 6d. per annum.

imagine that the benevolent toil thus unweariedly bestowed could be productive eventually of no lasting results, or that the seed so patiently sown should fail to take deep root, and to exhibit its fruits in some permanent improvement of the people.

For my own part I cannot reconcile myself to such a possibility, nor can I believe that convictions and principles which have been deeply impressed, and have already influenced, to some extent, the habits of thought and the social status of two generations, can ever be wholly obliterated, or that even were their inculcation and enforcement to be suspended, the good which has already been achieved would not continue for generations to come to exercise a salutary influence on the mental and moral development and on the material prosperity of the Tamils of Jaffna.

Before leaving Jaffna on the occasion of my visit to the stations of the American Mission, I felt it my duty to communicate to the Board at Massachusetts my own impressions of the course they had adopted and the success by which it was likely to be followed. I was the more anxious to make this communication, from having ascertained the fact that some discouragement had been felt and exhibited at the meagre returns of the number of converts as reported by them, and that some reduction of the Missionary establishments might possibly be apprehended in consequence. The following letter which I addressed to the Secretary at Boston expresses the impression which had been made on my mind by the inspection of their institutions and a careful observation of the result of their labours:—

Ceylon, 1848. Jaffna, March 23.

SIR,—Since my arrival in Ceylon, nearly three years ago, my duties as Chief Secretary to the Government prevented my visiting this important district of the island before the present month: but on many occasions the labours of the American missionaries had been previously brought to my notice in the most gratifying terms, not only in my official capacity as connected with the Civil Government and as President of the Commission of Education, but by the private reports of personal friends, whom business or inclination had led to visit the scene of their labours. Foremost amongst these I must place the generous testimony of the Bishop of Colombo, who, on his return from his visitation of the province last year (the first which his Lordship had made), brought back the most agreeable impression of the extensive good which had already been achieved and was still in progress through the instrumentality of your people.

Having at length visited in person all your stations; however unusual a spontaneous communication of this kind may be, I cannot resist the impulse to convey to you my strong sense of the sustained exertions of your missionaries, and of their unexampled success in this colony. Much as I had heard of their usefulness and its results, I was not prepared to witness such evidences of it as I have seen, not in their schoolrooms only or in the attainments and conduct of their pupils, but in the aspect of the whole community amongst whom they have been toiling, and the obvious effect which their care and instructions have been producing on the individual, social, and moral character of the surrounding population.

In their more immediate sphere as Christian ministers, though surrounded by the clergy of other denominations similarly engaged, and hemmed in on all sides by the priesthood of heathenism, they have so regulated their efforts, so tempered zeal by sound discretion, as to excite no rivalry, to disarm the opposition of any, and to conciliate the admiration of all. I have found here no sectarian jealousies amongst professing Christians, and no active hostility on the part of idolaters. The number of professing converts recorded by your people may be small, as compared with those occasionally announced by other missionaries or ministers in Ceylon, but the field of their labours presents to me the remarkable feature, as compared with all others in this island, that whilst in the other provinces we have multitudes of nominal Christians in ostensible connexion with our Churches, there is but too sad ground for believing that the vast majority are in reality still only heathens at heart, whilst at Jaffna, and more especially in the vicinity of your stations, even those of your pupils and hearers who still profess to be heathens exhibit a far advance towards Christianity in their conduct and life. Practically their ancient superstition has been shaken to its foundation, and the whole fabric will shortly totter to the ground, and give place to the simpler structure of pure and practical Christianity.

In the statistical returns of your mission this important result cannot yet assume a tangible form, or find a specific exposition; but I trust this my testimony to its existence, elicited by the heartfelt satisfaction with which I have made certain of the fact, may tend in some degree to prevent discouragement on your part, as you cannot be an eye-witness to what I have observed, or any diminution of that generous zeal which has so eminently characterized your exertions heretofore.

So much for your mission as an ostensible instrument for the immediate extension of Christianity, but in its other relation as a vehicle for the diffusion of Christian knowledge through the medium of education and general enlightenment, I thank God, its results require neither explanation nor apology; they are broad, palpable, and unsurpassed—matter, on our part, for gratitude to the Almighty, and deep acknowledgments to you as the instruments in His hand.

The whole appearance of this district bespeaks the efficacy of your system. Its domestic character is changing, and its social aspect presents a contrast to any other portion of Ceylon as distinct and remarkable as it is delightful and encouraging. Civilization and secular knowledge are rapidly opening the eyes of the heathen community to a conviction of the superiority of the external characteristics of Christianity, and thereby creating a wish to know something of the inward principles which lead to an outward development so attractive. Thus the schoolroom, operating simultaneously and in harmony with the pulpit and private counsel, is pioneering and preparing the way for the course of that spiritual enlightenment which, I firmly believe, will ere long pour forth in a flood irresistibly, and preserve its wide and calm career comparatively unimpeded, for every grosser obstacle will have been gradually but effectually removed beforehand.

I hope that this spontaneous tribute of mine will be regarded by you only with reference to the impulse which suggests it, of admiration of your labours, and, I may say, of astonishment at their success. As a private gentleman and a Christian, I could not witness without emotion the good which your faithful servants are so widely diffusing; and identified as I am by position with the Government of this rich and important portion of the Queen's dominions, I could not regard without gratitude to your Board the Christian liberality with which you are animating and directing a movement, the practical results of which have already manifested themselves in this province of Ceylon, in the moral elevation, the social enlightenment, the extended industry, and the spreading prosperity of our people.

I have the honour to be,
Sir,
Yours very faithfully,
(Signed) J. Emerson Tennent,
Colonial Secretary.

To the Rev. R. Anderson, D.D.,
Secretary A. B. C. F. Missions.

Missionary House of the American Board of Commissioners
for Foreign Missions, Boston, July 14, 1848.

SIR,—Your letter of March 23, 1848, is received by our Committee with much gratitude. Indeed it was a kind Providence which inclined you to write to us, just when and just as you did; for I ought to say, that we were beginning to have some doubts lest our method of operating in Jaffna was not as effective as it might be. Your spontaneous and decided testimony had the more weight by being so very opportune, and we cordially thank you for it.

The system of East India superstition appears to be bound together by bars of iron, requiring time and patience in those who would overturn it, beyond the superstitions of almost every other portion of the heathen world; and I have sometimes thought our faith would have failed, and that we should have given out in discouragement, had it not been for the protection and countenance we have so uniformly received from the Government of Ceylon. Our aim and desire have ever been to transform, through the blessing of God, the native population of Jaffna into an enlightened Christian community, which shall at length be competent of itself to support the institutions of the Gospel. This is the reason of our having gone so deeply into education. Our late doubts have arisen chiefly from the apparent failure of the mission in raising up a trustworthy native ministry, and of operating upon the masses of the people.

Your opinion as to the *general* influence of our mission on the community in which it is situated, meets a part of our difficulty, and gives countenance to the expectation that the results of missionary labours in India, though delayed, will at last be realized with apparent suddenness and with imposing magnitude. Perhaps, considering the immense influence of superstition, caste, and ancient custom, no other result could reasonably be expected. When the huge ancient mass comes down, it will be like the fall of some mighty arch.

The expenditure upon our missions among the Tamil people and the Mahrattas, which verges upon a hundred thousand dollars annually, is cheerfully borne by our community, in the belief that a corresponding amount of good is accomplished. The expenditure is much greater than it would be, in consequence of the security given to the results from the stable Protestant Government of the country. I think, however, that the *proportional* expenditure of the department of education is somewhat greater than we can afford to continue, as a permanent thing: but so long as we keep our eyes upon the establishment of a *self-sustaining* Christianity among the natives, we must not expect to secure that result in any other way, substantially, than it is secured in England

and America; that is, by a diffusion of correct and various theoretical and practical knowledge among the people. This involves a system of schools and the use of the press.

We have found a much greater scope for *experience*, in the prosecution of missions, than we expected. One thing was clear, indeed, at the outset; namely, that we were to preach the *essential* doctrines of the Gospel, as the grand means of spiritual renovation in man. But how to secure congregations for our preaching? How far our preaching should be controversial? How much time and money should be given to common schools? How far it is judicious to bring children into the seclusion of boarding-schools? How far our higher institution should approximate to the college in the nature of its studies? How far we should give employment, and consequently support, to our converts? What standard of qualification we should adopt for our native preachers, and how we should best introduce these preachers into the actual discharge of the sacred functions? These and many other similar questions are yet far from being satisfactorily resolved. We are applying the results of experience acquired in the thirty years past to these matters, but are afraid to do anything rashly.

You will ever find great readiness in our brethren to open their entire system of operations to yourself and to other members of the Government when among them, and we shall always esteem it a favour and honour to receive your suggestions.

I am, &c.,

(Signed) RUFUS ANDERSON,

Sec. of the A. B. C. F. M.

To Sir J. Emerson Tennent, &c. &c.
Colonial Secretary, &c. &c.

(B.)

THE MODERN ASTROLOGERS OF CEYLON.

FROM two native gentlemen, A. de Silva Mohanderam and L. de Soyza Mohanderam, I have collected the following particulars:—The profession of astrology among the Singhalese and Buddhists is not limited to any particular caste, but is practised alike by the highest and most humble, from the Vellales, or agricultural aristocracy, to the beaters of tom-toms, who have thus acquired the title of "*Nakatiyas*," or Astrologers. The attendance on particular ceremonies however, called *Balli*, which are connected with divination, belongs exclusively to the latter class. These practices and ceremonies are all borrowed from Hindooism, and although condemned by the religious precepts of the Buddhists as profane, the injunction has been disregarded, and some of the popular practitioners in the island are to be found amongst the priesthood of Buddhu. The ablest astrologers are said to reside in the districts of Matura and Galle; generally speaking their predictions are but meaningless repetitions applied almost indiscriminately to all visitors, and only a few of the more highly educated attempt astronomical calculations, or affect to understand the principles or expound the theory of their science.

Every Singhalese has his horoscope; and in the event of disease or dangerous illness, it is submitted to the nearest astrologer, who, after consulting his astrolabe and considering the probable planets by whom his disorder has been inflicted, proceeds to prescribe the Balli, or ceremony, by which these are to be propitiated, and which consist chiefly of songs and incantations chanted over images of consecrated clay, concluding as a matter of course with an offering of money to the diviners or Balli Adduras.

There are few events in the life of the natives and no works of importance on which they enter without a review of their horoscope. The services of the astrologers are thus employed, not only at the birth of an infant, but on the occasion of its being first carried into the sun; when it is permitted for the first time to eat rice; when its head is first shaved; when it commences its education; when the beard is first shaven in boys or the ears pierced in girls; before going a journey, erecting a house, or entering on any serious occupation of life. In contracting a marriage the horoscopes of the two parties are compared, and if they fail to present those accordances which astrology considers essential, the objection, at least amongst the uneducated, would be considered fatal to the proposed alliance.

The horoscope of an individual enters into the minutest predictions as to his future character and fortunes, his temperament and passions, his dispositions, his abilities and pursuits, with all minor incidentals as to health, pleasure, or disease, and similar particulars as to his future wife and their offspring.

The horoscope of the year is a still more popular and equally momentous document, foretelling before its commencement the character of the seasons, the success of the crops, the extent and value of the produce, the prices of articles of importance, and the still more engrossing topics of general health and disease, of wars, pestilence, and famine.

The nature of one of these documents will be best collected from the following horoscope for the years 1847-8 (the Singhalese new year commences in April), and the omens for the years 1848-9, by which it is followed. It will be seen that in their leading features they are not altogether dissimilar to compositions of the same kind which still find readers and belief even in England:—

TRANSLATION OF THE SINGHALESE HOROSCOPE FOR THE YEAR OF SAKA 1769 (A.D. 1847-1848).

The Name of the Year, &c.—The forthcoming year is called "Plawanga." It is the first year of the Iswara Vinsati (or the twenty years of Iswara in the cycle of sixty years).

The Appearance of the God of the Year.—He rides on a chariot of the *syām* (dark-blue) colour, half a *gow* in height, over which is placed a celestial yahana (seat), with a yāla (a measure) of dark-blue jessamine spread on it. Over this again is a celestial (piece of) silk which is covered with a yāla of dark-blue powdered pearl. His name is Mihingu, an incarnation of Iswara in the character of the god of the year. In height he will be thirteen cubits; his diadem is made of dark-blue pearl. A dark-blue-coloured shawl is his dress, with a girdle of the same colour round his loins. He satisfies his hunger by looking at milk-boiled rice of the *syām* (or dark-blue) colour. He performs his ablutions in the Vaidurya ocean. In his hand he bears a trident and a nosegay of celestial flowers. Flowers are his ornaments. He rests on a celestial yahane. His attendants will be the celestial musicians who spread the sound of music, vocal and instrumental, through the four cardinal points of the heavens. He places his chariot upon a bull, and manifests himself to this nether world as the god of the year, on the night of Sunday of the 12th Tithi (phase of the moon) of the dark half of the month of Medin in the year of Saka era, 1769, 18 Payas (hours) 13 Venadee (minutes) and 45 Tatpara (seconds) after nightfall, by the *hora* of Jupiter and the sign of Capricornus.

At which time the sun, assuming the form of a goat, issues out of a dark-blue-coloured garuda (a fabulous bird), and proceeds from west to east, or, in other words, the old year expires.

Good and Bad Effects of the Year.—As the god of the year proceeds from west to east, there will be little rain in those two quarters of the earth; sickness and affliction will prevail amongst people.

Because the name of the year is Plawanga, a deficiency of rain will ensue; crops of corn will fail; sickness will prevail among men. Great enmities will be cherished between man and man, and great destruction will come upon them all. The sun's assuming the form of a goat will make people sick and subject to attacks from robbers and enemies; the old year expiring on Sunday, and by the sign of Capricornus, will make kings and rulers oppressive to their people; fever, smallpox, and diseases caused by the bile will prevail; contentions and strife between one set of men and another will be on the increase.

As the nakat (lunar mansion) is *Siyawasa*, and the *hora* of Jupiter, and . . . . of moon, there will be an abundance of rain; crops of all kinds of grain will succeed well. Things brought in vessels (imports) will be abundant. People will enjoy freedom from sickness; cows and buffaloes will yield plenty of milk and ghee. As the old year expires at night, friendship will be maintained between people; weddings and social meetings will abound.

As the clouds are of the black kind, rain will fall; but seldom sickness will prevail over the country. Wars will arise; ministers and statesmen will not prosper. It will not be propitious to Sramanas (Buddhist priests), Brahmans, and learned men of the orthodox faith; but heretics, such as those of the Siva faith, will prosper. Infants and cattle will suffer from sickness.

Because Saturn is the lord of rain, many countries will suffer from want of rain. There will be wars and commotions in the different countries of the world; kings will suffer a diminution of prosperity. Trees and creepers will not yield much fruit. People will be in danger from thieves and enemies.

Because Moon is the lord of months and days, there will be good rain; in all countries crops of grain will succeed; countries will be flourishing; trees will yield fruit. People will be free from sickness; royal ministers will enjoy happiness; articles of merchandise will be abundant; cotton cloth will be cheap. There will be rain and high water.

Because Sun is the lord of clouds and lord of prices, there will be strife and enmity amongst people in general. Men as well as quadrupeds will suffer from sickness. There will be a middling quantity of red grain; precious things will be scarce. Trees and creepers of a red colour will yield much fruit.

Because Mars is the lord of grain, good grain will be little, bad in abundance.

Because Mercury is the lord of grain-crops, rain will be dispersed by the wind. Trees will put forth an abundance of leaves and flowers. Gems, pearl, gold, silver, and other articles will abound.

Because Mercury is in Pisces, there will be abundance of rain and wind; crops in low lands will fail, those in high lands will succeed. There will be wrecks of ships and vessels. Yams and other edible roots will grow well.

As Mars is in Capricornus, there will be war in different countries; cattle will suffer from sickness; there will be good rain, and people will enjoy health.

Because Saturn is in Aquarius, there will be little rain; it will be unpropitious to kings; crops shall wither, men will be sick, pregnant females will enjoy health; forest-trees will yield much fruit.

As Rahu and Kethu are in Virgo and Pisces, slaves, thieves, and others will be in danger of their lives. People will enjoy little happiness. Cows will give little milk. Those in prosperity will suffer a diminution of their enjoyments.

The good and bad results, as well as the rain and dearth of the year, after due calculation, will be in the following proportions:—

Good results	21
Bad ditto	20
Rain	21
Dearth	9

Those who wish to observe the ceremonies in connexion with the season, should eat and drink and leave off all manner of work for the old year by the evening of Sunday; and put a little rice on a pot over a hearth without extinguishing fire, as the old year expires at 18 *Payas* 13 *Venadees* and 45 *Tatparas* after the nightfall on that day. On the following Monday morning at twilight, the rice in the pot should be partaken of by all, with curries of dark-blue colour.

The ceremony of anointing the head with oil should take place on Saturday the 3rd of the bright half of the month of *Bak*, at 2 Pādas (footsteps) by the shadow of the sun. The ingredient for the purifying water of the head will be, leaves of Bo (Buddhu's) tree, those of the Banyan, Diuril, and Karandu trees; for cleansing the feet white Sandal, leaves of the Imbul tree should be taken. The head should be anointed with a mixture of the five different kinds of oil. Exchanges of money and visits to houses of friends as guests should also take place at the same time.

OMEN FOR THE YEAR 1848-9.

From the position of the planets as above described, the following will be the result of good and bad in the forthcoming year 1771 of the Saka era.

There will be famine and sickness throughout the world. Rain will fall but seldom. Crops will yield little. The people will suffer from thieves. There will be murrain among elephants and horses. But these ill effects will be more specially felt by the inhabitants of the countries of Kasala, Pandawa, Magadha, and Karnāta on the continent of Jamboodwepa. In the continents of Poorwawidhehe, Utturukurudewayena, and Aparagoyana, and the other countries of Jamboodwepa than those above named, the ill effects will be felt, but not so severely.

OMEN FOR THE YEAR 1848-9.

From the position of the planets as above described, the following will be the good and bad results of the forthcoming year 1771 of the Saka era.

As it is the Tiger's year, there will be abundance of rain and dangers from sickness. As Jupiter is in the sign of Cancer, gold will abound; kings will be angry; large trees will yield much fruit; cattle will increase; men will be industrious or enterprising. As the new year falls on a Wednesday, there will be rain; eatables and drinkables will abound, and the people will enjoy happiness. As the expiration of the old year takes place in the middle watch of the day, crops will yield little; good intentions of men will die away. In the last six months of the year the crops will be more fruitful; men will enjoy happiness, and attend to things that will tend to their welfare.

Shrine of the Sacred Tooth at Kandy. p. 235

CHAPTER V.

BUDDHISM AND DEMON WORSHIP.

National Character of the Singhalese — Indifference to all Religions — Buddhism and its Origin — Its Antiquity and Extended Influence — Story of the Life of Gotama Buddhu — His Incarnation — His Religion — Transmigration of Souls — Physical Science of Buddhism — Its Ideas of a Future State — Its Doctrine of Fate — Necessity — Its Priesthood — Their Privileges — Various Sects of Buddhists — Demon Worship — Its Origin — Practices — Priests.

CHAPTER V.

BUDDHISM AND DEMON WORSHIP.

FROM this sketch of Brahmanism, and of the efforts which have been made amongst the Tamils of Ceylon to supersede it by the faith of Christianity, I now turn to the purely Singhalese districts of the island, where the natives are of a different race and language, exhibit a different character, and profess a very different form of idolatry.

Whilst there is that in the tenets and genius of Brahmanism which proclaims an active resistance to any other form of religion, Christianity in the southern expanse of Ceylon has to encounter an obstacle still more embarrassing in the habitual apathy and listless indifference of the Buddhists. Brahmanism in its constitution and spirit is essentially exclusive and fanatical, jealous of all other faiths, and strongly disposed to persecution. Buddhism, on the other hand, in the strength of its self-righteousness, extends a latitudinarian liberality to every other belief, and exhibits a Laodicean indifference towards its own. Whilst Brahmanism is a science confided only to an initiated priesthood, and the Vedas and the Shastras in which its precepts are embodied are kept with jealousy from the profane eye of the people, Buddhism, rejoicing in its universality, aspires to be the religion of the multitude, throws open its sacred pages without restriction, and encourages their perusal as a meritorious act of devotion. The despotic ministers of Brahma affect to be versed only in arcana and mystery, and to issue their dicta from oracular authority; but the priesthood of Buddhu assume no higher functions than those of teachers of ethics, and claim no loftier title than that of "the clergy of reason."[1]

In the character of the Singhalese people there is to be traced much of the genius of their religion. The same passiveness and love of ease which restrain from active exertion in the labours of life, find a counterpart in the adjustment by which virtue is limited to abstinence, and worship to contemplation,

[1] The sect of the *Lao Tsen*, or "Doctors of Reason," whom Landresse regards as a development of Buddhism, prevailed in Thibet and the countries lying between China and India in the fifth and sixth centuries; and Fa Hian, the Chinese Buddhist who travelled from Sian-fou, through Tartary, Affghanistan, and India, and visited the Buddhist priesthood and their establishments in Ceylon in the year 412 A.D., always refers to them as the "*Clergy of Reason.*"—FOE KOUE KI, ou Relation des Royaumes Buddhiques, Voyage dans la Tartarie, dans l'Afghanistan, et dans l'Inde, exécuté à la fin du 4me Siècle, par CHY FA HIAN, traduit du Chinois par MM. Remusat, Klaproth, et Landresse. Paris, 1836. *Translated by J. W. Laidley, Esq. Calcutta*, 1848. Chap. xxxviii. pp. 334, 354, &c.

with only so much of actual ceremonial as may render visible to the eye what would be otherwise inaccessible to the mind. The same love of repose which renders sleep and insensibility the richest blessings of this life anticipates torpor, akin to extinction, as the supremest felicity of the next. In common with all other nations they deem some form of religious worship indispensable, but, contrary to the usage of most, they are singularly indifferent as to what that particular form is to be; leaving it passively to be determined by the conjunction of circumstances, the accident of locality, and the influence of friends or worldly prospects of gain. Still, in the hands of the Christian missionary, they are by no means the plastic substance which such a description would suggest—capable of being moulded into any form, or retaining permanently any casual impression—but rather a yielding fluid which adapts its shape to that of the vessel into which it may happen to be poured, without any change in its quality or any modification of its character.

From this unexcitable temperament of the people, combined with the exalted morals which form the articles of their belief, result phenomena which for upwards of three hundred years have more or less baffled the exertions of all who have laboured for the overthrow of their national superstition and the elevation of Christianity in its stead. The precepts of the latter, when offered to the natives apart from the divinity of their origin,[1] presented something in appearance so nearly akin to their own tenets that they were slow to discern the superiority. If Christianity required purity and truth, temperance, honesty, and benevolence, these were already discovered to be enjoined with at least equal impressiveness in the precepts of Buddhu. The commandment forbidding murder was supposed to be analogous to the Buddhist prohibition to kill;[2] and where the law and the Gospel

[1] Buddhism too aspires to a revelation as the authority not only for its doctrines, but for its history, and even the grammar of its sacred dialect, the Pali. See the origin of Kachchayano's Grammar in Turner's Introduction to the Mahawanso, p. xxvii.

[2] The order of Buddhu not to take away life is imperative and unqualified as regards the priesthood; but to mankind in general it forms one of his "*Sikshapada*," or *advices*, and admits of modification under certain contingencies. A priest who should take away the life of an animal, or even an insect, under any circumstances, would be guilty of the offence denominated *Pachitta*, and subject to penal discipline; but to take away human life, to be accessory to murder, or to encourage to suicide, amounts to the sin of *Parājika*, and is visited with permanent expulsion from the order. As regards the laity, the use of animal food is not forbidden, provided the individual has not himself been an agent in depriving it of life. The doctrine of prohibition, however, although thus regulated, like many others of the Buddhists, by subtleties and sophistry, has proved an obstacle in the way of the Missionaries; and, coupled with the permission in the Scriptures "to slay and eat," it has not failed to operate prejudicially to the spread of Christianity. The Buddhists, unlike the Brahmans, have no veneration for the cow more than any other living animal. Mountstuart Elphinstone says, "The Báudha religionists carry their respect for animal life much farther than the Bramins: their priests do not eat after noon,

alike enforce the love of one's neighbour as the love of one's self, Buddhism insists upon charity as the basis of worship, and calls on its own followers "to appease anger by gentleness, and overcome evil by good."[1]

Thus the outward concurrence of Christianity in those points on which it agrees with their own religion, has proved more embarrassing to the natives than their perplexity as to others in which it essentially differs; till at last, too timid to doubt and too feeble to inquire, they cling with helpless tenacity to their own superstition, and yet subscribe to the new faith simply by adding it on to the old.[2]

Combined with this state of irresolution a serious obstacle to the acceptance of reformed Christianity by the Singhalese Buddhists has arisen from the distinctions and differences between the various churches by whose ministers it has been successively offered to them. In the persecution of the Roman Catholics

nor drink after dark, for fear of swallowing minute insects; and they carry a brush on all occasions with which they carefully sweep every place before they sit down, lest they should inadvertently crush any living creature. Some even tie a thin cloth over their mouths to prevent their drawing in small insects with their breath. *Note.* The *laity* eat animal food without restraint: even the priests may eat it, *if no animal is killed on their account.*"—History of India, vol. i. b. ii. c. 4.

[1] From the Singhalese book, the '*Damma Padan*,' or Footsteps of Religion, portions of which are translated in '*The Friend*,' vol. iii. p. 149. Colombo, 1840.

[2] See Note B, end of the Chapter.

by the Dutch, the subsequent supersession of the Church of Holland by that of England, the rivalries more or less apparent between the Episcopalians and Presbyterians, and the peculiarities which separate the Baptists from the Wesleyan Methodists—all of whom have their missions and representatives in Ceylon—the Singhalese can discover little more than that they are offered something still doubtful and unsettled, in exchange for which they are pressed to surrender their own ancient superstition. Conscious of their inability to decide on what it has baffled the wisest of their European teachers to reconcile, they hesitate to exchange for an apparent uncertainty that which has been unhesitatingly believed by generations of their ancestors, and which comes recommended to them by all the authority of antiquity; and even when truth has been so far successful as to shake their confidence in their national faith, the choice of sects which has been offered to them leads to utter bewilderment as to the peculiar form of Christianity with which they may most confidingly replace it.

Of the BUDDHIST RELIGION it is difficult to attempt any condensed, and, at the same time, perspicuous sketch—a difficulty which arises not merely from the voluminous obscurity of its own sacred history and records, but still more from confusion in the variety of forms under which it exhibits itself in various localities, and the divergences of opinion which prevail as to its tenets and belief. The antiquity of its worship is so extreme, that doubts still hang over its origin and its chronological relation to the Brahmanical religion. Whether it took its rise in Hindostan or in countries farther to the West, and whether Buddhism was the original doctrine of which Brahmanism became a corruption, or Brahmanism the original and Buddhism an effort to restore it to its pristine purity,[1]—all these are questions which have

[1] Those early writers on the religions of India who drew their information exclusively from Sanskrit and Brahmanical sources incline to favour the pretensions of that system as the most ancient of the two. Of this opinion is Klaproth, a profound authority on such subjects; but in later times the translations of the Pali records and other sacred volumes of Buddhism in Western India, Ceylon, and Nepal, have inclined the preponderance of opinion, if not in favour of the superior antiquity of Buddhism, at least in support of its claim to the same origin, and perhaps a contemporaneous development, with the doctrines of the Brahmans. A summary of the arguments in favour of the superior antiquity of Buddhism will be found in the "Notes," &c., by Colonel Sykes, in the 12th volume of the Asiatic Journal—and in the 'Essai sur l'Origine des Principaux Peuples Anciens,' par F. L. M. Maupied, chap. viii. The arguments on the side of those who look on Brahmanism as the original, are given by Mountstuart Elphinstone in his 'History of India,' vol. i. b. ii. c. 4. "Admitting the common origin of the two systems which the similarity of their fundamental tenets would seem to prove, the weight of argument," he says, "appears to lean to the side of the Bramins; and an additional reason may perhaps be drawn from the improbability that the Báudha system could ever have been an original one." Mr. Elphinstone proceeds to argue that man would imbibe his first notions of a God from the perception of his power; that the idea of a *quiescent* deity would not

yet to be adjusted by the results of Oriental research.[1] It is, however, established by a concurrence of historical proofs, that many centuries before the era of

precede the worship of the sun or the elements; still less would man deify saints, sanctity being merely conformity to some religion already known. But, he continues, "the Hindu religion presents a more natural course: it rose from the worship of nature to theism; and then declined into scepticism with the learned, and man-worship with the vulgar. The doctrines of the Sankya school of philosophers seem reflected in the Atheism of Báudha; while the hero-worship of the common Hindus, and their extravagant veneration for religious ascetics, are much akin to the deification of saints among the Báudhas. We are led, therefore, to suppose the Bramin faith to have originated in early times; and that of Báudha to have branched off from it at a period when its orthodox tenets had reached their highest perfection, if not shown a tendency to decline." (History of India, vol. i., b. ii., c. 4.) The Rev. Mr. Gogerly, the most accomplished student of Buddhism in Ceylon, says its sacred books expressly demonstrate that its doctrines had been preached by the twenty-four Buddhists who had lived in succession prior to Gotama or Sakya, in periods incredibly remote, but that they had entirely disappeared at the time of Gotama's birth, so that he re-discovered the whole, and revived an extinguished or nearly extinct school of philosophy. (Notes on Buddhism by the Rev. D. J. Gogerly, Appendix to Lee's Translation of Ribeyro, p. 265.)

[1] The celebrated temple of Somnauth was originally a Buddhist foundation, and in the worship of Jaggernath, to whose orgies all ranks are admitted without distinction of castes, there may still be traced an influence of Buddhism, if not a direct Buddhistical origin. Colonel Sykes is of opinion that the Delada, or sacred tooth of Buddhu now preserved in the Temple at Kandy, was at one time deposited and worshipped in the great Temple of Kalinga, now dedicated to Jaggernath, by the Princes of Orissa, who in the fourth century professed the Buddhist religion. The tooth was not received in Ceylon till the year 311 A.D.

Christianity the doctrines of Buddhu were enthusiastically cultivated in central India, and at a still later period in Bahar, the *Magadha*, or country of the Magas, in the ancient geography of the Hindoos, and whose modern name is identified with the *Wihares* or monasteries of Buddhism. Thence its teachers diffused themselves extensively throughout the Indian continent, and the countries to the eastward; upwards of two thousand years ago it became the national religion of Ceylon and the Indian Archipelago; and its tenets have been adopted throughout the vast regions which extend from Siberia to Siam, and from the Bay of Bengal to the western shores of the Pacific.[1]

Looking to its influence at the present day over at least three hundred and fifty millions of human beings —exceeding one-third of the human race—it is no

(Colonel Sykes, Notes, &c., Asiatic Journal, vol. xii. pp. 275, 317, 420. See Note A, end of this Chapter.)

[1] Fa Hian, the Chinese priest of Buddhu, whose travels through Tartary to India and Ceylon in the fourth and fifth centuries have been already alluded to, declares that in the whole of that vast route, including Affghanistan and Bokhara, he found a Buddhist people and dynasty, with traditions of its endurance for the preceding thousand years. "As to Hindostan itself, he says, from the time of leaving the deserts (of Jaysalmeer and Bekaneer) and the river (Jumna) to the west, *all the kings of the different kingdoms in India are firmly attached to the law of Buddhu*, and when they do honour to the ecclesiastics they take off their diadems."—See also *Maupied*, Essai sur l'Origine des Principaux Peuples Anciens, chap. ix. p. 209.

exaggeration to say that the religion of Buddhu is the most widely diffused that now exists, or that has ever existed since the creation of mankind.[1]

[1] So ample are the materials offered by Buddhism for antiquarian research, that its doctrines have been sought to be identified at once with the Asiatic philosophy and with the myths of the Scandinavians. Buddhu has been at one time conjectured to be the Woden of the Scythians, at another the prophet Daniel, whom Nebuchadnezzar had created master of the astrologers, or chief priest of the Magi, as the title is rendered in the Septuagint—*Αρχοντα Μαγων*. This conjecture has no better basis than a similarity of sound between the words "Baal" and "Pali;" the latter the dialect of *Magadha*, the ancient name of Bahar, in which again is traced a fanciful coincidence with the Magi of Chaldea. (*See Letters of the Rev. Mr. Gilbert to Sir W. Colebrooke in the Ceylon Magazine*, 1840-1.) At the same time, so prolific is philological ingenuity, that a similar origin has been discerned for the Brahmanical system. The astronomy of the Hindoos has been traced to the star-worship of the Chaldees; the *Mithra* of their religion is associated with *Mitra*, the Sanskrit appellation for the sun; and the name of *Brahma* himself is presumed to suggest its own coincidence with that of Abraham. An antiquarian of Wales, in devising a pedigree for the Cymri, has imported ancestors for the ancient Britons from Ceylon; and a writer in the 'Asiatic Researches,' in 1807, as a preamble to the proof that the binomial theorem was familiar to the Hindoos, has traced Western civilization to an irruption of philosophers from India, identified the Druids with the Brahmans, and declared Stonehenge to be "one of the temples of Boodh." (Asiat. Res., vol. ii. p. 448.)

A still more recent investigator, M. Maupied, has collected, in his 'Essai sur l'Origine des Peuples Anciens,' what he considers to be the evidence that Buddhism may be indebted for its appearance in India to the captivity of the Jews by Salmanasar, 729 B.C.; to their dispersion by Assar-Addon at a still more recent period; to their captivity in Babylon, 606 B.C.; their dif-

It is a remarkable feature of Buddhism, as compared with the superstition of the Hindoos, that it draws a wide distinction between its own legendary and historical periods; ascribing to *tradition* the monstrous chronology and the miraculous minuteness which pervade its earlier annals, and claiming credence as *history* only for those records which it has carefully preserved from the time when Gotama became Buddhu. It admits the absolute mystification and obscurity of every legend anterior to the close of the sixth century before Christ, when Prince Siddhato, son of the sovereign of Magadha, or Bahar, commenced his reign of righteousness and wisdom, under the name and the character of Gotama Buddhu;[1] and though other Buddhus had previously

fusion over Media and the East, Persia, Bactria, Thibet, and China, and the communication of their sacred book to the nations amongst whom they thus became sojourners. He ventures even to suggest a possible identity between the names Jehovah and Buddhu: "Les voyelles du mot *Bouddha* sont les mêmes que celles du mot Jéhovah, qu'on prononce aussi *Jouva;* mais d'ailleurs le nom de Boudda a bien pu être tiré du mot *Jeoudda* Juda, le dieu de Joudda *Boudda.*"—Chap. ix. p. 235. To account for the purer morals of Buddhism, M. Maupied has recourse to the conjecture that they may have been influenced by the preaching of St. Thomas at Ceylon, and Bartholomew on the continent of India. "*Or il nous semble logique de conclure de tous ces faits que le Bouddhisme, dans ses doctrines essentielles, est d'origine Juive et Chrétienne; conséquence inattendue pour la plus de nos lecteurs sans doute.*"—*Maupied*, ch. ix. p. 257; ch. x. p. 263.

[1] Introduction to Turnour's Translation of the Mahawanso, p. xxviii.

reigned, their exploits are admitted to be utterly lost to authentic history. Gotama, or Sakya, the last who is adored as Buddhu at the present day, was born at Pataliputra, or Patna,[1] B. C. 623, attained the perfection by which he became Buddhu B. C. 588, and died at the age of eighty, in 543 B. C. He traversed the extent of India for the propagation of his faith, and twice visited Ceylon; but it was not till upwards of two centuries after his death, B. C. 307, that the island was permanently converted to his faith by the instrumentality of Mahindo (the great grandson of Chandragupta, or Sandracottus, the contemporary of Alexander the Great), previously to which time the religion of the Singhalese consisted chiefly in the worship of demons and serpents,[2] the former the most ancient form of superstition known to be practised by mankind. Between 104 B. C. and 76 B. C., the doctrines of Gotama were reduced to writing in Pali,[3] by the Buddhist priests of Ceylon, with a commentary in the vernacular language of the island; and these sacred volumes, the text of which has been preserved, are identical with the version which from time immemorial has been in use amongst the Buddhists of Burmah and Siam.[4]

[1] The Palibothra of the Greeks.

[2] Introduction to Turnour's Translation of the Mahawanso, p. xlv.

[3] The Mahawanso, c. 33, p. 207. See Note B, end of Chapter I.

[4] Amongst the Singhalese the ancient works in the history and

From the earliest period of Indian tradition, the struggle between the religion of Buddhu and that of Brahma was carried on with a fanaticism and perseverance which resulted in the ascendancy of the Brahmans, perhaps about the commencement of the Christian era, and the eventual expulsion some centuries later of the worship of their rivals from Hindostan; but at what precise time the latter catastrophe was consummated has not been accurately mentioned in the annals of either sect.[1]

That Buddhism thus dispersed over eastern and central Asia became an active agent in the promotion

philosophy of Buddhism are in Pali; but those of Nepaul, which Mr. Hodgson considers of still earlier origin, are in Sanskrit; in Ceylon all the treatises on the abstract and practical sciences, mathematics, astronomy, medicine, chemistry, and the arts, are composed in the latter. The historical books in Pali, commencing at a period of upwards of five hundred years before the birth of Christ, are continued in one uninterrupted series to the period of the Portuguese conquest. They present remarkable and confirmatory evidence of ascertained facts in the contemporary history of India; and after the most patient investigation and comparison of their contents, their able investigator Turnour has declared the sacred books of Ceylon to be "authenticated by the concurrence of every evidence which can contribute to verify the annals of any country; nor does there appear to be the slightest ground for questioning their correctness, even in minute respects."—Introduction to the Mahawanso, p. li., lvii.

[1] The final overthrow of Buddhism in Bahar and its expulsion from Hindostan took place probably between the seventh and twelfth centuries of the Christian era. Colonel Sykes, however, extends the period to the thirteenth or fourteenth (Asiatic Journal, vol. iv. p. 334).

of whatever civilization afterwards enlightened those races by whom its doctrines were embraced, seems to rest upon evidence which admits of no reasonable doubt. The introduction of Buddhism into China is ascertained to have been contemporary with the early development of civilization and the arts amongst this remarkable people, at a period coeval, if not anterior, to the era of Christianity.[1] Buddhism exerted a salutary influence over the tribes of Thibet; through them it became instrumental in humanizing the Moguls; and it would seem more or less to have led to the cessation of the devastating incursions by which the hordes of the East were precipitated over the Western empire in the early eras of Christianity.

[1] "Numerous texts prove in an incontestable manner the part which the Chinese took *two centuries* before our era in the events and commerce of Western Asia; . . . . . but it is to the religious communications established and entertained by Buddhism that they owe the most precious part of the knowledge they collected respecting foreign nations. The most ancient of these religious undertakings of which history preserves mention is that of the Lao tsen (or Doctors of Reason) to the west in the *sixth century* before our era. It is beyond all doubt that at extremely remote periods there was a kind of reciprocity in the importations into China of the doctrines of Buddhu and in the propagation beyond the limits of China of the precepts of the Lao tsen; and we cannot well deny the analogy which exists between the opinions of the Doctors of Reason and those of the Buddhists. A Buddhist priest of the name of Chi li fang arrived in Chan si in the year 217 B.C. Thus this province, where there is every reason to believe that Chinese civilization had its birth, was also the first to become acquainted with Buddhism."—See Colonel Sykes, 'Notes,' &c.; and M. Landresse, Introd. to Translation of Fa Hian.

The Singhalese, and probably the nations of further Asia, are indebted to Buddhism for an alphabet and a literature; and whatever of authentic history we possess in relation to these countries we owe to the influence of their religion. Nor are its effects limited to these objects alone: much of what is vigorous and manly in the character of its northern converts may be traced to the operation of its principles, in the development of their peculiar idiosyncrasy, which, unlike that of the unwarlike and timid Singhalese, rejected sloth and effeminacy to aim at conquest and power. Looking to the self-reliance which Buddhism inculcates, the exaltation of intellect which it proclaims, and the perfection of virtue and wisdom which it points to as within the reach of every created being, it can readily be imagined that, combined with other exciting causes, it must have wielded over those who were disposed to bow to its authority, a spell of unusual potency, and one well calculated to awaken boldness and energy in those already animated by schemes of ambition. In Ceylon, on the contrary, owing more or less to insulation and seclusion, Buddhism for upwards of 2000 years has remained as unchanged in all its leading characteristics as the genius of the people has remained torpid and inanimate under its influence. In this respect the Singhalese are the living mummies of past ages: they realize in their immoveable characteristics the Eastern fable of the city whose inhabitants were perpetuated in marble. If change has in any degree supervened, it has been from the corruption of the practice, not from any abandonment of the principles, of Buddhism; and in arts, literature, and civilization, the records of their own history, and the ruins of their monuments, attest their deterioration in common with that of every other nation which has not at some time been brought under the ennobling influences of Christianity.

In alluding to the distinctive doctrines of Buddhism, as it exists at the present day, my observations are to be understood as applying exclusively to the aspect under which it presents itself in Ceylon, and irrespective of the numerous forms in which it has been cultivated elsewhere. Even before the decease of the last Buddhu, schisms had arisen amongst his followers in India. Eighteen heresies are deplored in the Mahawanso within two centuries from his death; and four distinct sects, each rejoicing in the name of Buddhists, are still to be traced amongst the remnants of his worshippers in Hindostan.[1]

In its migrations to other countries since its dispersion by the Brahmans, Buddhism has assumed and exhibited itself in a variety of shapes. At the present day its doctrines, as cherished amongst the Jainas of Guzerat and Rajpootana,[2] differ widely from its mys-

[1] Colebrooke's Essays on the Philosophy of the Hindoos, sect. v. part 5, p. 401.

[2] An account of the religion of the Jains or Jainas, which holds a position intermediate between Buddhism and Brahmanism,

teries, as administered by the Lama of Thibet; and both are equally distinct from the metaphysical abstractions propounded by the monks of Nepal. Its observances in Japan have undergone a still more striking alteration from their vicinity to the Syntoos; and in China they have been similarly modified in their contact with the rationalism of Lao-tsen and the social demonology of the Confucians.[1] But in each and in all the distinction is in degree rather than essence; and the general concurrence is unbroken in all the grand essentials of the system.

Whilst Brahmanism, without denying the existence, practically ignores the influence and power of a creating and controlling intelligence, Buddhism, exulting in the idea of the infinite perfectibility of man, and the achievement of the highest attainable happiness by the unfaltering practice of every conceivable virtue, exalts the individuals thus pre-eminently wise into absolute supremacy over all existing beings, and attempts the daring experiment of an *atheistic morality.*[2] Buddhu himself is not worshipped as a deity,

will be found in Mountstuart Elphinstone's History of India, vol. i. b. ii. c. 4. They arose in the sixth or seventh century, were at their height in the eleventh, and declined in the twelfth.

[1] Details of Buddhism in China and Chin-India will be found in the erudite commentaries of Klaproth, Remusat, and Landresse.

[2] Colonel Sykes, in his Notes upon India, in the twelfth volume of the Asiatic Journal, pp. 263 and 376, has disputed the dictum that Buddhism is *atheistic;* and he has adduced, in support of his

or a still existent and active agent of benevolence and power. He is reverenced merely as a glorified remembrance, the effulgence of whose purity is to serve as a guide and incentive to the future struggles and aspirations of mankind. The sole superiority which his

views, opinions and allusions which occur in the Chinese writings of Fa Hian. But the passages which he refers to will be found on closer inquiry to present no direct contradiction to the expositions contained in this chapter of those metaphysical subtleties by which the Buddhistical writers have carefully avoided whilst they closely approach the admission of belief in a deity. I am not prepared to deny that the faith in a supreme being may not have characterised Buddhism in its origin, as the belief in a great first cause in the person of *Brahm* is still acknowledged by the Hindoos, although honoured by no share of their adoration. But whatever may have been the ancient constitution of Buddhism, it admits of little doubt that neither in the discourses of its priesthood at the present day nor in the practice of its followers in Ceylon is either the name or the existence of an omnipotent and eternal First Cause recognized in any portion of their worship. Maupied has correctly described Buddhism both in Ceylon and China as a system of refined atheism ('Essai sur l'Origine des Peuples Anciens,' ch. x. p. 277), and Mountstuart Elphinstone gives the weight of his high authority in the statement that "The most ancient of Báudha sects entirely denies the being of a God; and some of those which admit the existence of God still refuse to acknowledge him as the creator and ruler of the world. . . . . The theistical sect seems to prevail in Nepaul, and the *atheistical to subsist in perfection in Ceylon.*"—(History of India, vol. i. b. ii. c. 4.) An able writer in the fourth volume of the 'Calcutta Review' has also controverted the assertion of its atheistic complexion; but whatever truth may be developed in his views, their application is confined to Buddhism in Hindostan and Nepal, and is utterly at variance with the practice and received dogmas in Ceylon.

doctrines admit is that of goodness and wisdom; and Buddhu himself having attained to this perfection by the immaculate righteousness of his actions, the absolute subjugation of his passions, and the unerring accuracy of his unlimited knowledge, became entitled to the homage of all, and was required to render it to none.

Externally coinciding with Hindooism, so far as the avatar of Buddhu may be regarded as a pendant for the incarnation of Brahma, the worship of the former is essentially distinguished from the religion of the latter in the important particular that it regards that exalted being not as an actual emanation or manifestation of the divinity, but as a guide and example to teach that enthusiastic self-reliance by means of which mankind of themselves and by their own unassisted exertions are to attain to perfect virtue here and to supreme happiness hereafter. Both inculcate, but with diversified characteristics, the mysterious doctrine of the metempsychosis; but whilst the result of successive embodiments is to bring the soul of the Hindoo a step nearer to the final beatitude of absorption into the essence of Brahma and actual identification with the Creator, the end and aim of the Buddhistical transmigration is to lead the purified spirit to *Nirwana*,[1] a condition

[1] Nirwana is Sanskrit, *ni* (*r* euphon. causa) *Wana* desire. The Singhalese name Nirwana is also derived from Newanawa, to extinguish.

between which and utter annihilation there exists but the dim distinction of a name. Nirwana is the *exhaustion* without the *destruction* of existence, the *close* but not the *extinction* of being.[1]

In deliberate consistency with this principle of human elevation, the doctrines of Buddhu recognize the full eligibility of every individual born into the world for the attainment of the highest degrees of intellectual perfection and ultimate bliss; and herein consists its most striking departure from the Brahmanical system in denying the superiority of the "twice born" over the rest of mankind, in repudiating a sacerdotal supremacy of race, and in claiming for the pure and the wise that supremacy and exaltation which the self-glorified Brahmans would monopolize for themselves.

Hence the supremacy of "*caste*" is utterly disclaimed in the sacred books which contain the tenets of Buddhu; and although in process of time his followers have departed from that portion of his precepts, still distinction of birth is nowhere authoritatively recognized as a qualification for the priesthood. Buddhu being in fact a deification of human intellect, the philanthropy of the system extends its participation and advantages to the whole family of mankind, the humblest member of which it sustains by the assurance that by virtue and

[1] See Note C, end of this Chapter.

endurance he may attain an equality though not an identification with the supreme intelligence. Wisdom thus exalted as the sole object of pursuit and veneration, the Buddhists, with characteristic liberality, admit that the teaching of virtue may not be confined to their own professors alone;[1] especially when the ceremonial of others does not involve the taking of life. Hence in a great degree arises the indifference of the Singhalese as to the comparative claims of Christianity and Buddhism, and hence the facility with which, both under the Portuguese, the Dutch, and the British Government, they have combined the secret worship of the one with the ostensible profession of the other. They in fact admit Christ to have been a teacher, second only to Buddhu, but inferior, inasmuch as the latter, who was perfect in wisdom, has attained to the bliss of Nirwana.[2]

As regards the *structure of the universe*, the theories of the Buddhists, though in a great degree borrowed from the Brahmans, occupy a much less prominent position in their mythology, and are less intimately identified with their system of religion. Their attention has been directed less to physical than to metaphysical disquisitions, and their views of cosmogony

[1] See Note A, end of this Chapter.

[2] Sir John Davis, in his account of the Chinese, states that the Buddhists there worship the Queen of Heaven, a personage evidently borrowed from the Roman Catholics, and that the name of Jesus appears in the list of their divinities.—(Chap. xiv.)

have as little of truth as of imagination in their details. The basis of the system is a declaration of the eternity of matter, and its submission at remote intervals to decay and re-formation; but this and the organization of animal life are but the results of spontaneity and procession, not the products of will and design on the part of an all powerful Creator.

Buddhism adopts something approaching to the mundane theory of the Brahmans, in the multiplicity and superposition of worlds and the division of the earth into concentric continents, each separated by oceans of various fabulous liquids.[1]

Its notions of geography are at once fanciful and crude; and its chronology, again borrowing from the Shastras, extends over boundless portions of time, but invests with the authority of history only those occurrences which have arisen since the birth of Gotama Buddhu.

The Buddhists believe in the existence of lokas, or heavens, each differing in glory, and serving as the temporary residences of demigods and divinities, as well as of men whose etherialization is but inchoate, and who have yet to revisit the earth in further births and acquire in future transmigrations their complete attainment of Nirwana. They believe likewise in the existence of hells which are the abodes of demons or tormentors, and in which the wicked undergo a purgatorial imprisonment preparatory to an extended

[1] See Note D at the end of this Chapter.

probation upon earth. Here their torments are in proportion to their crimes, and although not eternal, their duration extends almost to the infinitude of eternity; those who have been guilty of the deadliest sins of parricide, sacrilege, and defiance of the faith being doomed to the endurance of excruciating deaths, followed by instant revival and a repetition of their tortures without mitigation and apparently without end.[1]

It is one of the extraordinary anomalies of the system, that combined with these principles of self-reliance and perfectibility, Buddhism has incorporated to a certain extent the doctrine of fate or "necessity," under which it demonstrates that adverse events are the general results of *akusala* or moral demerit in some previous stage of existence. This belief, which lies at the very foundation of their religion, the Buddhists have so adapted to the rest of the structure as to avoid the inconsistency of making this directing power inherent in any Supreme Being, by assigning it as one of the attributes of matter and a law of its perpetual mutations.[2]

Like all the leading doctrines of Buddhism, however, its theories on this subject are propounded with the usual admixture of modification and casuistry; only a portion of men's conduct is presumed to be

[1] Davy's Account of the Interior of Ceylon, p. 204.

[2] See Note E, end of this Chapter.

exclusively controllable by *fate*—neither moral delinquency nor virtuous actions are declared to be altogether the products of an inevitable necessity; and whilst both the sufferings and the enjoyments of mortals are represented as the general consequences of merit in a previous stage of existence, even this fundamental principle is not without its exception, inasmuch as the vicissitudes are admitted to be partially the results of man's actions in this life, or of the influence of others from which his own deserts are insufficient to protect him. The main article, however, which admits neither of modification nor evasion, is that neither in heaven nor on earth can man escape from the *consequences* of his acts; that morals are in their essence productive causes, without the aid or intervention of any higher authority; and hence forgiveness or atonement are ideas utterly unknown in the despotic dogmas of Buddhu.

Allusion has already been made to the subtleties entertained by the priesthood, in connexion with the doctrine of the *metempsychosis*, as developed in their sacred books; but the exposition would be tedious to show the distinctions between their theories, and the opinions of transmigration entertained by the mass of the Singhalese Buddhists. The rewards of virtue and the punishment of vice are supposed to be equally attainable in this world; and according to the amount of either, which characterizes the conduct of an individual in one stage of being, will be the elevation or degradation into which he will be hereafter born.

Thus punishment and reward become equally fixed and inevitable: but as retribution may be deferred by the intermediate exhibition of virtue, and an offering or prostration to Buddhu, or an aspiration in the fervour of faith in his name, will suffice to ward off punishment for a time, and even produce happiness in an intermediate birth; so the most flagitious offender, by an act of reverence in dying, may postpone indefinitely the evil consequence of his crimes, and hence the indifference and apparent apathy which is a remarkable characteristic of the Singhalese who suffer death for their offences.[1]

To mankind in general Buddhu came only as an adviser and a friend; but, as regards his own priesthood, he assumed all the authority of a lawgiver and chief. Spurning the desires and vanities of the world, he has taught them to aspire to no other

[1] Et vos barbaricos ritus, moremque sinistrum
Sacrorum Druidæ positis repetistis ab armis.
Solis nosse deos, et cœli numina vobis
Aut solis nescire datum: nemora alta remotis
Incolitis lucis: *vobis auctoribus umbræ*
Non tacitas Erebi sedes Ditisque profundi
Pallida regna petunt: regit idem spiritus artus
Orbe alio, longæ (si canitis cognita) vitæ
Mors media est, certi populi quos despicit Arctos
Felices errore suo, quos ille timorum
Maximus haud urget leti metus.

Lucan, l. i. 450 et seq.

reward for their labours than the veneration of the human race, as teachers of knowledge and examples of benevolence. Taking the abstract idea of perfect intelligence and immaculate virtue for a divinity, Buddhism accords honour to all in proportion to their approaches towards absolute wisdom, and the extinction of all the desires and passions of humanity; and as the realization of this perfection is regarded as almost hopeless in a life devoted to secular cares, the priests of Buddhu, on assuming their robe and tonsure, forswear all earthly occupations; subsist on alms, not in money, but in food; devote themselves to meditation and self-denial; and, being thus proclaimed and recognized as the most successful aspirants to Nirwana, they claim the homage of ordinary mortals, acknowledge no superior upon earth, and withhold even the tribute of a salutation from all except the members of their own religious order.

The *priesthood* comprises two orders—those who have obtained the first rank of ordination as *Samanaros*,[1] and those who, after a long interval, are

[1] It is remarkable that this name, which to the present day is preserved as the designation of the Buddhist priesthood in Siam and Ceylon, should be the same by which the *Samaneans*, or Buddhists of Bahar, are described by Megasthenes, who, B.C. 300, was an ambassador from Seleucus to their king; and whose lost work, on the state of India at that period, is quoted by Strabo and Pliny. The same designation for the priesthood, Samana, is applied equally by Clemens Alexandrinus in the second century, and by Porphyry in the fourth.

further invested with the dignity of Upasampada or "attainment." The rules of their religion enjoin poverty, abstinence, the tonsure of the head, and the use of a particular habit, *the yellow robe* which is assumed by the neophyte on admission; and thenceforth, unless deliberately laid aside as an abandonment of his rank, it becomes not merely the distinguishing emblem of his calling, but an integral portion of his priesthood. The sacerdotal robe is presumed to be lent by Buddhu to his servant, who can possess no property of his own. It can at no period of life be dispensed with; to lay it aside is to lay down the sacred character of his order; and even if by violence a Buddhist priest were to become deprived of his robe, or by accident to lose it, and be compelled to cover himself momentarily with any other garment, his ordination would be cancelled by the act, and could only be restored by a fresh conferment from a chapter of the Order.[1]

Independently of the absence of any sanctity derivable from exaltation of caste, there are numerous other peculiarities attached to the priesthood of Buddhu, and inherent in the constitution of their order, which are unfavourable to the growth of their power as a hierarchy, and inconsistent with any pre-

[1] The robe of the Buddhist priesthood, and the fashion in which it is borne, are represented in the vignette at the close of this volume.

tension to social ascendancy in the state. In their case the priestly character is not indelible; it is assumed for a variety of objects, and laid aside as they become gratified. The majority, when yet children, have been dedicated by their parents to the service of the temple, and desert it in manhood from weariness, or a fancy for some other pursuit. Others assume the sacerdotal character from a love of study and seclusion, and abandon it to return to active life under the influence of satiety or a restlessness for change. Some forsake the priesthood to inherit paternal lands, or to marry; and as each can resume his secular pursuits without reproach or loss of honour, such changes are perpetual, and serve to weaken, to a great extent, the association in the minds of the people of any thing peculiar and exclusive with the spiritual character of the priests.

Generally speaking, the Buddhist priests in Ceylon adhere in practice to the rule of poverty imposed on their order, and although a few acquire property clandestinely, and some connected with the larger temples derive rich incomes from their endowments, the majority are wretchedly poor; and thus solely dependent on the offerings of the people, they may be said to follow, rather than to lead, popular feeling. In point of education, they rise little above the average information possessed by the better class of peasants; but so far as religious sincerity is concerned, it is unquestionable that they themselves are the veriest slaves of the superstition which it is their calling to teach.

In spite of the injunctions of Buddhu to show reverence to his priests, all these circumstances conspire to diminish their consideration in the eyes of the people. They honour them with all external respect so long as they wear the yellow robe; but, at the same time, they take every opportunity to make it known that *the robe*, and not the wearer, is the real object of their veneration.

Conscious of the dubious and evanescent nature of their influence, the priests occasionally resort to other expedients to sustain it; and combining the practice of medicine and astrology with their spiritual profession, the superstitious mystery with which these are enveloped contributes somewhat to the object desired. But from what sources soever their influence may be derived, it is seldom that an instance occurs of its abuse; and in their intercourse with the Christian missionaries, I have rarely heard of an occasion on which the ministrations of the latter had been either denounced or obstructed by the priesthood of Buddhu.

To mankind in general the injunctions of Buddhu prescribe *a code of morality* second only to that of Christianity itself, and superior to every heathen system that the world has ever seen, not excepting that of Zoroaster. It forbids the taking of life from even the humblest animal in creation, and it prohibits intemperance and incontinence, dishonesty and falsehood—vices which are referable to those formidable assailants, *rago* or concupiscence, *doso* or malignity, and *molo*, ignorance or folly.[1] These, again, involve the prohibition of all their minor modifications—hypocrisy and anger, unkindness and pride, ungenerous suspicion, covetousness in every form, evil wishes to others, the betrayal of secrets, and the propagation of slander. Whilst all these offences are forbidden, every conceivable virtue and excellence are simultaneously enjoined—the forgiveness of injuries, the practice of charity, a reverence for virtue, and the cherishing of the learned; submission to discipline, veneration for parents, the care for one's family, a sinless vocation, contentment and gratitude, subjection to reproof, moderation in prosperity, submission under affliction, and cheerfulness at all times. "Those," said Buddhu, "who practise all these virtues, and are not overcome by evil, will enjoy the perfection of happiness, and attain to supreme renown."[2]

Buddhism, it may be perceived from this sketch, is, properly speaking, less a form of religion than a school of philosophy; and *its worship*, according to the institutes of its founders, consists of an appeal to the reason, rather than an attempt on the ima-

[1] The Rev. Mr. Gogerly's Notes on Buddhism. Lee's Ribeyro, p. 267.

[2] Discourse of Buddhu entitled Mangala.

gination through the instrumentality of rites and parade. "Salvation is made dependent, not upon the practice of idle ceremonies, the repeating of prayers or of hymns, or invocations to pretended gods, but upon moral qualifications, which constitute individual and social happiness here, and ensure it hereafter."[1] In later times, and in the failure of Buddhism by unassisted arguments to ensure the observance of its precepts and the practice of its morals, the experiment has been made to arouse the attention and excite the enthusiasm of its followers by the adoption of ceremonies and processions; but these are declared to be only the innovations of priestcraft, and the Singhalese, whilst they unite in their celebration, are impatient to explain that such practices are less religious than secular, and that the Perrehera in particular, the chief of their annual festivals, was introduced, not in honour of Buddhu, but as a tribute tothe Kandyan kings as the patrons and defenders of the faith.[2]

[1] Col. Sykes, Asiat. Journ., vol. xii. p. 266.

[2] So early as the fifth century, Fa Hian describes the processions of Buddhists which he witnessed in the kingdom of Khotan, and which much resemble the modern processions of the Brahmans in India: the roads swept, watered, and decorated; the houses hung with tapestry and banners, and the images drawn upon a four-wheeled car, "18 feet high, in the form of a moveable pavilion, ornamented with hanging curtains and covertures of silk." And it is not a little remarkable, along with the image of Buddhu were associated those of the Brahmanical deities *Indra*

In its formula, whatever alterations Buddhism may have undergone in Ceylon are altogether external, and clearly referable to its anomalous association with the worship of its ancient rivals the Brahmans. These changes, however, are the result of proximity and association rather than of incorporation or adoption; and even now the process of expurgation is in progress with a view to the restoration of the pristine purity of the faith by a formal separation from the observances of Hindooism. The Malabar kings, who at an early period had acquired the sovereignty of Ceylon, on the failure of the native dynasty introduced the worship of Vishnu and Shiva into the same temples with that of Buddhu. The innovation has been perpetuated; and to the present day the statues of these conflicting divinities are to be found within the same buildings:[1] the Dewales of Hindooism are erected

and *Brahma*, the *Lha* of the Thibetans and the *Toegri* of the Moguls.

Fa Hian describes a similar procession at the capital of the King of Central India, with twenty decorated cars, carrying figures of Buddhu, accompanied by theatrical representations, feats of wrestlers, concerts of music, and illuminations at night.

[1] See note B, end of this chapter. It is remarkable that the Buddhists in China have been equally accommodating in this particular, and have admitted into their Pantheon a large assemblage from the Hindoo mythology. M. Remusat enumerates *twenty* so enrolled, including Brahma, and Indra, and Iswara. In one of the curious diaries of the Ambassadors sent from the Burman Empire to Pekin, and published by Colonel Burney (Journal of the Asiatic Soc. of Bengal, vols. vi. vii.), the writers state that they found the Chinese temples filled with figures of naats or spirits, and that

within the same inclosure as the Wihares of the Buddhists; and the Kappoorales of the one religion officiate at their altars, almost beneath the same roof with the priests and neophytes of the other. But beyond this parade of their emblems, the worship of the Hindoo deities throughout the Singhalese districts is entirely devoid of the obscenities and cruelty by which it is characterised on the continent of India; and it would almost appear as if these had been discontinued by the Brahmans in compliment to the superior purity of the worship with which their own had become thus fortuitously associated. The exclusive prejudices of caste were at the same remote period partially engrafted on the simpler and more generous discipline of Buddhu; and it is only recently that any vigorous exertions have been attempted for their disseverance.

Some of the Singhalese kings, who in later times recovered the sovereignty of the island, sent ambassadors to Siam in the eleventh century, with a view to the reform and restoration of the national faith,[1] but apparently with no appreciable success. In 1684, the Dutch government took an extraordinary share in a similar project at a moment when some apprehensions were entertained for the reviving influence of Portugal through the activity of the

they did not see a single figure of Buddhu between the frontiers of Ava and Pekin.—Colonel Sykes, Asiat. Jour., vol. xii. p. 289.

[1] Turnour's Mahawanso, p. lxv.

Roman Catholic priesthood. From the effects of civil war and confusion, the highest order or *Upasampada* priests had become almost extinct in Ceylon; and as they alone could confer ordination on the inferior rank of *Samanaros*, the Dutch lent their assistance in dispatching a mission to Arracan, who brought back a number of duly-qualified dignitaries to restore the worship of Buddhu, and oppose a more effectual barrier to the increasing influence of the Church of Rome. A similar embassy was dispatched a century later to Siam, by the King of Kandy, Kirti Sree Raja Singha, A. D. 1753, when a similar emergency required a fresh importation of Upasampada priests; but although the order was a second time restored, the chief corruptions of the religion remained unreformed. The Kandyan kings, strongly embued with the prejudices of the Brahmans, upheld the doctrines of polytheism and caste; and in conformity with the practice of the Hindoos, none below the rank of Vellales were admitted to the higher order of the priesthood.

In 1798, the low-caste priests of the maritime districts, and especially the Challias of the southern province, indignant at this unrighteous exclusion, organized a fresh expedition to the orthodox Buddhists of Burmah, with a view to the restoration of the faith. Their mission was eminently successful; the Sanga Raja at Amarapoora, the head of the national religion of Burmah, received them with singular favour: the emperor caused their ordination to be celebrated with all the pageantry of royalty; and five Burmese ecclesiastics returned with them in 1802 to Ceylon, where they became founders of the "Amarapoora sect," who have since maintained the most vigorous exertions for the suppression of the heresies and corruptions incorporated in the national worship with the sanction of the priesthood of Siam.[1]

The animosity is extreme between these two sections of Buddhism in Ceylon, each ascribing the most fatal errors to the other, and denying to their rival the possible attainment of Nirwana. The Amarapoora priests have, however, made considerable way in the maritime provinces, as well as in the mountainous district of Saffragam, which, from its vicinity to the sacred mountain of Adam's Peak, has from the earliest period been a stronghold of superstition. The reforms on which they insist are the expulsion of the Hindoo worship from their temples, the extinction of caste, and the exclusion of the priesthood from secular occupations, such as physic and astrology. They reject the authority of the sovereign or the civil power to introduce novelties in worship; they deny the supremacy of the chief priests in the Kandyan colleges; they read and expound the sacred books indiscriminately to the people, whereas the Siamese expound a few passages only to the Upasam-

[1] For a curious account of the reception and ordination of the Singhalese priests in Burmah, see note F at the end of this chapter.

pada priests; they affect a style of dress different from their rivals, by wearing the yellow robe over the entire of the person, instead of leaving one shoulder uncovered; and in many minor points they dissent from the practice and ritual of Siam.[1] In the particulars above enumerated their differences of opinion may seem unimportant, but they are sufficient to widen and perpetuate a schism, even when on other and more essential matters both sections cordially concur.

On comparing this system with other prevailing religions which divide with it the worship of the East, Buddhism at once vindicates its own superiority, not only by the purity of its code of morals, but by its freedom from the fanatical intolerance of the Mahomedans and its abhorrent rejection of the revolting rites of the Brahmanical faith. But mild and benevolent as are its aspects and design, its theories have failed to realize in practice the reign of virtue which they proclaim. Beautiful as is the body of its doctrines, it wants the vivifying energy and soul which are essential to ensure its ascendancy and power. Its cold philosophy and thin abstractions, however they might exercise the faculties of anchorets and ascetics, have proved insufficient of themselves to arrest man in his career of passion and pursuit; and

[1] For a minute account of the two Singhalese sects, see a curious Paper by De Silva Mohanderam, in the Appendix to Lee's translation of Ribeyro.

the bold experiment of influencing the heart and regulating the conduct of mankind by the external decencies and the mutual dependencies of morality unsustained by higher hopes and a faith that penetrates eternity, has proved in this instance an unredeemed and hopeless failure. The inculcation of the social virtues as the consummation of happiness here and hereafter, suggests an object sufficiently attractive for the bulk of mankind ; but Buddhism presents along with it no adequate knowledge of the means which are indispensable for its attainment. In confiding all to the mere strength of the human intellect and the enthusiastic self-reliance and determination of the human heart, it makes no provision for defence against those powerful temptations before which ordinary resolution must give way; and it affords no consoling support under those overwhelming afflictions by which the spirit is prostrated and subdued, when unaided by the influence of a purer faith and unsustained by its confidence in a diviner power. From the contemplation of the Buddhist all the awful and unending realities of a future life are withdrawn—his hopes and his fears are at once mean and circumscribed; the rewards held in prospect by his creed are insufficient to incite him to virtue; and its punishments too remote to deter him from vice. Thus, insufficient for time, and rejecting eternity, the utmost triumph of his religion is to live without fear and to die without hope.

Both socially and in its effects upon individuals, the result of the system in Ceylon has been apathy almost approaching to infidelity. Even as regards the tenets of their creed, the mass of the population exhibit the profoundest ignorance and manifest the most irreverent indifference. In their daily intercourse and acts, morality and virtue, so far from being apparent in practice, are barely discernible as the exception. Neither hopes nor apprehensions have proved a sufficient restraint on the habitual violation of all those precepts of charity and honesty, of purity and truth, which form the very essence of their doctrine; and in proportion as its tenets have been slighted by the people, its priesthood are disregarded, and its temples universally neglected and in ruin.[1]

[1] Sir John Davis represents Buddhism throughout China to be in a similar state of neglect and decline. "Its present condition," he says, "is very far from flourishing, and the extensive and magnificent establishments which had been founded in former times are evidently in a state of dilapidation and decay. It is rarely that one meets with any of their pagodas in tolerable repair, though one or two occur in every landscape. Between Macao and Canton there are no less than four or five nine-storied pagodas on elevated points by the river-side, and every one of them in a state of ruin."—The Chinese, chap. xiv.: Religion.

M. Maupied traces the decay of Buddhism universally to its abandonment of the belief in a supreme being and its lapse into atheism: "Les mômes résultats se sont manifestés dans les phases du Bouddhisme hors de l'Inde: à Ceylan, où il est demeuré, dans le nord de l'Asie et à la Chine, il a fini par arriver à une sorte d'athéisme spéculatif, qui non-seulement a arrêté son prosélytisme, mais qui le tue chaque jour, et finira par le détruire entièrement." —Chap. x. p. 275.

No national system of religion, no prevailing superstition that has ever fallen under my observation presents so dull a level, and is so pre-eminently deficient in popular influences, as Buddhism amongst the Singhalese. It has its multitude of followers, but it is a misnomer to describe them as its *votaries*, for the term implies a warmth and a fervour that is unknown to a native of Ceylon. He believes, or he thinks he believes, because he is of the same faith with his ancestors; but he looks on the religious doctrines of the various sects which surround him with a stolid indifference which is the surest indication of the little importance which he attaches to his own. The fervid earnestness of Christianity, even in its most degenerate forms, the fanatical enthusiasm of Islam, the proud exclusiveness of Brahma, and even the zealous warmth of other Northern faiths, are all emotions utterly foreign and unknown to the followers of Buddhism in Ceylon.

Yet, strange to tell, under all the icy coldness of this barren system, there burn below the unextinguished fires of another and a darker superstition, whose flames overtop the icy summits of the Buddhist philosophy, and excite a deeper and more reverential awe in the imagination of the Singhalese. As the Hindoos in process of time superadded to their exalted conceptions of Brahma, and the benevolent attributes of Vishnu, those dismal dreams and apprehensions which embody themselves in the horrid worship of Shiva, and in invocations to propitiate the destroyer, so the followers of Buddhu, unsatisfied with the vain pretensions of unattainable perfection, struck down by their internal consciousness of sin and insufficiency, and seeing around them, instead of the reign of universal happiness and the apotheosis of intellect and wisdom, nothing but the ravages of crime and the sufferings produced by ignorance, have turned with instinctive terror to propitiate the powers of evil, by whom alone such miseries are supposed to be inflicted, and to *worship the demons* and tormentors to whom their superstition is contented to attribute a circumscribed portion of power over the earth.

DEMON WORSHIP was the prevailing practice of the Singhalese before the introduction of Buddhism by Mahindo. Some principle akin to it seems to be an aboriginal impulse of uncivilized man in his first and rudest conceptions of religion, engendered, perhaps, by the spectacle of cruelty and pain, the visitations of suffering and death, and the contemplation of the awful phenomena of nature—storms, torrents, volcanoes, earthquakes, and destruction. The conciliation of the powers which inflict such calamities, seems to precede, when it does not supplant, the adoration of the benevolent influence to which belong the creation, the preservation, and the conferment of happiness on mankind; and in the mind of the native of Ceylon this ancient superstition has maintained its ascendancy, notwithstanding the introduction and ostensible prevalence of Buddhism; for the latter, whilst it admits the existence of evil spirits, has emphatically prohibited their invocation, on the ground that any malignant influence they may exert over man is merely the consequence of their vices, whilst the cultivators of virtue may successfully bid them defiance. The demons here denounced are distinct from a class of demigods, who, under the name of *Yakshyos*, are supposed to inhabit the waters, and dwell on the sides of Mount Meru, and who are distinguished not only for gentleness and benevolence, but even by a veneration for Buddhu, who, in one of his earlier transmigrations, was himself born under the form of a Yakshyo, and, attended by similar companions, traversed the world teaching righteousness. One section of these demigods, however, the *Rakshyos*, are fierce and malignant, and in these respects resemble the Yakkas or demons so much dreaded by the Singhalese, and who, like the *Ghouls* of the Mahomedans, are believed to infest the vicinity of grave yards, or, like the dryads and hamadryads of the ancients, to frequent favourite forests and groves, and to inhabit particular trees, whence they sally out to seize on the passer by.[1] The Buddhist priests connive at

[1] Travellers from Point de Galle to Colombo, in driving through the long succession of gardens and plantations of cocoa-nuts which the road traverses throughout its entire extent, will not fail to observe numerous fruit-trees of different kinds, round the

demon worship because their efforts are ineffectual to suppress it, and the most orthodox Singhalese, whilst they confess its impropriety, are still driven to resort to it in all their fears and afflictions.

Independent of the malignant spirits or Yakkas, who are the authors of indefinite evil, the Singhalese have a demon or *Sanne* for each form of disease, who is supposed to be its direct agent and inflicter, and who is accordingly invoked for its removal; and others, who delight in the miseries of mankind, are to be propitiated before the arrival of any event over which their pernicious influence might otherwise prevail. Hence, on every domestic occurrence, as well as in every domestic calamity, the services

stem of which a band of leaves has been fastened by the owner. This is to denote that the tree has been devoted to a demon; and sometimes to Vishnu or the Kattregam dewol. Occasionally these dedications are made to the temples of Buddhu, and even to the Roman Catholic altars, as to that of St. Anne of Calpentyn. This ceremony is called *Gok-bandeema*, "the tying of the tender leaf," and its operation is to protect the fruit from pillage till ripe enough to be plucked and sent as an offering to the divinity to whom it has thus been consecrated. There is reason to fear, however, that on these occasions the devil is, to some extent, defrauded of his due, as the custom is, after applying a few only of the finest as an offering to the evil one, to appropriate the remainder to the use of the owner. When cocoanut palms are so preserved, the fruit is sometimes converted into oil and burned before the shrine of the demon. The superstition extends throughout other parts of Ceylon; and so long as the wreath continues to hang upon the tree, it is presumed that no thief would venture to plunder the garden.

of the *Kattadias* or devil-priests are to be sought, and their ceremonies performed, generally with observances so barbarous as to be the most revolting evidence still extant of the uncivilized habits of the Singhalese. Especially in cases of sickness and danger, the assistance of the devil-dancer is implicitly relied on: an altar, decorated with garlands, is erected within sight of the patient, and on this an animal, frequently a cock, is to be sacrificed for his recovery. The dying man is instructed to touch and dedicate to the evil spirit the wild flowers, the rice, and the flesh, which have been prepared as the *pidaneys* or offerings to be made at sunset, at midnight, and the morning; and in the intervals the dancers perform their incantations, habited in masks and disguises to represent the demon which they personate, as the immediate author of the patient's suffering. In the frenzy of these orgies, the Kattadia having feigned the access of inspiration from the spirit he invokes, is consulted by the friends of the afflicted, and declares the nature of his disease, and the probability of its favourable or fatal termination. At sunrise, the ceremony closes by an exorcism chanted to disperse the demons who have been attracted by the rite; the devil-dancers withdraw with the offerings, and sing, as they retire, the concluding song of the ceremony, "that the sacrifice may be acceptable and the life of the sufferer extended."

In addition to this Yakka worship, which is essentially indigenous in Ceylon, the natives practise the invocation of a distinct class of demons, their conceptions of which are evidently borrowed from the debased ceremonies of Hindooism, though in their adoption they have rejected the grosser incidents of its ritual, and replaced them with others less cruel, but by no means less revolting. The Capuas, who perform ceremonies in honour of these strange gods, are of a higher rank than the Kattadias, who conduct the incantations to the Yakkas, and they are more or less connected with the Dewales and temples of Hindooism. The spirits in whose honour these ceremonies are performed, are all foreign to Ceylon. Some, such as Kattregam and Pattine, are borrowed from the mythology of the Brahmans; some are the genii of fire and other elements of the universe, and others are deified heroes; but the majority are dreaded as the inflicters of pestilence and famine, and propitiated by rites to avert the visitations of their malignity.

Their ceremonies consist of a variety of forms for the recovery of the sick[1]—*daana*[2] or "the food offering," the *harvest-home* of the Singhalese, and *horn-pulling*, a rite in honour of Pattine, performed to drive away pestilence. But the principal, and that

[1] Kaphiltaweema.

[2] Dana-deema. There is also a ceremony called *Kiri-eleema*, or the overflow of milk—when the liquid of the cocoanut is boiled till it runs over, as an emblem of plenty and a land "flowing with milk."

which seems to incorporate the worship of the whole corps of these infernal divinities, is the ceremony of the *Dewol-madoowa*, which is celebrated on a larger scale, and frequently performed on behalf of a whole village or district which has been afflicted by cholera or the fever so much dreaded by the natives. It takes place in a Madoowa, or temporary building constructed of branches, and decorated with white cloths and garlands; and it generally lasts throughout seven days, on each of which offerings are made of wild flowers and fruit, together with rice and money; which latter the Capuas profess is afterwards taken by the temple elephants to the mountain where the treasury of the demons is concealed.

Preparatory to its commencement, the priests and their attendants undergo a purification by abstinence from prohibited food, (the list of which is nearly identical with the unclean animals interdicted to the Jews,) and on the appointed day the rites are initiated by ablutions, and sprinkling with water tinted with saffron; after which, day after day, the same ceremonies are repeated with incantations and dances, and the placing of offerings on the various altars, amidst the rolling of tom-toms and the burning of resin, to imitate lightning and thunder. With these are intermingled games which combine emblematical representations of various secular employments, such as the catching of elephants, the binding of buffaloes, the weaving of mats, and other village occupations; and as each of these is concluded, a benediction is pronounced upon the art which has been represented; and after a succession of performances half devotional and half ludicrous, the Dewol-madoowa is concluded by carrying the sacred poonawa (an earthen vessel) to the nearest river, where it is broken by the Capuas, and the fragments cast into the stream.

The ascendancy of these superstitions, and the anomaly of their association with the religion of Buddhu, which has taken for its deity the perfection of wisdom and benevolence, present one of the most signal difficulties with which Christianity has had, at all times, to contend in the effort to extend its influences throughout Ceylon. The Portuguese priesthood soon discovered that, however the Singhalese might be induced to profess the worship of Christ, they adhered with timid tenacity to their ancient demonology. The Dutch clergy, in their reiterated lamentations over the failure of their efforts for conversion, have repeatedly recorded the fact, that however readily the native population might be brought to abjure their belief in the doctrines of Buddhu, no arguments or expedients had proved effectual to overcome their terror of the demons, or check their propensity to resort on every emergency to the ceremonies of the Capuas, the dismal rites of the devil-dancers.[1] The Wesleyans, the Baptists, and

[1] See also Hough, Hist. Christ. in India, vol. iv. b. xii. ch. v. p. 558.

other missionaries, who in later times have made the hamlets and secluded districts of Ceylon the scene of their unwearied labours, have found, with equal disappointment, that to the present hour the villagers and the peasantry are as powerfully attracted as ever by this strong superstition, bearing on their person the charms calculated to protect them from the evil eye of the demon, consulting the astrologers and the Capuas on every domestic emergency, solemnizing their marriages under their auspices, and requiring their presence at the birth of their children, who, together with their mother, are not unfrequently dedicated to the evil spirits, whom they dread.[1] A large proportion of these nominal Christians, who have been excommunicated by the missionaries for relapses to paganism, have been betrayed into apostacy in times of sickness and alarm; when, in the nervousness of their terror, and in compliance with the entreaties of those around them, they have assented to the employment of the devil-dancers, and the celebration of rites for their recovery. In health they have strength to reject such delusions, but in the prostration of mind and body by disease, they become overpowered by the recurrence of early associations, and return helplessly to superstitions, which in the manlier vigour of frame and intellect they had spurned. Nor is there

[1] Harvard's History of the Wesleyan Mission in Ceylon, Introd., p. iii.

a surer test to the missionary of the active power of Christianity over the minds of his converts, than the evidences presented in the instances of those who, when beset by fears and expostulations at such a moment, have adhered firmly to their faith, and resolutely resisted the interference of the Kattadias.

NOTES TO CHAPTER V.

(A.)

THE SHRINE OF THE SACRED TOOTH.

THE *Delada*, or sacred tooth of Buddhu, is the most devoutly worshipped relic of their religion which is possessed by the natives of the East. Long before the Christian era it was adored by the Buddhist sovereigns of Orissa, and was originally deposited in the great temple of Jaggarnath, then a Buddhist foundation. Its history and vicissitudes for fifteen hundred years since its first deposition in Ceylon in the fourth century of Christianity, are minutely recorded in the Mahawanso and other sacred books of the priests; and to the present day pilgrimages and offerings come from the remotest parts of India, Burmah, and Siam to the sacred shrine in which it reposes at Kandy. Some doubts of its authenticity, and a tradition of the original relic having been destroyed by the Portuguese, are of course disregarded, as is also the still more striking fact that the *delada* itself, so far from being the tooth of a prince, is a piece of discoloured ivory, about two inches in length, which resembles still more closely both in shape and dimensions the tusk of a boar. It is kept in a small temple of elegant construction, adjoining the ancient palace of the Kandyan kings, and guarded with peculiar care not merely from respect for the sacredness of the relic, but out of regard to the costly jewels which decorate the chamber in which the precious tooth is enclosed. The room is hung with cloths of golden tissue, gifts from the Buddhists of Chin-India; and a table of massive silver, richly chased, supports the sacred kurundus or caskets, in the innermost of which the tooth is deposited, amidst the leaves of a golden lotus. The outer shrine, which is in the form peculiar to all dagobas (*Dhatu garba*, the "hollow" for a "relic"), that of a slender obelisk placed on the summit of a semicircular dome, is hung with a profusion of gold chains and other ornaments, heavy with all the jewels peculiar to Ceylon; sapphires and emeralds of unusual dimensions, cat's-eyes, which the Singhalese prize almost equal to brilliants, rubies, amethysts, and pearls. The chamber is never opened except in the presence of the Dewa Nilleme, a chief of the highest rank in the Kandyan kingdom, who is associated with the high priests in the custody of the sacred tooth and its property; and for the protection of the latter, one key of the temple has hitherto been kept by the chief civil officer of the province, the Government Agent at Kandy.

In addition to their veneration for the *delada* as a relic of their founder, the Buddhists of Ceylon have a tradition that the tooth is a palladium, the possession of which is inherent only in the rulers of Ceylon, and that whoever can succeed in retaining it must of necessity become the sovereign of the country. A drawing of the shrine and its chamber, by Mr. Nicholl, will be found at the title to Chap. V. of this volume.

The adoration of a *tooth* of Buddhu is not peculiar to the Singhalese, as Fa Hian the Chinese traveller mentions amongst the precious relics worshipped in the fifth century by the Buddhists of Ladak *a vase in which Buddhu had spat*, and one of his *teeth;* and in honour of the latter of which a tower had been raised by the king. Another tooth was similarly cherished by the king of Nakia, in Affghanistan, eastward of Ghuzni. In an adjoining monastery the monks preserved the cuttings of his hair and nails. But of all the sacred relics which Fa Hian describes in his journeys none was so extraordinary as a *shadow* of Buddhu, which he states to have been shown to him at Nakia, though he candidly admits his inability to describe the process of its preservation.

(B.)

THEORY WHICH RECONCILES THE BUDDHISTS TO PROFESS TWO RELIGIONS.

"In morals the Buddhists look on their own religion and that of the Christians as identical, so that without formal hypocrisy they fancy they can find themselves justified in making a profession of both. The doctrine of Christ shedding his blood for the redemption of men is not in opposition to their previous habits of thought; for they are taught by their own books that if all the blood lost by Buddhu himself in his different transmigrations for the benefit of sentient beings were collected, it would be more than the waters of the ocean. Until Christianity assumed a decidedly opposing position, even the priests looked upon that religion with respect, and upon its founder with reverence. I have seen it stated in a controversial tract, written by a Buddhist priest of Matura not fifteen years since, that probably Christ in a former state of existence was a God residing in one of the six heavens (a position which they represented Gotama as having occupied immediately previous to his birth as Buddhu); that animated by benevolence he desired and obtained a birth as man, and taught truth so far as he was acquainted with it. That his benevolence, his general virtue, and the purity of his doctrines rendered him worthy of reverence and honour. If, therefore, the supremacy of Buddhu and the absolute perfection of his system were conceded, they saw nothing inconsistent in respecting both systems,—Buddhism as the perfection of wisdom and virtue; Christianity as an approximation to it, though mingled with many errors."—*From a MS. by the Rev. D. J. Gogerly.*

A curious illustration of the prevalence of this disposition to conform to two religions was related to me recently. A Singhalese chief came a short time since to the principal of a government seminary at Colombo, desirous to place his son as a pupil of the institution, and agreed, without an instant's hesitation, that the boy should conform to the discipline of the school, which requires the reading of the Scriptures and attendance on the hours of worship and prayer; accounting for his ready acquiescence by an assurance that he entertained an equal respect for the doctrines of Buddhism and Christianity. "But how can you," said the Principal, "with your superior education and intelligence, reconcile yourself thus to halt between two opinions, and submit to the inconsistency of professing an equal belief in two conflicting religions?" "Do you see," replied the subtle chief, laying his hand on the arm of the other, and directing his attention to a canoe, with a large spar as an outriggér, lashed alongside, in which a fisherman was just pushing off upon the lake, "do you see the style of these boats, in which our fishermen always put to sea, and that that spar is almost equivalent to a second canoe, which keeps the first from upsetting? It is precisely so with myself: I add on *your* religion to steady my *own*, *because I consider Christianity a very safe outrigger to Buddhism.*"

(C.)

BUDDHIST DOCTRINE OF THE TRANSMIGRATION OF SOULS AND NATURE OF NIRWANA.

The general mass of the Buddhists in Ceylon are not orthodox in their views of transmigration, as they believe that the same soul migrates into different bodies. But this is contrary to the teaching of Buddhu, and of this the learned priests are fully aware; but they do not attempt to correct the error, regarding the subject as too difficult to be understood by the unlearned. His doctrine is that of *a series of existences*, which he illustrates by the metaphors of a tree and a lamp. A tree produces fruit, from which fruit another tree is produced, and so the series continues. The last tree is not the identical tree with the first, but it is a result, so that if the first tree had not been, the last tree could not have existed. Man is the tree, his conduct is the fruit, the vivifying energy of the fruit is *desire*. While this continues, the series will proceed: the good or evil actions performed give the quality of the fruit, so that the existence springing from these actions will be happy or miserable as the quality of the fruit affects the tree produced from it. According to this doctrine the present body and soul of man never had a previous existence, but a previously existent being under the influence of desire performed virtuous or vicious actions, and in consequence of these upon the death of that individual a new body and soul is produced. The metaphor of the *lamp* is similar. One lamp is lighted from another; the two lamps are distinct, but the one could not have been lighted had not the other existed. The nature of Nirwana, or cessation of being, is obvious from this. It is not the *destruction* of an existent being, but the *cessation of his existence.* It is not an absorption into a superior being, as the Brahmans teach; it is not a retreat into a place of eternal repose, free from further transmigration; it is not a violent destruction of being, but a complete and final cessation of existence. (See Notes on Buddhism in the Appendix to Lee's translation of Ribeyro's Ceylon, by the Rev. D. J. Gogerly, p. 264.)

"It has been questioned whether *annihilation*, or what other condition short of such absolute extinction, is meant by the happy state to which perfect saints attain. The term which the Bhuddhists as well as Jainas more particularly affect is Nirvána—profound calm. In its ordinary acceptation it signifies "extinct," as a fire that has gone out. Its etymology is from *vá*—to blow—as wind, with the preposition *nir* used in a negative sense. It means calm and unruffled. The notion which attaches to the word is that of *perfect apathy*. Other terms distinguish different gradations of pleasure, joy, and delight; but a happy state of *imperturbable apathy* is the ultimate bliss to which the Indian aspires; and in this the Jaina as well as the Bauddha concur with the orthodox Vedanten."—COLEBROOKE's *Essays on the Philosophy of the Hindus*, sect. v. c. v. p. 401.

(D.)

THE MUNDANE THEORY OF BUDDHISM.

THE Sakwala, or mundane system, is a vast circle; the outward boundary, or circumference, being a zone of rocks, ascending 82,000 yoduns above the sea (a yodun is 16 Singhalese miles, between 13 and 14 English miles): this zone measures 3,610,350 yoduns.

In the centre is Maha Meru, 84,000 yoduns covered by the sea, 84,000 yoduns in height above the sea, 84,000 yoduns long, and the same in breadth.

Seven series of concentric rocks, each half the height of the preceding one, surround Maha Meru. Thus Yugandhara is half the height of Maha Meru (or 42,000 yoduns); these are separated from each other by seas, and are inhabited only by gods and demons.

Between the seventh and last circle and the Sakwala Gala, or rocky circumference, are four continents; the southern one, Jambudwipa, being that which we inhabit.

There are six heavens; one, the starry, having the altitude above the earth of Yugandhara, or 42,000 yoduns; one on the summit of Maha Meru, and four above it, ascending by stages: above these, one higher than the other, are the sixteen Brahma worlds; above these four Arupa worlds.

Below the earth, the sea and Maha Meru, are the abodes of the Asuras or Titans, that of the Nāgas and the hells. Below the solid earth is an ocean 480,000 yoduns deep, and below this an atmosphere 960,000 yoduns deep. This is the lowest part of the Sakwala, the Arupa world being the highest.

(E.)

BUDDHIST DOCTRINE OF FATE AND NECESSITY.

THE Buddhist doctrine of fate or necessity presents something of the following character:—Matter, and the whole series of beings who have been formed from it, are supposed to be eternal and subjected to destruction and reproduction in successions without end. In one of their religious books of high authority, '*The Questions of Milinda*,' all things are divided into four classes: 1, all sentient beings, from the minutest insect to the most exalted intelligence, whose stages of existence are influenced by moral causes; 2, the elements, plants, &c., which are controlled by natural causes; 3, the earth, the water, the air, the mountains, &c., which are affected by the seasons and their changes; and 4, those which are "uncaused," such as the immensity of space and the condition of Nirwana, which is an end of all causation. All unorganized substances, the universe, the earth, and the atmosphere, are subject to dissolution at the end of a Kalpa, and to reconstruction, not by any active agency or external influence, but by their own inherent impulse, inseparable from and eternal like themselves. The argument of the referability of the earliest of these changes to some pre-existent cause, is evaded by the sophism of action in a circle, represented by the entirety of a ring,[1] which presents neither end nor beginning. In like manner the re-production of plants from their seeds, and the never-ending series of their re-appearance, is referred to this same doctrine of necessity inherent in their nature; and the succession of sentient beings only differs from the others in this particular, that, whilst the matter from which they are formed is eternal, the sensation by which they are animated is finite, and consciousness on the

[1] The *wheel* forms a prominent object in the Buddhistical sculptures and inscriptions throughout Continental India. It was used as an emblem of the perpetual succession and eternity of matter; and served likewise another purpose in the corruptions of Buddhism. *Prayers* were pasted on it by the priests, who then put the wheel into rapid revolution. *Each turn had the efficacy of an oral repetition*; and the faster it revolved the more rapidly was the devotee approaching the ultimate bliss of Nirwana.

attainment of Nirwana must for ever become extinct. King Milinda, in the work from which this is taken, in answer to his inquiry whether a *commencement* of being was a thing ascertained or possible? received for answer that no existing thing can be produced from nonentity, but re-produced from some pre-existing matter, as a house may be re-constructed from its former materials, or a plant from its seed. The doctrine of a Creator is thus distinctly repudiated;[1] and the maintenance of a succession of existences, and even of the first of the series (if the phrase is admissible when the existence of a first is ignored), is accounted for by the theory of "desire" as the great motive cause. *Ignorance of the truth*, by producing a "desire" for existing objects, is thus the cause of the perpetuation of transmigrations, till the series becomes suspended by the attainment of that perfect *knowledge which extinguishes desire* and ushers in Nirwana. So long as any degree of ignorance of the perfect teaching of Buddhu remains, actions will be unavoidably performed, meriting respectively either happiness or suffering.

Upon death a new consciousness is evolved as light from a newly-kindled lamp, the moral state of the previous existence becoming the kindler of the new, and determining its quality. "Here is the peculiar feature of the system, that moral causes are efficient, and that the results are inevitable from the mere necessity of the case, without the intervention of the will or the acts of any other being, that 'necessity' being an occult power and irresistible in its operation."[2] If the moral state has been good, it becomes the germ of subsequent happiness; if bad, the result will be suffering proportioned to the intensity of the evil. Whether these states of existence are to be in one of the hells in an endurance of torture, or a birth upon earth as an insect, a man, or a hero, is inevitably fixed and determined by the moral quality of all previous existences—as the nature of a tree is pre-determined by the properties of its seed.

[1] "Buddhu, who appears to have been conversant with the Hindoo philosophy, affirms in the *Brahma jata*, that Brahma himself was a being in course of transmigration, and in no sense the creator of any being."—MS. of the Rev. Mr. Gogerly.

[2] Ibid.

(F.)

CURIOUS ACCOUNT OF THE RECEPTION AND ORDINATION OF THE SINGHALESE PRIESTS AT AMARAPOORA.

THE following account of their reception at Amarapoora and of the ceremonial of their ordination, is translated from the epistle of the Sanga Rajah, or Hierarch of Burmah, addressed to the Buddhist priesthood of Ceylon, and brought back by the Mission on its return from Amarapoora.

"Perceiving the gradual decline of the religion of the teacher of gods and men, in the island of Lanka, in former times honoured by the presence of myriads of deified saints, illuminated by the three-branched Saddhamma (the sacred writings of Buddhu), and being profoundly afflicted at this state of things, I was thus revolving in my own mind, 'O! when shall it be granted to me to be an humble instrument in re-establishing the religion on a firm basis in the island of Tambapanni?' While I was thus meditating and groaning in spirit for the religious welfare of Lanka, on the full-moon day of the month of Wésák'ha (April—May), in the two thousand three hundred and forty-fourth year from the death of the Supreme Buddhu, there arrived from Lanka (Ceylon) six Samanaro priests, with their lay devotees, at the great city of Amarapoora. Having inquired their names, their teachers' names, and the names of their teachers' teachers, their tribe and the object of their mission, I have welcomed them like so many relations coming from a distance. Announcing also the joyful event to our most gracious Sovereign, I have caused the strangers to be duly supplied with all necessaries, to be lodged in the upstair apartment designed for the reception of illustrious strangers. In the same year, on the commencement of the 'Wassa season,' the six Samanaros were re-ordained by me, supplied with robes of cotton and silk, and above all, gladdened with religious instruction and advice.

"At the close of the 'Wassa season' I have informed our

Sovereign King Mahá Dhamma, lord of the white elephants, whose silvery brightness resembles the water-lily, or moonbeams in the spring season, of the fitness of the six candidates for the *Upasampada* order, and the candidate for the Samanaro order, to enter into those orders respectively. Whereupon his most righteous Majesty—presenting them with bowls of refection, yellow robes, and other priestly requisites, causing them to be arrayed in tunics of royal (white) cloth, and adorning them with ornaments of various kinds, coronets, ear-ornaments, bracelets, gold chains, pearl necklaces, &c. &c., to rival the dress of a universal monarch, or the king of gods, placing them in golden howdhas fit for the use of a king whose dominions extend to the extremity of the ocean, and (causing) two superb umbrellas, brilliant like a couple of morning orbs of the sun, to be held over each of them—sent them in procession through the streets of Amarapoora, with all the insignia of royalty carried in procession before them, accompanied with vocal and instrumental music of various countries, dancers and other indications used on joyous occasions; attended by thousands of functionaries of various grades, ministers of state, generals of the army, together with an immense crowd of people. Having thus paraded through the city of Amarapoora, which resembles another *Amarawati* (the celestial metropolis of India), they were next conducted to the Mangaluchhanagara pavilion at the Royal Palace, where his Majesty King Mahá Dhamma Rajadhi Raja—of the Sakya dynasty, descended in an unbroken line from the renowned Maha Sammata, the abode of faith, piety, knowledge, munificence, and other virtues, lord of the white elephants, who had (previously) supplied their temporal and spiritual necessities, aspiring (by this meritorious act) to attain (in a future state of existence) the supreme Buddhahood, sitting in the midst of the four constituent hosts of his military array (chariots, elephants, cavalry, and infantry), escorted by his body-guard, surrounded by the sub-king, the princes of the blood royal, the queen and ladies of the Court, ministers of state and the provincial Rajahs—blessed them by pouring water from a golden vase like unto the proboscis of an elephant of the Ch'haddanta species. The candidates were next conducted in the aforesaid order of procession, to the 'three-storied' royal golden-hall, called *Saddhamma*, situated within the citadel, to the north-west of the king's palace, and there delivered over to the priesthood by the king, saying, 'Let these persons be admitted into the holy orders of *Pabbajja* and *Upasampada*.'"

The Sacred Bo Tree. p. 334.

CHAPTER VI.

MORAL AND SOCIAL CHARACTER OF THE SINGHALESE.

Traced to the Influence of their Religion — Progress of Christianity — The Missions of the Baptists — The Wesleyan Mission — The Mission of the Church of England — Results — And future Prospects.

CHAPTER VI.

MORAL AND SOCIAL CHARACTER OF THE SINGHALESE AS INFLUENCED BY THE BUDDHIST RELIGION.

It will at once be seen that in Buddhism, imperfectly as it has here been sketched, the Christian missionary in the south of Ceylon has a very different form of heathenism to overcome from the Brahmanical type which prevails amongst the Tamils of Jaffna and the north of the island. In addressing himself to his task, it becomes therefore necessary to adjust the process to the subject; and in looking to the system of the missionaries amongst the Singhalese Buddhists, it presents a marked distinction from that adopted with the same object in the northern province.

The difference consists mainly in the relative positions assigned to preaching and education as the basis of the operations relied on in each. The reasons have been already detailed why the latter appeared the more suitable for exposing the physical and historical errors which form the foundation of the Brahmanical faith; but with the Buddhists, whose belief rests less on physical than on metaphysical fallacies, whilst a prominent place has been given to education and to secular teaching, a still more advanced position has been assigned to argument and expostulation; to preaching throughout the scattered villages; and to the universal diffusion of publications designed to expose the delusions of idolatry, and exhibit the principles and divine origin of Christianity.

In this contest for ascendency over the Buddhist superstitions, the most formidable difficulty which the missionary has to overcome is the listlessness and indifference to all religion engendered by the feeble moral sense of the Singhalese themselves. Even the civilizing rudiments of their own social creed they are deplorably ignorant of; and amongst the priesthood of Buddhu the proportion is small of those who have sufficiently studied their sacred books to qualify them to act as the leaders of those who are helplessly reliant on them for guidance. Beyond some imperfect formulæ the teachers are as destitute of information as the taught; and in the hands of these illiterate exponents the treasures of ineffable wisdom, professed to be contained in their divine books, have proved as ineffectual "for reproof and correction" as they are essentially insufficient "for instruction in righteousness."

A sense of abstract right and wrong is a moral element of human nature; and there are few in whom it can be said to be altogether silent and numbed; but in none are its dictates more perverted, more torpid, and uninfluential than amongst the unenlightened Singhalese. Conscience in them can scarcely be said to be seared, for its impulses are but imperfectly awakened; and even when excited they fail to echo to the appeals of truth, or but imperfectly respond to them. Shame and compunction are sensations comparatively unknown; the senses rather than the soul become the monitors of the man; the spiritual and the remote suggest no motive impulses; and virtue and vice are terms which acquire relation only through the interests and passions of the moment.

In the development of their moral character there is to be traced all the negative results of this deficiency of moral sense. To strangers the mass of the Singhalese people appear courteous and mild; they seldom fail to exhibit in their outward demeanour the evidences of sympathy, benevolence, and gratitude; but to those who have penetrated their secluded villages, and become to some extent domesticated in their communities, their genuine character presents itself with traits and features far less pleasing. Jealousy, slander, litigation, and revenge prevail to an unlooked-for excess. "Every household has its internal differences, every circle its unconcealed feuds and animosities. The women especially cherish the spirit of discord, and rise in furious passions against each other, which are vented by railings, loud, virulent, and obscene. They are addicted to few disgusting vices or brutalizing crimes;

but in a Singhalese village licentiousness is so universal that it has ceased to be opprobrious, and hatred so ungovernable that murders are by no means rare."[1]

Falsehood, the unerring index of innate debasement, is of ubiquitous prevalence; and even in the courts of law, the testimony of every magistrate is concurrent that perjury on both sides is so habitual, that the duty of the judge is to conjecture the truth from the incidents rather than the evidence; and the difficulty of those who conduct suits, either for the Crown or individuals, is to avert the obstruction of justice by the impatience of their own witnesses to corroborate truth by invention.

Theft, which is merely falsehood in action, is equally prevalent with prevarication; and deceit in every conceivable shape, in forgery and fraud, in corruption and defamation, is so notorious and habitual amongst the uneducated mass, that the feeling of confidence is almost unknown; and in the most intimate arrangements of domestic life, the bond of brotherhood or friendship, of parent and of child, inspires no effectual reliance in the mutual good faith and honour of the interested parties.

The censure passed by Epimenides on the Cretans[2] might with little modification be applied equally to the uneducated population of Ceylon; and yet this revolt-

[1] MS. Note of the Rev. J. Davies, Baptist Missionary.

[2] Κρῆτες ἀεὶ ψεῦσται. Titus i. 12.

ing propensity to prevaricate is more or less referable to a political origin, and presents some curious modifications in particular relations; for although in one class of cases detection may expose the liar to rebuke, there is another and an extensive one which enjoys a licence within which falsehood is held by the Singhalese to be, if not commendable, at least exempt from condemnation. Whilst its universality is ascribable to the passive dispensation under which it luxuriates and expands, its origin is not wholly without reference to the national conjunctures of the race; to the despotism beneath which from the remotest ages they have groaned under their native sovereigns, and even, I regret to add, in many respects to their political position under their Christian rulers. Their subjection to the absolute feudalism of their chiefs and headmen, and the expedients by which the revenues of the Government have been heretofore raised, from jealous monopolies and arbitrary assessments levied off the produce of their lands, have driven the Singhalese to devices and cunning for their common protection, and rendered a lie, when its tendencies would be conducive to the general interests, not only venial but chivalrous in the eyes of the community. Prevarication to a superior, or successful deception practised on the Government or its officers, are acts not of baseness, but of duty. Deceit, or frauds attempted towards each other, may be treated with Lacedemonian leniency; but the man would be scorned by his community who would venture to tell the truth to a representative of authority, if it militated against the general interests of his village.[1]

Between themselves, however, in their secret relations there does exist a certain amount of truthfulness, without which the whole fabric of their social system, imperfect as it is, would fall asunder; and besides, its existence is indispensable for the maintenance of their common cause against their rulers.[2] This germ of integrity is occasionally so far

[1] In many particulars the character of the Singhalese in regard to falsehood and deceit is assimilated to that of the Hindoos as sketched by Mountstuart Elphinstone:—"Their most prominent vice is want of veracity, in which they outdo most nations of the East. They do not even resent the imputation of falsehood; and perjury, which is only an aggravated species of falsehood, naturally accompanies other offences of the kind. It is in people connected with Government that deceit is most common; but in India this class spreads far, as, from the nature of the land-revenue, the lowest villager is often obliged to resist force by fraud. To take a bribe in a good cause is almost meritorious; and it is a venial offence to take one when the cause is bad. Pecuniary fraud is not thought very disgraceful; and if against the public, scarcely disgraceful at all. Even in corrupt transactions it is seldom that men will not rather undergo punishment than betray those to whom they have given a bribe. The villagers are everywhere an inoffensive, amiable people, affectionate to their families, kind to their neighbours, and, *towards all but the government*, honest and sincere."—Hist. India, b. iii. c. xi.

[2] A native gentleman of rank, a Kandyan by birth, of a chief's family, and with the style of *Banda*, which is nearly equivalent with the Singhalese to that of a nobleman, was recently convicted by

developed and partially extended to their mutual intercourse, that falsehood becomes to a certain extent censurable; and however feeble may be the impulse of honour in the individual, the odium of society imposes a modified obligation to truth. It has been found by experience that the man who would lie without limit to a stranger at a distance from his village, and who would perjure himself without scruple or passion in a court of law, will still shrink when confronted with his village associates, whose presence serves to elicit a scintillation of truth, when the influence of authority and even the terror of punishment have been exerted in vain to extort it. But even such instances are rare; they form merely the exception; falsehood as the rule is all but universal; and whilst its frequency destroys all moral sense within, its veniality produces an indifference to opinion and external repute, which aggravates the general humiliation of the national character, and complicates the difficulty of establishing an ascendancy for Christianity and its influences.

Coupled with this disheartening obstacle, opposed

the Supreme Court of perjury in a case in which he had no further interest than his desire to assist the claims of a suitor who happened to be his friend. He was sentenced to the usual punishment of fine and imprisonment: the former he expressed his readiness to pay, but petitioned the Governor for enlargement, on the ground that his offence was so venial, prevarication and falsehood being the well known characteristics of his countrymen and never regarded by them as a crime.

by the debasement of the national mind, is another and almost equally formidable obstruction, *in the obtuseness and torpor of the intellectual faculties* engendered by ages of neglect, and confirmed by a combination of physical and social causes, unfavourable to exertion of any kind, and destructive of energy both mental and physical.

The Singhalese are lethargic and slothful to an excess beyond even the extreme of most southern Asiatics. The industry of man will always be the complement of the liberality of nature; where she confers or refuses everything, exertion loses either its impulse or its reward, and man alike degenerates in ease or despondency. But in that bounteous mean where the earth yields or withholds her gifts in proportion as they are sought for and elaborated, men, under the conjoint influence of necessity and hope, mature the intellectual and physical powers on which invention and energy are dependent, but which lie dormant and undeveloped when the lavish luxuriance or the hopeless sterility of nature withdraws the motive or the recompense, and renders labour respectively superfluous or vain.[1]

[1] Sir John Davis has the following passage in applying this theory, but in a different development, in relation to the Chinese: —"An attentive survey of the tropical regions of the earth, where food is produced in the greatest abundance, will seem to justify the conclusion that *extreme* fertility has been rather prejudicial to the progress of the human race; or at least that the industry and advancement of nations have appeared in some measure to depend

The natives of Ceylon have been placed by Providence in the first of these extremes; for them nature has done so much, that man in sluggish satisfaction

on a certain *proportion* between their necessities and their natural resources. Man is by nature an indolent animal; and, without the stimulant of necessity, will, in the first instance, get on as well as he can with the provision that nature has made for him.

"In the warm and fertile regions of the tropics, or rather of the equinoctial, where lodging and clothing (the two necessary things after food) are rendered almost superfluous by the climate, and where food itself is produced by little exertion, we find how small a progress in most instances has been made; while on the other hand a different result is apparent in the whole of Europe and by far the greater part of China, which are situated beyond the northern tropic. If again we go *farther north*, to those arctic regions where man exists in a very miserable state, we shall find that *there he has no materials to work on:* in other words, the *proportion* is destroyed; the equinoctial regions are too spontaneously genial and fertile—the arctic too unkindly barren—and on this account it would seem that industry, wealth, and civilization have been principally confined to the temperate zone, where there is at once *necessity* to excite to labour and *production* to recompense it."—Sir John Davis's China, Introd., p. vii.

Mountstuart Elphinstone thus applies the same theory to the native tribes of India. The defects of the Hindoos "no doubt arise chiefly from moral causes, but they are also to be ascribed in part to physical constitution and in part to soil and climate. Some races are certainly less vigorous than others; and all must degenerate if placed in an enervating atmosphere. Mere heat may not enervate; if it is unavoidable and unremitting, it even produces a sort of hardness like that arising from the rigours of a northern winter. If sterility be added, and the fruits of hard labour are contested among scattered tribes, the result may be the energy and decision of the Arab. But in India a warm temperature is accompanied by a fertile soil, which renders severe labour unnecessary, and an extent of land that would sup-

aspires and labours for no more. Every want and almost every wish is provided for by the gentleness of the climate and the spontaneity of the soil. Civilization has created no artificial wants; over-population has not interfered with the gratification of those which nature has implanted; and man is energetic and industrious only in those rarer instances in which accident has divested his situation of the advantages which neutralize or supersede exertion. Amongst the great mass of the people in Ceylon there have never yet been awakened those emotions of enterprise, emulation, and ambition which elsewhere have supplied a stimulus to intellect, and organized the march of improvement. Their country presents no vestiges of art, and their literature no achievements of mind; and voluminous and minute as are the records of their history from the earliest times, they chronicle few events

port an almost indefinite increase of inhabitants. The heat is moderated by rain, and warded off by numerous trees and forests; everything is calculated to produce that state of listless inactivity which foreigners find it so difficult to resist. The shades of character that are found in different parts of India tend to confirm this supposition. The inhabitants of the dry countries in the north, which in winter are cold, are comparatively manly and active; the Maharattas, inhabiting a mountainous and infertile region, are hardy and laborious; while the Bengalese, with their moist climate and their double crops of rice, where the cocoanut-tree and the bamboo furnish all the materials for construction, unwrought, are more effeminate than any other people in India." —History of India, vol. i. book iii. ch. xi.

except the vicissitudes of their national superstition, and no exploits beyond the brute labour expended upon gigantic tanks and canals for the irrigation of rice-lands.

Even the energy and combination which were essential for the formation of these, and the narrow amount of intelligence which was required for their construction, have long since disappeared. The very labour required to arrest their ruin has been since withheld,[1] and those prodigious remains, which still astonish the traveller as the monuments of an extinct civilization, have converted into pestilential swamps extended districts once teeming with human life, and still retaining the traces of former fertility and toil.

The decrease of inhabitants in Ceylon, which appears to have been progressive from a period now remote and uncertain, has facilitated the easy supply of all the wants of recent generations. The popu-

[1] It is a striking illustration of the want of energy and industry on the part of the Singhalese, that although portions of the island, the Wanny, Neura-kalawya, Tamankadua, and others, abound with tanks on which the very existence of the population depends, and the majority of them are in ruins, their repair is seldom or never undertaken by the Singhalese; but parties of Tamils, who devote themselves to this employment, make annual excursions from Jaffna at the proper seasons, carrying with them tools and mattocks, and are employed by the Singhalese villagers in the repair of their tanks. For an account of some of the gigantic tanks and artificial lakes of Ceylon see an extract from my Journal, Note A, end of this chapter.

lation at the present day are subjected to no pressure which can impel them to improvements, and hence indolence has become a habit to which their intellect has conformed—inveterate, hereditary, and almost insurmountable. Low intrigue for the promotion of their pecuniary interests, or artifice for their protection, seem almost the highest effort of which their minds are susceptible—their perceptions, keen and subtle so far as their domestic and social transactions are concerned, seem to collapse when applied to higher or more profound ideas. Beyond the narrow range within which they have been accustomed to confine their thoughts, they exhibit an incredible obtuseness, and, with the exception of the inhabitants of the towns, whose faculties have been sharpened by collision with Europeans, it seems almost impossible to lodge permanently in their minds the impress of the simplest truth.[1]

Such mental debasement is unfavourable in the last degree to the access of Christian truth. Christianity reveals doctrines of the loftiest sublimity based upon truths of the sublimest comprehension, and to induce their reception, but still more to effect it in substitution of ancestral delusions, implies an exercise of thought and an exertion of intellectual power which seems almost beyond the capacity of the lethargic Singhalese. There must be volition

[1] MS. Notes of the Rev. J. Davies, Baptist Missionary.

and effort in such a process, and not mere passiveness and plasticity; he that would "find" must first exert the energy to "seek;" and looking to the reluctance and almost compulsion with which the Singhalese can be induced even to *listen*, the task to an ordinary observer appears all but impracticable, to awaken their interest and excite the operation of reflection and inquiry by which the unwilling auditor may, in process of time, become the deliberate student and the convinced and reconciled Christian.

The scope and the soil for missionary labour in the East at the present day is in many respects, but especially in this particular, widely different from that cultivated by the first Apostles of Christianity. Mankind, in the area within which their earliest efforts were made, had been already awakened to inquiry from the long torpor of an exhausted superstition. The philosophy and the ethics of Greece had shed their light over the regions of Western Asia, and disturbed the rude mythology of the Romans and their tributaries. The long stagnation of the human mind was at length moved. Philosophy had given a noble expansion to intellectual power, and diffused an energetic contempt for the absurdity of pagan rites. Satire had directed its shafts in ridicule of popular delusion; and rhetoric had roused whilst science directed an impulse to the exposure of error and the search after truth. Contemporary with these great social phenomena, two powerful auxiliary movements were in active operation to aid the extension of Christianity — the dispersion of the Jews with their sacred books and antiquities over every region of the Western world, and the diffusion of the literature and language of the Greeks (the vernacular of the Apostles and probably of their august Master himself[1]) over all the southern dominion of Rome, where the Greeks, before their final submission, had planted their numerous colonies, from the shores of the Hellespont to the confines of the Atlas.

Co-extensive with the march of the Apostles, therefore, were the facilities which they found already prepared for the triumph of their mission; but these facilities their humbler followers throughout the East at the present day have in every instance slowly and laboriously to create, amidst difficulties more obstructive and influences more adverse than the dangers which beset the path of the Apostles, or the active persecution which overtook their earliest disciples. Instead of the strife of theology, they have to overcome the apathy of indifference, and experience has proved that they encounter a more formidable opponent in the stupor of ignorance than in the dialectics of scepticism.

In opposition to these discouraging obstacles, the expedients of the missionaries amongst the Buddhists of Southern Ceylon have been the same, though combined in different proportions, as those adopted

[1] Diodati de Christo Græcè loquente.

by their fellow-labourers amongst the Hindoos of the north—*education, exhortation,* and the *press.* Of these the latter has been hitherto a comparative failure; but before recording the general success of the others, it is necessary to advert to those causes in the peculiarities of the people by which the variation in the process, as well as the extent of success in the results, have been more or less influenced.

As an instrument of conversion to Christianity, *the press* has hitherto been productive of but limited success in Ceylon; but the causes of this are neither remote nor obscure. Till the Baptist missionaries established themselves at Serampore, printing for the use of the natives in the numerous languages of India had never extended beyond the publication of grammars and elementary works of no very important character. In Ceylon the Church of England missionaries and the Americans introduced the use of the printing-press amongst the Tamils of Jaffna,—the Wesleyans were the first to employ it in the Singhalese districts, and it was not till 1841 that it was established by the Baptists in Kandy, where its manipulation excited a lively interest amongst the chiefs and the natives who crowded to witness the process. But the moral results have been limited and unsatisfactory, although industriously applied to the multiplication of the Scriptures and Scriptural tracts, and to the preparation of school-books for the educational establishments.

To one important function of the press, attention has as yet been but inadequately turned—*the formation of a Singhalese literature* in supersession of the extravagant legends and unsatisfactory treatises written on olahs,[1] and disseminated under the sanction of the Buddhist priesthood. National superstitions have ever found their surest allies in a national literature, with which their traditions and tenets are almost imperceptibly blended. This was the case with the Chaldæans and the Egyptians, with the Greeks and the Romans, with the literature of the Arabs, and in the later times with that of Hindoostan and Burmah, of China, and of Ceylon; and no more essential service can be rendered to the march of Christianity in the latter island than the encouragement of a popular literature in which the tenets and the morals of the Gospel might be made familiar to the ideas and prepossessions of the Singhalese.

Although the success of these attempts has been obstructed by many local impediments, the press, even in its imperfect efforts, has done much to lay the foundation of intelligent piety, and erect a bulwark for the future against the encroachments of error; but consisting almost unavoidably of translations from European languages, the works hitherto communicated in their own dialect to the natives of Ceylon have not only abounded in ideas totally

[1] Prepared leaves of the palm-tree, to be written on with an iron style.

foreign to their customs and their habits of thought, but in idioms and forms of expression neither familiar nor intelligible. No people of the East are more critical as to style or more fastidious as to terms than the natives of Ceylon, and the harmonious arrangement of sentences has an allurement for them far more attractive than any interest in the sense. Unfortunately, hitherto this inducement has been but imperfectly supplied, and the strangers who have made a study of their tongue, with a view to its employment in translation, have failed to master that peculiar tone and those graces of style by which alone the natives are attracted.

In the preparation of the Church of England version of the Scriptures and the Book of Common Prayer an innovation has likewise been admitted, to which it will be long before the ear and the taste of the Singhalese will be thoroughly reconciled. So pliant is their dialect, and so artistically has it been inflected to adapt it to the relative station of the personages addressed, that in one particular alone, the variations of a single pronoun, a native of Ceylon is enabled to apply with delicate propriety no less than ten or twelve degrees of respect, each appropriate to the recognised rank of the individual addressed, and ranging from a familiarity expressive of contempt to a degree of awe and veneration with which in their ideas of worship the Supreme Being alone should be approached. In the version of the

Scriptures translated by the Church of England missionaries of Cotta all these distinctions have been equalized: they have omitted the use of the honorific "*wohanse*," and addressed the Deity throughout with the ordinary appellative of "*to*" or thou. The alteration has given rise to the most vehement remonstrances on the part of the higher class of natives and of the many who, like them, have been reared in that national veneration for rank which the Buddhists have substituted somewhat inartificially for the prohibited distinctions of "caste." They have protested, as *blasphemous*, against the application to the Supreme Being of epithets which would be felt as an insult if addressed to one of themselves. They lately rose in a body and retired from a church when the obnoxious version was introduced, and they have intimated an intention, should an innovation so offensive be persevered in, to seek in some other communion of the Christian church that respect for their feelings which they conceive has been disregarded in their own.[1]

[1] The proceedings of the Singhalese on this occasion are strangely illustrative of the deep tenacity with which, notwithstanding their long familiarization with Christianity, the upper classes still maintain their attachment to caste and its distinctions. After retiring in a body from the church in which the obnoxious version of the Scriptures was sought to be used, they addressed a remonstrance to the Bishop of Colombo in which the following passage occurs:—

"When language absolutely insulting, and in our opinion degrading, to our God and Saviour is used, we can only testify

Another incident which has unavoidably retarded the usefulness of the press, is a natural result. of the

our abhorrence of it by withdrawing from the sound thereof; or inexpressibly grieve our minds, and substitute for feelings of devotion very different and opposite feelings, by remaining to hear that which we conscientiously believe to be little short of blasphemy."

This remonstrance failing to procure from the Bishop a declaration that, till some authorized version should have been promulgated, each congregation should be permitted to select that which best accorded with their own ideas of devotion and worship, a memorial was presented, in terms equally strong, and accompanied with an intimation of the determination of those whose feelings it represented to attach themselves to some other body of Christians, rather than continue in the Church of England with their earnest entreaties disregarded:—

"It is with sorrow and surprise we find in your Lordship's communication of the 21st of November a rule altogether different, mentioned as that referred to by your Lordship in your letter of the 7th—a rule having no direct concern with *congregations*, but with *clergymen*—a rule, we most respectfully submit, perfectly unnecessary, unless it be supposed that a clergyman has not himself the power (if he choose to exercise it) of preventing objectionable doings in his own church by another clergyman.

"What we have from the commencement, and without any variation, sought for, is a declaration from your Lordship, recognizing and enforcing the rule your Lordship found in existence when you arrived in Ceylon; a rule which in effect declared that a clergyman, when ministering in any Singhalese church, be it his own or not his own, should use that version which the congregation prefers, and not that which he himself wishes to adopt—or may even find compulsorily adopted—against the known wishes and expressed remonstrances of the people. We would also most respectfully submit, that we cannot be justly charged, by implication or directly, with needless agita-

scarcity of books, that the natives, from want of practice and familiarity, read with so much slowness

tion, when we only lawfully seek to be protected from having what we believe a blasphemous version of Scripture and of the Liturgy thrust upon us, and when we as lawfully assist others of our countrymen, who required our advice, in attaining the same object.

"We would also further most respectfully urge, that while we seek no imposition upon others of that version which we prefer, and which they may not prefer, we only entreat, until the Church has set forth authorized versions, that even-handed justice may be dealt out to all parties; whereas, your Lordship, with heartfelt sorrow we observe in your letter, would deny to us laymen that liberty which you would freely allow to others, who, though clergy, are no more alone *the church* than we, the laity, are alone *the church*. This cannot promote the things that make for peace, and must have the effect of perpetuating discord instead of bringing about union.

"As matters now stand, according to the rule laid down by your Lordship, were our respected chaplain to die to-morrow, or to be induced to use the blasphemous version of Cotta, no remedy is provided for us.

"We owe it to your Lordship, as well as to ourselves, our countrymen, and to our posterity, to declare explicitly that matters cannot remain thus. If your Lordship cannot grant our reasonable prayer, we must appeal to the higher powers in Church and State, and, if need be, even to the highest; and should such appeal (which God in his mercy forbid) prove in vain, your Lordship will drive us to the necessity of seeking Christian privileges in some other branch of the Church Catholic, which will not impose on us, as terms of communion, a version of the Scriptures and of a Liturgy abounding (as we conscientiously aver the Cotta version does abound) in blasphemous expressions towards our Creator, Redeemer, and Sanctifier.

"We implore your Lordship—who cannot possibly know our language as we know it—to save us from this only alternative

and difficulty as to diminish the enjoyment and to render reading an effort, to overcome which the interest or the idiom of such works as we have hitherto supplied them with scarcely present a sufficient allurement. Many who can read with comparative ease their own books, which are written with an iron style upon olahs, are embarrassed by the same letters when impressed upon paper; and it is a curious illustration of the temperament of the lower orders, that the belief is not unfrequent amongst them that reading is an operation of magic, by which ideas are invoked and come from some distant quarter on naming the mysterious signs which have been previously traced upon the page.

Reading is, in fact, a drudgery to the Singhalese; and the same, I apprehend, may be said of the majority of Asiatics, including the Chinese. Even the most successful pupils of the missionary schools seldom devote themselves to it as a voluntary pursuit; and it cannot be concealed that the impulsive taste for study, either as an enjoyment or a relief, has yet to be created in Ceylon. That it has struck root on the continent of India may be inferred from the circumstance of the establishment of native presses in Hindoostan; but before such a manifestation can

open to us, *by declaring that until the Church shall have set forth authorized versions of the Bible and Book of Common Prayer, each congregation shall be left in peaceable possession of that version of both which it conscientiously prefers.*"

be looked for amongst the Singhalese, we must await the diffusion of education and the multiplication of books.

No one who has had opportunities of observation and experience of the results of missionary exertions amongst uncivilized races can hesitate to record his conviction that the means which have proved most effective for conversion to Christianity have been the conjoint influences of *education* and *preaching*, not conducted as independent operations, but as subsidiary, co-operative, and mutually sustaining. Preaching is doubtless the original and the ordained means of diffusing the Gospel; but however unqualified the terms in which it was enjoined on or recommended to the Apostles, those who would follow their example, whilst adapting that means to the end, must not overlook the diversity of circumstance which characterizes respectively the scenes of the Apostles' labour and their own. For the former, the way was already prepared by anticipation; and they were relieved from the necessity to educate as well as to preach. The Jews were no doubt inferior to their Greek and Roman audiences in the elements of general knowledge; but they were by no means inferior to the teachers who arose amongst themselves to announce the new dispensation. The modern missionary, on the contrary, goes forth from the most enlightened regions to illuminate the most benighted. This superiority implies a duty, distinct, though identified with the main object of his mission; and wherever that mission has been successful, civilization has become more or less synonymous with Christianity. Even where the results of the alliance have been less striking, the process, though incomplete, is inchoate; and civilization has not merely prepared the way for the reception of the truth, but has laid that solid foundation which is essential to the stability and permanence of the structure. Where schools have never effected a single conversion amongst the natives, they have nevertheless served to diffuse preliminarily that general intelligence which is its surest forerunner; and even in this secondary relation their social importance is extreme. The objection to merely secular education may be so far well-founded that in insulated instances it may render the individual more accomplished as an evil-doer, and refine his sagacity for mischief; but education has never yet been productive of these effects upon a general scale—never aggravated the defection of a nation, or precipitated the general deterioration of a community: on the contrary, whilst ignorance gives eternity to vicious custom and perpetuates depravity, education, by arousing the energies and stimulating the improvement of the few, leads eventually to the enlightenment and social elevation of the mass.

But as more immediately affecting the interests and diffusion of Christianity itself, the condition of ignorance is of all others the most unfavourable to its reception, and the least congenial to its permanent ascendancy; and those who aim at having it embraced most intelligently, most effectually developed, and most abidingly established, must be prepared to pioneer its path by the toil of education, and the improvement of the social condition of its recipients. It is more or less by secular and scientific education that we can eventually hope to undermine the false philosophy which forms the basis alike of the Buddhist and Brahmanical systems. They are so intimately intermingled, and so familiarized in the minds of the people, that they must be swept away by education before a standing-place can be formed for the truth of Christianity; and, on the other hand, to confirm the victory of the latter, and establish its permanent dominion over error, education alone can confer the ability to investigate its evidences, and teach them like the Jews of Berea to examine for themselves, and "search the Scriptures whether these things are so."

Christianity began its career in the most polished circles, and amongst the most enlightened community of the age. Its behest was to "teach all nations;" and the line of its march was most triumphant where the progress of instruction had been the most marked and successful. Its first churches were planted in the educated circles of Asia Minor and of Greece; and in remoter districts and villages its progress was so comparatively slow that four centuries after the birth of its founder the last refuge of parting idolatry was amongst the *pagani* and rustics.

But not only are the most civilized races the first to receive Christianity; they are likewise the most enduring and consistent in retaining and preserving it in its pristine integrity. Neither history nor more recent experience can furnish any example of the long retention of pure Christianity by a people themselves rude and unenlightened. In all the nations of Europe, embracing every period since the second century, Christianity must be regarded as having taken the hue and complexion of the social state with which it was incorporated, presenting itself unsullied, contaminated, or corrupted in sympathy with the enlightenment, the ignorance, or debasement of those by whom it had been originally embraced.[1]

At the period of the Reformation the progress of the purified faith was coeval with the restoration of letters, and concurrent with the advancement of learning, a result which had not escaped the perspicuous foresight of Luther, and which inspired that importance which he uniformly attached to the diffusion of knowledge.[2]

[1] The rapid and universal degeneracy of the early Asiatic churches is associated with the decline of education and the intellectual decay of the communities amongst whom they were established.

[2] D'Aubigné, b. iv. c. 9.

In Ceylon, and in India, after all that has been achieved by the influence of Europeans, and the exertions of missionaries, there exists between the religion of the native converts and their social and intellectual condition an incongruity which cannot be permanent. Either Christianity in their hands will degenerate to the level of its guardians, or their own national character must be elevated till it approaches the standard of their religious profession. Christianity amongst them is at the present moment preserved in its purity, only by the presence and the vigilance of the strangers who implanted it; but looking to the probable arrival of a period when the support derived from Europe by foreign missions may cease, and the natives of India may be left to their own unaided efforts and guidance, the question becomes of paramount importance,—to whose guardianship and culture is Christianity in India to be hereafter entrusted? —whether to be committed to a people debased below the condition of other Asiatics, amongst whom it has heretofore declined and disappeared, or elevated by education towards that pitch of enlightenment which characterizes the nations of Europe, by whom it has been cherished for nearly 2000 years, retaining more or less of the integrity and purity in which it was communicated to mankind by its divine Author and his disciples?

In more than one passage I have already alluded to those distinctive peculiarities in the relative structure of the Brahmanical and Buddhist superstitions, which, while both are accessible to the conjoint influence of *education* and *preaching*, have rendered it expedient to adjust these two great engines of intellectual power in such different proportions as are best suited for their intended effect upon each. The basis of this distinction is the greater degree in which the religion of the Brahmans professes to repose on the exact and physical sciences, and the larger admixture of false philosophy and fable with which its most important tenets have been copiously blended. Buddhism, whilst affecting a similar association with subjects so profound, has in the long lapse of time not only admitted innovations into its physical and historical structure; but, enamoured of its metaphysical subtleties, it has given to its code of ethics and morals a prominence of position beyond that which is affected by the religion of the Brahmans and Hindoos, and which renders the latter system comparatively more assailable by the agency of argument.

In addition to this, so universal is the ignorance of the Buddhist population, that although the terms of their scientific absurdities may be familiar to their ear, so little do they cultivate their study, and so imperfectly are they acquainted with their theories and combinations, that even successful demonstration of their errors in such particulars would fail in the majority of instances to destroy the polypus vitality of their tenacious faith in the remainder. The same amount of exposure as to its scientific fallacies which would be fatal to the belief of a Hindoo, would prove less effective in shaking the confidence of a Buddhist, and hence the greater reliance which the missionaries in Ceylon have reposed in the efficacy of preaching when sustained and associated with the agency of the school-room and the seminary.

But disconnected with the pulpit, the results of mere education in India, even under the most favourable circumstances, have been deplorably meagre in relation to conversion from the native superstitions. It has undoubtedly done much to prepare the way for the Gospel; it has shaken erroneous systems, checked the further ascendency of superstition, diffused an elementary knowledge of Christianity, and prepared a more intelligent audience for the voice of the truth; but as a means of direct and actual conversion, unassisted education has most signally failed. A large proportion of native converts have no doubt been trained in the schools of the various missions; but the fact is a coincidence, and by no means a result, conversion in such instances having been the effect of a separate agency.

In Jaffna, while the educational labours of the American mission have produced almost a social revolution throughout the province, the number of their nominal converts has barely exceeded 600 out of 90,000 pupils. Of these perhaps less than one-half could trace the change to the unaided instrumentality of instruction; and instances are not rare in which the scholars reared by these devout and untiring men, so far from returning their care by an alliance with their objects, have proved by their scepticism and infidelity more dangerous enemies to the truth than even heathenism itself.[1]

[1] The Rev. Howard Malcolm, of Boston, U.S., who in 1836 made a tour of the Missions in Hindoostan and Burmah, in Siam, Malaya, and China, after describing the extent to which education has been carried in their Christian institutions, has thus summed up the inadequate success by which all its labours have been followed as regards conversion to Christianity:—"The proportion of conversions among this mighty host of scholars is certainly very small. It was stated by the late Rev. Mr. Reichardt, of Calcutta, who laboured long in the service of the Church Missionary Society, that of the many thousand boys instructed by this Society, only five or six had been converted. At Vepery, a suburb of Madras, where for a hundred years this species of labour had been largely bestowed by the Christian Knowledge Society, the results are scarcely more encouraging; nor at Tranquebar, where schools have been maintained for a hundred and thirty years. In all Madras, where several thousands have been constantly taught in Missionary schools, there are not known to be half-a-dozen converted natives. At the Anglo-Chinese College at Malacca, which has existed for twenty years, only a few have been converted, though some twenty or thirty have been brought over to Christianity. In Ceylon, where schools have been conducted for twenty-six years, and generally with more attention to religion than is common in India, few conversions occurred before 1830; and those since that time have been rather the effect of protracted meetings and especial pastoral effort, than the school system. Out of the Scotch General Assembly's School in Calcutta, which for six years has had an average of 400 scholars and the entire and

The conclusion is irresistible, that the schoolmaster of himself is not calculated, nor is he expected, to supersede the missionary; and education does not forfeit its esteem because it has failed to realize what it was never relied on to achieve. As preparatives and auxiliaries, the value of schools can scarcely be overrated; as independent agencies they can be but productive of disappointment; and *preaching* as the grand momentum of conversion can find no adequate substitute in mere educational discipline. Even were schools universal and books multiplied without end, the living voice would be still indispensable to awaken attention and apply general truth to the ever-changing relations of life.

constant attention of two Missionaries, there have been but five or six conversions. The Baptist schools in Bengal, numbering thousands of scholars, for more than thirty years past have produced very few conversions. That at Chittagong, taught by a Missionary in person every day for sixteen years, with an average of 200 pupils, has witnessed but two of the scholars brought to a knowledge of the truth. In Arracan no conversion has yet occurred in the schools. Among all the Burmans I know of no Christian who is regarded as the fruit of schools. Among the Karens many scholars have been converted; but the primary and daily object of these schools has ever seemed to be the conversion rather than the education of the scholars. In places where schools have most abounded and for the longest time, a considerable number of pupils have rejected Heathenism without embracing Christianity, and are now conceited infidels, worse to deal with than pagans. Many of them by means of their education have obtained offices under government, or in commercial houses, and exert a considerable influence against religion."

Preaching was founded on no peculiar adaptation to the existing state of society in that portion of Asia in which it took its rise. It is suited to the capacity of human nature in every condition of society, in every quarter of the universe, and in every vicissitude of times, wisely founded as it is on the nature of religion itself, as well as on the nature of man. Of all expedients it has proved the most effectual in arousing the interest and directing the inquiries of an illiterate and uncivilized people; and, strange to say, from the earliest period preaching has been the special practice of the Buddhist priesthood themselves. Every temple has its pulpit, round which an audience is collected, to whom the sacred books of their religion are expounded; by the reading of a passage from the Pali, followed by a commentary in Singhalese, by another officiating priest. With the natives, the ease of listening to such discourses not only relieves them of the effort to read, but they evince an interest in the operation which has more or less disposed them to attend to public exhortations from the Christian missionaries who have visited their villages. And small as has been the result of their labours, it may safely be said, that of the whole number of real conversions in Ceylon, *five* at least have been made by means of preaching for one by the influence of schools, or any other instrumentality.[1]

[1] The instance of the Moravians in Greenland is a striking

But in using the accustomed phrase of *preaching* to the heathen, a very different idea is associated with the practice in Ceylon from that which is conveyed by the same familiar term to the ear of an European. The preaching of a missionary has little of the form and ceremonial of an address to a congregation elsewhere. It is with difficulty that a native audience can be induced either by curiosity or entreaty to attend. Even then they do not exceed an assemblage of some ten or twenty persons, to whom the subject is not only so new but so incomprehensible that it is seldom they will listen, and rarely, indeed, that attention is followed by either reflection or inquiry. The life of the jungle missionary of

illustration of the failure of education as a substitute for preaching in the case of a Christian mission:—"The Moravians tried both methods; they tried the preparatory system of instruction and civilization under most favourable circumstances and with surprising perseverance, but it totally failed in reclaiming a single savage from his rude and hideous superstition; the Greenlanders refused to be moved by the Missionaries' pre-arranged plans of conversion, and after years of fruitless toil they varied this experiment, they began to preach the Gospel in plain and perspicuous terms, and the effect was instantaneous. Preaching and its influences were successful in transforming these northern savages into humble and docile beings; and amongst the Cingalese, strange as it may sound to those who have had no practical intercourse with unenlightened races, yet it is a fact that when spoken to on the subjects of sin and salvation, of time and eternity, their attention is more readily arrested, and their resistance more easily subdued, than when addressed on the more ordinary topics of moral and economical instruction."—MS. Notes of the Rev. J. Davies.

Ceylon is one of privation and fatigue, of exposure and sickness, of disappointment and repulse; nor can it be more faithfully described than in the words of one of the most apostolic teachers who has ever visited India, the late Baptist missionary, Mr. Daniel, who, to the close of a long and useful existence, made the hamlets and forest villages the scene of his toilsome but not unsuccessful labours. After describing,[1] in touching terms, the discouraging repulse of every ordinary attempt to obtain a hearing from the villagers, where there is nothing to excite, amuse, or astonish; and after describing the ridicule and frequent insults by which such invitations are usually answered, Mr. Daniel thus tells of his daily life and pursuits in exploring these secluded spots in the jungle:—"I enter a village, and, proceeding from house to house, I sit down on a seat, if I can procure one, or if not, I spread a mat upon the ground, and endeavour, in the plainest language, and with the most familiar illustrations, to explain the way of salvation. Sometimes, in answer to my invitations to attend, the Singhalese ask, 'What will you pay us to do so? Will you give us arrack, if we listen to you?' If not thus coarsely insolent, they will invent some excuse to get away; and if sent to ask their friends to attend, they go, but do not return. We proceed to another house; and having thus spoken the word

[1] In a letter to the Baptist Committee in London, July 8, 1840.

in one village, we pass on to the next. We often meet with little but contempt, opprobrium, and laughter; and each day in the week (except Saturday, which is devoted to study) is employed in these exertions, and in the journeys connected with them. Oh! that I could tell you of success in proportion; but for the present this is denied us. But those who sow in tears have the promise that they shall reap in joy; and probably we are now depositing the seed which at no distant day will spring into a glorious harvest."

The good man who wrote this was attached to the first mission that, after the British conquest, commenced its labours in Ceylon—that of THE BAPTISTS, who, early in 1792, formed themselves into a society for the propagation of the Gospel beyond the British islands, and whose career on the continent of India is one which must be ever memorable in the annals of Christianity. They have carried the Gospel into numerous countries of the East; they have translated the Bible into forty-five languages; they have printed a million copies of the Scriptures, and thirty millions of other Christian publications, for distribution to idolaters; and at this moment they have nine thousand children under instruction, and thirty-eight thousand converts, members of their church in various lands of the heathen. They made their first visit to India in 1793; and twenty years later they sent their earliest representative to Ceylon, in the person of Mr. Chater, whose memory has been perpetuated as one of the first who made the attempt to systematize the study of Singhalese for Europeans,[1] with a view to the future dissemination of the Scriptures.

In 1814, the Baptist missionaries were followed by those of the Wesleyan Methodists; in 1816, by the Americans; and in 1818, by those of the Church of England. In selecting the scene of their labours, each of these bodies appears to have chosen its position so as least to interfere with the operations of the others, contented that each in his own sphere should make known the great truths of Christianity, with an absence of all rivalry or sectarian distinctions. The Americans took their way to Jaffna, and commenced their career amongst the Tamils of the North. The Baptists, who had already commenced their labours amongst the Buddhists of the South, fixed their head quarters at Colombo, and thence gradually extended their operations throughout the surrounding villages, and eastward till they reached to Kandy, and the rich valley of Matelle.[2] The Methodists chose the line of the sea-coast, from Negombo, southward, to Matura. The Church of

[1] His Singhalese Grammar is still one of the best that has appeared. In addition to which he took a share in the Singhalese translation of the Bible, in 3 vols. 4to., made a translation of the New Testament into Portuguese, and innumerable tracts explanatory of the Christian religion.

[2] The Baptists have also a station in the Southern Province at Matura.

England clergy established themselves a little more inland at the villages of Baddegamma, a few miles northward of Galle, and at Cotta, the ancient capital of the low country:—at both points they devoted themselves to education as a leading feature in their operations; and at the latter especially they founded one of the most important normal seminaries in the island for the training of teachers, and the instruction of native assistants for the ministry.

The singular fact has already been stated of the almost total disappearance amongst the Buddhist population of every trace of Christianity within a very few years from the retirement of the Dutch from Ceylon; and so strong was the re-action, that on the arrival of the English missionaries, the natives could not be persuaded to listen to their first addresses, and even after three years of exertion and discouragement, not one Singhalese had admitted his distrust in idolatry.

A Buddhist priest who had been converted by the Baptists, and took the name of Theophilus, was the first to embrace Christianity, and a few years later his example was followed by a second who had been attached to one of the Kandyan temples.[1] These were men of acuteness and comparative intelligence, and the missionaries have recorded it as the result of their subsequent observation and experience, that

[1] From a MS. account of the Baptist Mission in Ceylon, by the Rev. Mr. Dawson and the Rev. J. Davies.

in proportion as the Buddhists exhibit an acquaintance with the doctrines of their own religion, they evince also a spirit of inquiry into the tenets of Christianity—a characteristic which affords higher hopes of their ultimate conversion than can possibly be entertained of their more listless and phlegmatic fellow-countrymen. Amongst them, too, the influence of the press has been found most attractive, and much good has resulted from the circulation of a valuable work by Mr. Gogerly, of the Wesleyan mission, *On the Evidences of Christianity, adapted to the Use of the Buddhists.*[1] This is another encouraging trait in the character of the Singhalese, and its existence is confirmed by the fact of the prodigious circulation of Christian tracts and translations throughout the island, amounting in 1848 to upwards of five million pages, of which 3,657,300 have been printed at the press of the Baptist mission in Kandy, and the rest procurable elsewhere.

Notwithstanding these indications, however, of an inclination to inquire, the progress of conversion through the instrumentality of the Baptists was slow and circumscribed; and after ten years of toil and anxiety, they could boast of but three small village congregations and eight schools with less than three hundred pupils in attendance. Even here, too, the peculiar genius of the Singhalese was a serious obstacle

[1] The title of the work, which is still in the course of publication, is '*Christiana Prag-nyapti.*'

to their progress· Those in the vicinity of the towns do not undervalue education, especially if it include such an amount of English instruction as may qualify them for public employment; but even this they will not receive without some scruples as to the hands by whom it is offered. Caste, though distinctly denounced by their sacred books, and ostensibly disavowed by the Singhalese themselves, still exists in their veneration for rank, whether hereditary or adventitious. Thus every district and every village has its little leader, a pre-eminence accorded to birth rather than property, and by a descending scale certain members of the community in right of relationship or connexion assume an undefined superiority, and are tacitly admitted to the exercise of what is technically called an "influence." In the hamlets so universal is this feeling amongst the natives, so habitual the impulse to classify themselves, and to *look up tosome one* as their superior in the scale of society, that the custom descends through every gradation of life and its occupations, and in some of the villages the missionaries found it necessary to appoint two schoolmasters, even when there was less than occupation for one—"influence," as well as ability to teach, being an essential qualification; and if the individual did not possess the former, it was indispensable to associate with him some other who did.[1] Again, if a village could not furnish a master com-

[1] MS. Account of Baptist Mission.

petent to teach, it was in vain to procure one from a distance; his "influence" did not extend to that locality, and no pupils could be got to attend. Nor was caste itself without the open avowal of its force; the children of a *Vellala* or high caste family being on no account permitted to enter the schoolhouse of a lower caste master. These are obstacles which prevail in all their original force even at the present day; and in the purely Singhalese districts, such as Matura, the prestige of caste is so despotic, that no amount of qualification in all other particulars can overcome the repugnance to intercourse with those who are deficient in the paramount requisite of rank.

Mr. Chater, after a long career of usefulness, died in 1829, and was succeeded by the excellent man to whom allusion has already been made, Mr. Daniel. Even then the amount of success which had been bequeathed to him by his indefatigable predecessor was so small as almost to occasion despondency; and the number of pupils under instruction barely exceeded *four hundred.* Mr. Daniel's first impulse was to attempt the conversion of the Moormen of Colombo, and for this purpose he prepared a Manual of Christianity for their especial instruction:—"But no perceptible good was the result. The more respectable Mahomedans met the offer of the tract with a dignified refusal; the lower classes rejected it with contempt; and to the present day no decided conversions from Islamism have ever been made in Ceylon."[1]

For ten years this good man laboured in preaching the Gospel, and establishing schools and congregations in the villages around Colombo. Female education in particular was found to be of no less importance amongst the Buddhists and Singhalese than amongst the Tamils of Jaffna. The social position of women amongst the Singhalese, although they are not altogether excluded from intercourse, is entitled to no higher approval than a faint expression of its superiority to that assigned them amongst the Hindoos. The female peasantry are utterly destitute of education, and those of the wealthier classes receive only a smattering of instruction in the merest elements of knowledge. Secluded in their own houses, and with no means of observation beyond the narrow circle of the few females which form a Singhalese hamlet, they know comparatively nothing of the universal scepticism around them. They cling tenaciously to the attractive precepts of Buddhism; they are the earnest patronesses of the priesthood; and almost universally they are in possession of rude images of their divinity, which are

[1] MS. Account of Baptist Missions. Harvard, in his narration of the Wesleyan Mission, records the conversion of one Mahomedan, who was converted in the Fort Church of Colombo in 1814, and baptized by the name of Daniel Theophilus. Ch. viii. p. 160.

worshipped with fervour as the penates of the household.

Their early marriages, the mere bargains by which they are contracted, and the extreme facility with which they are dissolved,[1] their low status in the families of their husbands as well as in their own, all tend to confirm their social degradation even in the highest ranks; whilst in the villages and hamlets the females do all the drudgery of the house and of the field, they are the messengers to the bazaar and the drawers of water from the wells, they collect the firewood, cook the food, and wait on the males of the family whilst they eat; and in the intervals of their employment they assist in the labours of the rice-grounds, plunge through the mud of the irrigated fields, weed the paddy as it rises above the water, and assist to sever and carry home the collected crop during harvest. The indefatigable Baptist missionary saw the value of enlightenment amongst a class so unequally circumstanced, and within three years after his landing in the place, Mr. Daniel had succeeded in establishing female schools in several of the villages around Colombo, and one of higher pretensions near the Fort, which being designed to in-

[1] A pithy, but correct, picture of the institution of marriage amongst the Buddhists, was given by the late Queen's Advocate, Sir Arthur Buller, in one of the discussions in the Legislative Council, when he said that the marriages of the Singhalese were generally arranged by a "come hither," and dissolved by "a kick."

struct the more affluent natives, was superintended in person by the ladies of his own family.

The remainder of his story is like that of too many of these devoted men, who have done honour to Christianity and their country in the East. In the midst of a career of usefulness, the health of his children declined; a return to England was inevitable; his wife died upon the voyage, and the bereaved old man, as if nerved for still bolder exertion by these disasters, shortly after changed the scene of his labours from the civilization of the capital to the solitudes of the forest. He spent two years in incessant wanderings from village to village, throughout the maritime provinces to the east of Colombo, the toils and discouragement of which he has narrated in a passage already quoted from his correspondence.[1] He returned to Colombo, resumed his educational labours, his attention to preaching and the press, and in 1844 he died full of years and honour; his last moments cheered by the affection of all good men in the island, and his name endeared to the Singhalese by the remembrance of his toils and benevolence.

At the time of his death, so successful had been his exertions, and those of others who had been associated with him in the ministry, that 1000 pupils were under instruction in 44 schools of his mission; but after upwards of thirty years' preaching little more than 200 converts were in the immediate

[1] Page 28.

membership of the church. In the interval that has since elapsed, the same good work has been progressing with an impulse acquired from its own increasing success, the press has been sending forth its perennial streams of instruction, a normal seminary for the training of native ministers has been founded in addition to the numerous schools of the mission, and the preaching of Christianity has been carried into every accessible hamlet. It has penetrated the awful retreats into which the lepers have retired to conceal their mutilations from the shuddering glance of mankind; and it has found an audience and an echo in the repulsive community of the Gahalyas—the hereditary executioners under the Kandyan kings; a whole village of whom have from time immemorial been established on the farther banks of the Mahavillaganga, a few miles distant from Kandy, their presence being too polluted to be permitted within the gravets[1] of the capital.

The successors of Mr. Daniel were Mr. Dawson

[1] This term, which is applied to the space outside the principal Forts in Ceylon, has puzzled some of the military engineers. The Singhalese word, *Cada-wetta*, describes the enclosure or boundary of a temple or city, or a royal chase. It was adopted by the Portuguese, after the erection of these fortresses, to define the limits of the lands they had been permitted by the native princes to appropriate, and the word Garvetta is still used in the patois of the Portuguese burghers. When the Dutch seized the Forts the word passed into *Gravette*, which appears on their records, and from the British in turn took the present term Gravets.

and Mr. Davies, the latter from Horton College, near Bradford.[1] Under their auspices the progress of the mission has been uninterrupted. At present it occupies 130 villages of the Singhalese; employs three European and eleven native missionaries; maintains 35 schools, with an average attendance of 830 pupils, and has enrolled as communicants 451 converts to Christianity. Over these who from time to time have been admitted as members of their communion, they exercise the greatest caution as to baptism and the reception of professions; looking to conduct rather than conformity as the genuine test of conversion, and hence the proportion of their converts who have relapsed into heathenism has been comparatively small, whilst numbers have lived worthy of their profession, and died unshaken in their faith.

The greatest detriment to success has arisen from the example and influence of the merely nominal Christians whose life has been an insult to their profession, and whose acts have deterred others from adopting it. But of these who have received their earliest instruction at their hands, and been taught

[1] Since this passage was written this excellent and amiable man has breathed his last—a victim to the fearful epidemic scourge of Ceylon, dysentery. It was my privilege to know him intimately; a more enlightened Christian I never met, and a more benevolent spirit never winged its way from a scene of earthly usefulness to an eternal reward.

by them the principles and the precepts of Christianity, there are many Singhalese now filling places of honour and emolument in the public service, and engaged in private professions, who, though they have not openly made any avowal of Christianity, have been instrumental in disseminating amongst their countrymen that respect and veneration for its precepts which they have been taught to imbibe not less by the lives than by the lessons of the Baptist missionaries.

Next in order of time to the Baptists the Wesleyan missionaries engaged in similar works amongst the Singhalese Buddhists. On their arrival in 1814 they were welcomed by the clergy of the Church of England who had preceded them in the capacity of chaplains; and the Government, hopeful through their instrumentality to counteract the universal apostacy of the natives, assigned them salaries as teachers, and sanctioned their dispersion throughout the island, for the purpose of opening schools at the principal stations in the northern and western provinces. In pursuance of this arrangement, they established themselves amongst the Tamil population of Jaffna, Trincomalie, and Batticaloa; and so early as 1819 they had opened schools in the principal villages along the western coast, from Negombo to Galle. For twenty years the Wesleyan missionaries carried on the work of general education in the maritime provinces, which was afterwards taken up by the

Government in 1834. They did not aspire to the communication of the higher branches of learning, which had already been provided for in the seminary of Colombo (an institution maintained by the Government for the education of the sons of the chiefs and higher order of the natives); but in the principal villages to which they extended their operations the children of the peasantry were instructed by the Wesleyans in the principles of Christianity and the essentials of elementary knowledge.

The usual objection was at first urged to females learning to read;[1] but this was soon overcome; and at a very early period the attention of the missionaries was directed strongly to an object which has since been kept steadily in view, the education of the Singhalese through the medium of their own vernacular tongue.

Until taken up by the Wesleyans, this important department had been exclusively in the hands of the priesthood, who occupied themselves in every pansela and temple, in teaching to write upon olas, and

[1] In speaking of the influence of females the Missionaries observe, "If, as is frequently the case at the commencement of a new work, the congregation consists only of school-children and men, then we feel that as yet little good has been achieved; *but so soon as the females feel interested and attend*, we have good hopes: and when an equal or even a larger proportion of the congregation consists of them, we begin to regard our cause as likely to be eventually successful."—MS. Account of the Wesleyan Mission.

read from the legendary books of the Buddhists. In their hands education was of the lowest description; and the priests themselves were but a stage in advance of their pupils. Science forms no feature in their own education; history is confined to the events connected with religion and its movements; medicine is culled from the imperfect notices of their ancient Sanskrit authorities; and astronomy, degraded into the mere dreams of astrology, is affected to be studied by the priests, who, by a singular anomaly, share its cultivation with the *tom-tom beaters* or *berrawayos*, one of the lowest and least respected castes in Ceylon.

Vernacular education was begun by the Wesleyans in 1817, in the hope of superseding the Buddhist priesthood in this department; and so successful was the effort, that before the close of the year upwards of 1000 scholars were in attendance; twelve months after the number increased to 4000; and during thirty years that the system has been in operation, upwards of 21,000 pupils, females as well as males, have from time to time been instructed in the numerous schools of the mission.[1] No religious test is required for admission; and no compulsion is exerted to enforce participation in the Christian services of the schools. The objections of parents are at once respected, if advanced; but the instances have been rare

[1] MS. Account of the Wesleyan Mission in Ceylon, by the Rev. D. J. Gogerly, Colombo.

in which any scruples have ever been urged, either by the priesthood or the people, to any portion of the system.

But laborious and extended as have been these efforts of the Wesleyans, the tenor of their observation and experience has produced a conviction, that however efficient education may have proved amongst the Buddhists as a pioneer and precursor for the introduction of Christianity, its value is but secondary as compared with preaching to adults, and awaking the native mind through the instrumentality of the pulpit and the printing-press.[1] Under this conviction the Methodists have been at all times the closest investigators of Buddhism, the most profound students of its sacred books in the original, and the most accomplished scholars both in the classical and vernacular languages of Ceylon.

The information thus acquired has been sedulously employed by them in the preparation of works in Singhalese, demonstrative of the errors of the Buddhist religion, and illustrative of the evidences and institutes of Christianity. To the value of these publications and the influence exercised by their promulgation throughout Ceylon, the missionaries of other churches who labour in the same field with the Methodists have borne their cordial and concurrent attestation.

[1] MS. Account of the Wesleyan Mission in Ceylon, by the Rev. D. J. Gogerly, Colombo.

But the most important of all missionary labour amongst the natives, that by which the knowledge of Christianity is most successfully implanted, and its practice is most effectually encouraged, is the *pastoral visitation by the native clerical assistants.* The individual selected for this duty spends his days amongst the villagers; he is their adviser on all occasions, their companion in all pursuits; he becomes their umpire in differences, their friend in every emergency; he gains their confidence by his superior knowledge, and he retains their affections by the discharge of all kindly and gentle offices. I have conversed with men of this class, whom I have sometimes encountered in my journeys, and from no sources have I been able to glean the same accurate knowledge of the people and their customs, their social habits and their wants. Nor is there any agency, however energetic, to which we can look with equal confidence, not only for the extension of Christianity throughout the island, but for the inculcation of those principles and an example of those morals and rules of conduct which win respect for religion even amongst those who are themselves slow to admit its influence and truth.

As to the general success of their labours, the Wesleyan clergy speak with the same modesty and caution which so strongly distinguishes the records of the modern missions from the deceptive and self-delusive statements of the Portuguese and the Dutch.

The total number of native Christians admitted to actual membership with their *church* is something over 1000; but they draw a strong line of distinction between these and the mere members of their *congregations*, who are infinitely more extended. From the latter no other demonstration is required than an outward avowal of Christianity, and a respectful attendance on its worship; but from those received into actual communion there must be such a practical demonstration of its power as leads not only to a renunciation of heathenism, but to a life and conduct such as becomes adherents of the truth.

As regards the ostensible number of their converts, although a proportion of impostors must be expected, there is yet something in the circumstances of the Methodists and Baptists, as a church, that reduces the probability of such practices to the lowest possible amount. They can hold out no pecuniary inducements as a lure to conformity; they have no appointments in their gift which might operate as incentives to deceit; and so far as rank or respectability might operate as motives to profession, these could only be anticipated in relation to the other churches whose ostensible connexion with the Government is usually associated in the minds of the natives with patronage and power.[1]

[1] It may be taken as demonstrative evidence of a certain amount of sincerity in avowed converts, when they attest it by their willingness *to contribute from their pecuniary resources* to

Opposite p. 298.

THE CHURCH OF ENGLAND MISSION began its labours in Ceylon in 1818, and from that time to the present upwards of twenty ordained clergymen have devoted their labours, and some of them their lives, to its promotion. Its success amongst the Singhalese and Buddhists of the south has not been less remarkable than amongst the Tamils of Jaffna, though qualified by the difficulties which are peculiar to the national religion and social habits of the people.[1]

At the same time that the first Church missionaries

the support of the form of Christianity which they have embraced —and this is extensively the case with the congregations of the Baptists and Wesleyans. They lend their assistance readily to the construction of places of worship and sheds for preaching in the villages, which are erected by their labour or their contributions either in money or in gifts of timber and materials, and they unite in paying the expenses of servants and other charges attendant on these simple forms of worship.

Trifling as may be the aggregate amount of these contributions, the spirit and intention with which they are offered are all important as identifying the natives with Christianity as a national and local institution, and thus giving them a personal interest in what they are sometimes disposed to undervalue when performed for them gratuitously, or pressed on them only by foreigners and strangers. The Roman Catholic converts are by far the most willing to contribute from their own means to the support of their clergy and churches, and their donations for these purposes are on a scale of extreme liberality.

[1] A detailed account of the first establishment of the Church of England Mission in Ceylon will be found in *Recollections of Ceylon*, &c., by the Rev. JAMES SELKIRK; himself one of the zealous ministers by whom the first mission was reinforced in 1826. London, 1844: p. 195.

formed their settlement amongst the Hindoos of the northern province, two equally energetic men, Mr. Mayor and Mr. Lambrick (the latter the translator of the Cotta version of the Scriptures in Singhalese), established themselves respectively among the Buddhists of Point de Galle and Colombo, whence the latter removed to Kandy in 1818, to commence the work of re-introducing Christianity into that ancient kingdom, which had recently fallen under our dominion, and throughout which its knowledge, and almost its remembrance, had been extinguished since the expulsion of the Portuguese from the island in A.D. 1658.

In no part of Ceylon has the progress of Christian instruction been so slow, or the obtuseness and indifference of the people been so disheartening, as amongst the peasantry of the Kandyan hills: even secular and scientific education, which has been elsewhere welcomed in the lowlands as a qualification for active employment, has failed to present any attraction to these mountaineers; and it is a singular fact that at the present moment, out of a population of 200,000 persons who inhabit the Kandyan highlands, there are but 159 pupils in all the Government schools;[1] and of these only twenty-three are the children of Kandyans, the remainder being Malays, Moors, or Singhalese, or of European descent.

[1] This is of course exclusive of the schools of the several missions.

It was four years after the arrival of the first Church of England missionary in Kandy before there was sufficient encouragement for the building of a school-house, even in the capital of the new province, and that was attended not by the children of natives, but by strangers and settlers, attracted by prospects of trade. The first objects of ministerial care were the Caffre soldiers attached to the Ceylon Rifle Corps, and the Singhalese prisoners who were confined in the Kandy gaol; and it was rarely, and with difficulty, that any Kandyan listener could be induced to attend their preaching.

Ten years had elapsed before any encouraging symptoms were manifested; and even then, although some few schools had been opened in the villages around Kandy, the number of pupils was but small, and the slightest cause was sufficient to interrupt their attendance. In these lofty mountain-ranges the fall of the tropical rains is a phenomenon almost unimagined by an European, as regards their frequency and volume: the exhalations from the Arabian Sea and the broad Gulf of Bengal, attracted by the elevated peaks of Ceylon, descend in sudden bursts, which swell every streamlet to a torrent, and spread wide inundations over the valleys. During these rains, or even in apprehension of a sudden shower, the Kandyan peasantry have the extremest aversion to exposure; hence their children at all such times are prohibited leaving the houses, and the schools in the villages are in consequence deserted.

At other seasons the collection of the rice crop and the various occupations in the field afford sufficient excuses for non-attendance; and these accidents, when assisted by the open hostility of the Buddhist priesthood, presented incessant discouragements to the first efforts of the Church of England Mission.

From causes more profound, the progress of conversion was, if possible, still more slow and discouraging. The Kandyan kings had been at all times the most energetic defenders of the Buddhist faith; and their jealous policy had so effectually excluded European intercourse, that the confidence of the natives had been in no degree shaken in their ancestral superstitions. The boundaries of the Kandyan territory were defended by dense forests, which those who dwelled within were compelled to keep impenetrable by the annual plantation of a particular species of palm,[1] which is densely covered with thorns; whilst every opening was carefully thickened by training those wonderful climbing plants which abound in the Ceylon forests, covered with knobs, from the points of which protrudes a spike as strong and sharp as the beak of a hawk.[2]

These and numerous other shrubs similarly pro-

[1] Caryota horrida. [2] Todalia aculeata.

vided by nature with weapons of defence[1] formed the natural fortifications of the Kandyan border, and at every pass from the low country to the mountains watches were stationed beside gates of thorns, which swang upon a pivot, and were only raised to allow the passage of the king's people.[2] From the low country

[1] Phoberos Pusilla, the Acacia latronum, Acacia tomentosa, &c.

[2] KNOX, the most authentic historian and narrator of the ancient kingdom of Kandy, has given a quaint account of these "thorn-gates" and defences; he was himself a captive within them for nineteen years; and after making his escape and returning to England, he published his '*Historical Relation of the Island of Ceylon*,' in the year 1681. In his chapter on "the King's Strength and Wars," he says:—"It remains now that I speak a little of the king's *military affairs*. His power consists in the *natural* strength of his country, in his watches, and in the *craft* more than the *courage* of his soldiers. He hath no artificial *forts* or *castles*, but nature hath supplied the want of them. For his whole country of *Cande Uda* standing upon such high hills, and those so difficult to pass, is all an impregnable fort; and so is, more especially, *Digligy-neur*, his present palace. These places have already been described at large, and therefore I omit speaking any further of them here. There are constant watches set in convenient places in all parts of the country, and *thorn-gates*—but in time of danger, besides the ordinary watches, in all towns, and in all places, and in every cross-road, exceeding thick, that 'tis not possible for any to pass unobserved. These *thorn-gates*, which I here mention, and have done before, are made of a certain *thorn-bush*, or *thorn-tree*, each stick or branch whereof thrusts out on all sides round about, sharp prickles, like iron nails, of three or four inches long; one of these very thorns I have lately seen in the *Repository of Gresham College*. These sticks or branches being as big as a good cane, are platted one very close to another, and so being fastened or tied to three

all the paths towards their passes led by circuitous windings, and beneath heights which commanded them; and even so lately as the year 1815, the only road from Colombo to Kandy made a detour of many miles towards the south, and lay across rivers abounding in alligators, and which were only to be passed on the single trunks of trees. Within these gloomy confines Europeans were seldom permitted to enter; and down to the year 1818 the British Government discouraged the attempt of Christian ministers to penetrate the interior from their consciousness of the want of power to assure them adequate protection.

Thus shielded from interference, the priesthood of Buddhism exerted an undisputed influence over the minds of the Kandyans; and the latter, withdrawn from any contact with other religious teachers, preserved a rigid conformity to all the teaching and observances of their own national faith. The Kandyans to the present hour are exclusively Buddhist in

or four upright spars, are made in the fashion of a door. This is hung upon a door-case some ten or twelve feet high (so that they may and do ride through upon elephants), made of three pieces of timber, like a gallows, after this manner II; the *thorn-door* hanging upon the transverse piece like a shop window, and so they lift it up or clap it down, as there is occasion, and tie it with a rope to a crossbar. But especially in all roads and passages from the city where the king now inhabits are very strict watches set, which will suffer none to pass not having a *passport*, which is the print of a seal in clay."—KNOX, *Relation*, &c., part 2, c. vi. p. 54.

belief; and amongst them there exists little of that laxity of profession which enables the low-country Singhalese to avow themselves the disciples of two creeds, and to rejoice in the anomalous title of "Christian Buddhists." Ignorant and uninstructed themselves, the Kandyan peasantry, on the arrival of the Christian missionaries, were apparently insensible of any advantages to their children derivable from education; and as Christianity found no access to their villages, it became impracticable to establish schools with adequate hopes of success, as no Christian teachers could be found to officiate; and no stranger, however eligible, could have compassed the attendance of a single Kandyan class.[1] Besides this, the population of each hamlet is too small to support an establishment of its own, and the villages themselves too remotely scattered to admit of the children for a group being assembled at one central point.

In 1823, the number of schools was but five, and the number of pupils 127; but so persevering were the missionaries, and so progressive their success, that in 1839 the number of schools had been increased

[1] "In 1830 the number of persons in Kandy who attended public worship, Portuguese and Singhalese, was less than 200. In March 1831, the Bishop of Calcutta visited the station and confirmed 36 persons belonging to the congregation. After the examination of some of the schools in his presence, the Bishop said '*We had enough to encourage, but nothing to elate us.*'"— Selkirk, pp. 205-6.

to thirteen, and the number of scholars to something close on *four hundred.*[1]

Under such difficulties the attempt to introduce that most important branch of all, the *education of females*, must have appeared all but hopeless. Amidst all these obstructions and discouragements, the education of boys was never utterly neglected by the Kandyans, who sent their sons to the temples to be instructed by the Buddhist priests; but even this imperfect attempt at cultivation was unavoidably withheld from the girls, who were inadmissible to such tuition, and unable to find any female teachers to supply its place. In Kandy, the capital town of the province, it was upwards of ten years from the first commencement of the mission before the Church of England missionaries could venture to open a school for the instruction of females; and one of them has recorded the fact, "That learning was at so low an ebb amongst the females, and so uncommon, that when one little girl went to a village sixteen miles from Kandy, the females of the place were so astonished to hear her read that at first they came in crowds to listen to her."[2]

The attempt was, however, made, and not without success. A school for girls was established in 1830, and in 1838 it was attended by between twenty and thirty pupils; but of these very few were Kandyans,

[1] Selkirk, p. 210. [2] Ibid., p. 212.

the rest being of different races, and the majority of European descent. It continues to the present time, and with steady and unceasing usefulness, Mr. Oakley, the present missionary, and his lady, having devoted to it an unremitting attention for the last fifteen years.

With an intimate knowledge of the native language the Church Missionaries and their catechists have perambulated the country and explained the doctrine of Christianity to the Kandyans in their secluded villages. By the captivation of its morals, actively exhibited in the blameless lives and examples of its ministers, a mutual confidence amounting to personal friendship has grown up between the peasantry and their benevolent teachers; yet such is the ascendancy of the priesthood, sustained by the influence and authority of their native chiefs, that although belief in their own religion has been shaken, a few only have come forward to avow their conviction of the truth of Christianity.

It is likewise a curious feature in the case that the most numerous and apparently the most ingenuous inquirers into the doctrine of Christianity have been the priesthood themselves. Mr. Oakley has been in the habit of visiting their temples, and to assemblies of fifty of their priests at a time he has had opportunities of expounding the tenets and divine authority of the Gospel. They have come in numbers to his residence to ask for still further information, but the result has tended to show that their inquiries were directed rather by theological curiosity than by alarm for their own religion, or any serious doubts as to its authenticity.

The labour of instruction, however, advances and expands; at the present moment the native teachers who instruct the villagers are numerous; schools are scattered in various directions, where the people have evinced a disposition to encourage them; and although the proportion of native Kandyans is still small in their attendance, the stream of knowledge has commenced to flow, and it is steadily finding its way in all directions.

European settlers have, during the last ten or twelve years, established themselves extensively throughout the Kandyan hills, and converted into wide plantations of coffee the ancient forests which had been heretofore the haunts of the wild elephant and the elk. Civilization has thus been carried to the border of every Kandyan village, and simultaneously with this, education has sprung up into unexpected importance, owing to the demand which has suddenly been created for intelligent natives as the assistants and servants of the planters.

Such a social revolution, although productive in many particulars of irritation to the Kandyan peasants from this intrusion on their privacy and the consequent disruption of their habits, has been naturally accompanied by more than compensating advantages.

It has presented at once a pathway and protection for missionary enterprise; and, even more rapidly than enlightenment has made its way amongst the low-country Singhalese, I anticipate its progress amongst the mountaineers of Kandy, endowed as they are by nature with greater energy both of intellect and frame.

Of the establishments of the Church of England Mission amongst the *low-country Singhalese*, the first in order of time, though not of magnitude and importance, was that of Baddegamma, a village in the southern province, about ten miles north of Point de Galle. Notwithstanding the presence of Europeans for upwards of three hundred years, this portion of the island is remarkable to the present day for the tenacity with which its inhabitants have adhered to their own superstitions. The district of Matura, to the Eastward of Galle, is still the stronghold of Buddhism,[1] and in that to the north the practice of demon worship and devil dancing prevails to an extraordinary degree, and has been a source of continued embarrassment to the missions of every Christian denomination, Portuguese and Dutch as well as British.

In this unpromising district the Church of England Mission erected the first Episcopal Church that had ever been built in Ceylon for the exclusive use of the Singhalese. It was consecrated in 1824

[1] See ante, c. ii. p. 47.

by Bishop Heber; and Baddegamma, the village in which it is situated, has been for upwards of thirty years the scene of the unintermitted toils of its ministers.

In addition to their own schools they undertook the superintendence of those provided by the Government; and thus with increased power of usefulness, derived from their more extended access to the natives, they have given an added impulse to the exertions of others, whilst their own operations have been conducted with marked vigour and success.

In 1822 they had *one hundred and sixty* pupils under training, of whom upwards of one-third were females, and these within the seven years which followed were increased to *two hundred and seventy-five.* Of these a proportion were maintained as boarders in the institution, and so successful was their course of education, that some of the most remarkable students who have distinguished themselves at the Collegiate Seminary of Cotta have been scholars from the elementary school of Baddegamma.[1] Bishop Turner, who visited the settlement in 1831, was irresistibly struck by that astonishing quickness which characterizes the Singhalese in early youth, but which, to a great degree, disappears as they approach manhood; and the missionary who conducted him over the establishment has recorded his pithy remark that the pupils were "as sharp as

[1] Selkirk's Recollections, &c., p. 243-4.

needles," and gave singular grounds of hope for the rising generation of the province.

The social changes which followed, as the result of these exertions, were as remarkable in this locality as in other portions of the island. A system of nominal education had existed under the care of the Government, but previous to the arrival of the Missionaries it had been superficial and unsound—the salaried masters neglected for other duties the obligation to teach; and the instruction and training of females was so utterly unknown that "before the missionaries came among them a needle had never been seen in the district."[1] Within fourteen years from their arrival elementary education had been extended throughout the surrounding villages; printed books were read by the pupils as freely as the native characters upon olahs; five hundred children were in daily attendance at the schools; many thousands had been made acquainted with the essential principles of Christianity; and so expert had the pupils in the female seminary become, that the sale of their needlework contributed in part to defray the ordinary expenditure of the establishment.[2]

The Moodliar, or native headman of the district, in speaking of this remarkable improvement, observed in 1840, that "although the people were

[1] Report of Mr. Tremnell. See Selkirk's Recollections, &c., page 245.

[2] Ibid., p. 246.

still ignorant and careless, and quite satisfied with declaring that one religion (Christianity) was as good as another (Buddhism), still a striking change for the better had taken place among them; those who have been educated, though they do not *turn out religious*, yet build better houses, know better manners, are more industrious, and more respected by the people around than those who are not—while with respect to the girls they almost all of them get better husbands, and are much more kindly treated than before."[1]

Still, notwithstanding all these preliminaries to conversion, the number of actual converts were few; inquiry was nevertheless active, and the Buddhist priesthood, like those of the Kandyan Wihares, continued to resort to the missionaries and invited their attendance at the temples, to furnish answers to their interrogatories as to the proofs and principles of Christianity; but the avowals of innate conviction were rare, and the proportion of communicants small compared with the large numbers who ordinarily assembled to listen to the preaching of the missionaries.

Of the Church missionary establishments in Ceylon the most important is that of Cotta, a populous district within a few miles of Colombo, once the residence of a line of princes, who held the sovereignty of this portion of the low country prior to the arrival

[1] See Selkirk's Recollections, &c., page 268.

of the Portuguese in the sixteenth century. Amidst the thick jungle in the vicinity there are still to be traced the ruins of their palaces and buildings, whilst the dense population once attracted to the seat of government still exhibits its numbers in the many villages and hamlets which are congregated about the spot. The priesthood, encouraged by the protection of the kings of Cotta, formed several establishments in the neighbourhood of their court. Many of these remain to the present day, the priests are still numerous, and Buddhism in that locality exhibits more activity and earnestness than is generally met with in the Western section of the island. The population of the surrounding plain are as usual "baptized Buddhists," professing what they designate the *sopremada agama* or "Government religion."[1]

[1] Mr. Lambrick, the first Church of England missionary at Cotta, recounts that he one day asked a native of Cotta of what religion he was; and the answer was, "Buddha's." "So then you are not a Christian?" "Oh, yes, to be sure I am; I am a Christian, and of the *reformed Dutch religion too!*"—SELKIRK, Recollections, &c., p. 312.

The embarrassing anomaly of administering *baptism* to the children of heathens, and the still more embarrassing difficulty of withholding, was pressed on the attention of Bishop Heber by the clergy of Cotta in the year 1825. They applied to him for authoritative advice upon the subject, and in reply to their inquiries he addressed to them a letter expressive of his views on that point as follows:—

"To your questions respecting baptism, I reply—

"1st. We are not, as I conceive, allowed to baptize the in-

More or less influenced by these circumstances, and decided by the prospects of usefulness which

fant child of heathen parents when there is reason to fear that such child will be brought up in heathenism.

"2nd. We may not even baptize the infant child of heathen parents on the promise of such parents to procure for it a Christian education, unless security of some kind is actually given for its adoption, and removal from its parents' corrupt example, by its sponsor, or some other Christian.

"3rd. We may, I apprehend, baptize the children of a Christian father by a heathen mother, though they are living together *unmarried*, provided the father declares his intention of giving his child a Christian education, and there are sufficient sponsors to add their promises to that of the parent. My reason for this decision is, that, as no professed Christian, however wicked his life, is beyond the outward means of grace, and the Lord may, for all we know, have still merciful purposes concerning him, so we cannot, for the father's sin, exclude the child from that promise which is made to the children and the children's children of believers. But where the mother is Christian, and not the father, it is doubtful whether she may have sufficient property in, or authority over her child, to insure it a Christian bringing up. Nor is it a point on which the promise of a heathen father can be received as sufficient; its actual adoption, therefore, by some Christian friend or sponsor, must in this last case be stipulated for.

"4th. The same principle appears to apply to cases when one only of a *married* couple is a professing Christian: though here some latitude of discretion may be allowed, in case of danger of death, of extreme maternal solicitude, of known good character on the believing mother's side, and the known probability that may exist that her wishes, and the endeavours of the sponsors, will not be frustrated in her infant's education.

"5th. The case of nominal Christians notoriously addicted to heathen practices must depend, in part, on the nature and extent of the evil; and still more on the character and sufficiency of

they presented, Cotta was selected as the seat of missionary operations in 1823. The scenery is peculiarly

the sponsors. Mere idolatrous or superstitious habits in the parents, if not attended with open apostacy, cannot exclude the infant when properly vouched for from another quarter. The parent, however blinded and sinful, has not lost the external privileges of Christianity, and the infant cannot be deprived of a privilege which the parent has not forfeited.

"6th. The same rule will apply yet more strongly to Christians of whom we know no further harm than their ignorance and neglect of public worship.

"7th. It will have been already seen, that we have no right to refuse baptism to children actually adopted by Christians, provided those or other Christians become their securities.

"8th. With regard to the case of children thus adopted, when past the age of six years, and on the marks of conversion which may then be required in them, it appears that at this age a child who has not, from its earliest infancy, enjoyed a Christian education, can seldom know much of Christianity. Such may be admitted as infants, with proper sponsors, and it may very often be desirable thus to admit them. It is not easy to fix an age at which infancy ceases, which must depend on intellect, opportunity, and many other considerations. 'In subjects capace,' conversion is doubtless required; and where capacity may be soon expected, it is generally desirable to wait. But in cases of sickness, or where any good or charitable end is answered by the immediate baptism of such children, and where, as before, sufficient securities are present, it appears that we are not warranted in denying them God's ordinance.

"9th. The Church of Rome, though grievously corrupted, is nevertheless a part of the visible Church of Christ; we may not therefore repel the children of such parents from baptism, if they are vouched for by their sponsors in the words of our service; which it may be noticed are wisely so framed as to contain nothing but those points on which all Christians are agreed. The direction at the end to teach our Church Catechism is a

attractive: the present village is situated on the verge of the vast gardens of cinnamon by which Colombo is surrounded; and a branch of the river which flows through the plain here expands into a placid lake, surrounded by natural forests, and interspersed with plantations of spices and groves of the cocoa-nut palm.

counsel from us to the sponsors, no engagement entered into by them. It follows that we are not to refuse baptism to the children of Roman Catholic parents, with sufficient Protestant sponsors; I even doubt whether we are at liberty even with sponsors of their parents' sect.

"But in all these questions I cannot forbear observing, that we may remark the wisdom of that primitive institution (which our Church has wisely retained) of godfathers and godmothers, as affording a way of receiving into the flock of Christ those children for whose education their own parents cannot satisfactorily answer. An ignorant or immoral father may be himself, for the present, irreclaimable; but we may always insist that the sureties whom he adduces should be competently informed, and of a life not openly immoral. And though the decay of discipline in our own country has grievously impaired the value of such sponsors, yet a missionary among the heathen both may and ought in this respect to exercise a sound discretion, both examining with mildness, informing with patience, and with firmness and temper deciding on the knowledge, faith, and holiness of those who themselves undertake to be the guides of the blind, and to sow the seeds of knowledge, holiness, and faith, in the hearts of the young candidates for salvation.

"That God, my reverend brethren, may increase and strengthen you in these and all other gifts of his Spirit through his Son, and that both here and hereafter his blessings may largely follow your labours, is the prayer of

"Your affectionate friend and servant,

"REGINALD CALCUTTA."

Here the mission commenced its labours, by the opening of schools, and the expounding of the Christian religion to the natives throughout their hamlets. So early as 1828 they had 297 children under instruction; and the first successful effort was to establish a school for females, with an attendance of five-and-twenty pupils. The first obstacles to success were as usual presented by the obtuseness and listlessness of the adults, who were equally unmoved by the most appalling denunciations, and unencouraged by the most captivating promises of the Gospel;[1] and as the profession of Christianity was not required as qualification for admission to the village-schools, the attendance of their children was perpetually interrupted by the recurrence of village festivals, and the attraction of the frequent ceremonies at the Buddhist temple and *dewales*.

In 1834, the number of pupils had increased to upwards of 350, of whom one-sixth were girls; and so sensibly did the people themselves begin to discern the value of female instruction, that several schools for girls were opened in villages in the neighbourhood, to which the natives gave a willing encouragement; and in which they were instructed not only in elementary knowledge, but taught for the first time to sew and make lace, with such other training and acquirements as were essential for the conduct of their ordinary domestic duties. So remarkable was the

[1] Selkirk, Recollections, &c., p. 311.

result of these several undertakings that within sixteen years from the commencement of the mission upwards of 900 boys were in daily attendance on the schools, and 400 girls,—a total of 1300 children throughout twenty-nine hamlets, in the immediate vicinity of Cotta. In 1840, the numbers had increased to *seventeen hundred* pupils, and the schools to *twenty-seven*; and at the present time, after the perseverance and toil of the missionaries for twenty-six years, their schools number seventy-one, and their scholars exceed *two thousand*, of whom 500 are females.[1]

In connexion with the mission, and as indispensable to its success, a collegiate institution was founded in 1827, for the higher instruction of native teachers, and the training of assistants destined for the ministry. The students were to be selected from the most promising pupils at all the other stations; and the curriculum of study was designed to include all ordinary branches of a liberal education. The foundation was laid by Sir Edward Barnes; and in 1829 the seminary commenced its operations with an attendance of only ten students.

[1] December, 1844. Schools at Cotta . . 71

Boys in attendance . . .	1855
Girls	535
	2390

—*MS. Notes on the Church of England Mission, by the* REV. A. DOUGLASS GORDON.

From that time to the present the "CHRISTIAN INSTITUTION" of Cotta has maintained a career of usefulness unsurpassed, and exhibited a success the most remarkable. Its pupils have been received from the remotest parts of the island, wherever the missionaries have established themselves. The Tamils of Jaffna, the Singhalese of the low country, and the young Kandyans from the hills, have all been congregated here to collect their stores of truth and enlightenment, and return laden with intelligence to communicate their knowledge to their own countrymen. I have attended the annual examination of the more advanced classes, and my own emotions have been not more those of gratification than of astonishment at the results which it has been my good fortune to witness: the students of this oriental college exhibiting an extent of scientific knowledge and a proficiency of historical and classical attainment rarely surpassed in collegiate institutions of much higher pretensions in Europe.

The clergy who for nearly thirty years have devoted themselves to these objects have contributed from time to time the result of their own studies and investigations into the languages and literature of Ceylon; and some of the most eminent scholars in these departments have been amongst the Church of England missionaries. The press has lent its aid to the school-room; and a printing establishment, second in magnitude only to that of the Americans at Jaffna, has long existed at Cotta, where the natives have been supplied with millions of pages full of truth and instruction.

Hence there issued the translation of the Scriptures known as the "*Cotta version*," to which allusion has been already made; the idiom of which has so seriously wounded the feelings of the higher caste natives, by the exclusion of the honorific terms by which the structure of their language enables them to adapt its expression to every conceivable gradation of rank.[1]

The system of the Church of England mission amongst the Singhalese, as amongst the Tamils, includes the maintenance of both English and vernacular schools, as well as boarding establishments in which the education is of a much higher range, and is designed to qualify pupils for admission to the collegiate foundation at Cotta. So marked has become the change in the sentiments of the natives as to the value of instruction, that in lieu of that indifference, which at first rendered it difficult to procure even ordinary attendance, the parents are now eager to pay a fee for their children; and the extent to which such institutions might be multiplied is only limited by the means which have been placed at the disposal of the mission.

Active hostility can scarcely be said to be mani-

[1] See ante, p. 265.

fested either by the Buddhists or their priesthood; and although more energetic exertions have been recently made by the latter, in the erection of banamaduas, the holding of pinkamas, and ceremonies, their efforts have been directed less to the discouragement of the Christian religion than to the extension of their own. Gross immoralities are perceptibly declining amongst the villagers, not only in the vicinity of Cotta, but within the range of missionary influence generally; and it has been remarked by one and all, that whilst intoxication and other excesses have come to be regarded with a measure of scorn, the prevalence of theft has diminished, and falsehood has received a check, from a sense of shame, the result of the newly-developed feeling of contempt for those betrayed into it.[1]

Marriage as a permanent union was previously unknown amongst the Singhalese; and polyandry, which is now confined to the remoter districts and

[1] The effects of this moral improvement have been strikingly illustrated by a recent analysis of the education and moral bearing of the prisoners confined in the criminal gaol at Colombo. Of these the number who could read was 16, who could read and write 63, and who could do neither 221. Of 300 prisoners, 30 were Protestant Christians, 40 Roman Catholics, 33 Mahomedans, 39 Hindoos, and 158 Buddhists.

Of 200 prisoners admitted to the gaol *who could all both read and write*, 31 had been educated in Government schools, 26 in the schools of the missionaries, 5 in the schools of other persons, and 138 by private native schoolmasters, or by priests in the Buddhist temples.

the Kandyan kingdom, was within a comparatively recent period universal in the maritime provinces. Though still of a mercenary and degraded character, marriage has now come to be regarded as a lasting and solemn obligation; divorced wives and deserted children have become rare; and the endearments of domestic life have attained a respect and appreciation unknown to the ancestors of the present generation.

The industrial and material improvement of the Singhalese in the vicinity of Christian communities is undoubted; but as this is most apparent in the vicinity of the European settlements, its acceleration must be conjointly ascribed to other influences besides those of Christianity—although it cannot be concealed that the instrumentality of the latter has been in too many instances neutralized and perverted by the laxity of morals and the pernicious example of unscrupulous Europeans.

In regard to the personal comforts and physical advancement of the Singhalese people, British capital and enterprise have done much; and from the towns and plantations that influence has extended to the secluded hamlets of the interior: new careers of occupation have been opened up, and new energies called into exertion; every missionary from north to south of the island has had occasion to mark the change produced by such causes; but there are other changes incident to the same classes which are directly ascribable to missionary agency. The missionaries have taught the Singhalese industry, to avail themselves of these opportunities; frugality in the husbandry of their gains, and rational enjoyment in lieu of frivolous objects to which to devote their expenditure. One singular peculiarity of the Singhalese is the universality of their proneness to run into debt; and it is no exaggeration to say that half their time is devoted to borrowing money in one quarter, in order to satisfy the claims of another. The two great occasions in which they plunge into this vice are through marriages and feasts, on which sums so disproportionate are lavished, that the entertainer runs the risk for the remainder of his life of one continuous struggle with creditors and notaries, with extravagant rates of interest rapidly accumulating, embarrassment, lawyers, lawsuits, and ruin. This inveterate habit the missionaries have done much to discourage, by enforcing economy upon all within their influence, and by discountenancing in every instance unreflecting extravagance and disproportionate expenditure. Christianity has thus proved itself not less conducive to the political improvement than to the spiritual elevation of the people; it has taught them that habits of thought and observation are the best allies of industry, has supplied them with new motives and incentives to labour, and given value and security to the produce of their toil. It has lowered the pride of pretension, and raised the self-respect of the degraded. Before its influence the aversion to change has given way to the spirit of improvement; and there is no missionary station in the interior in the neighbourhood of which we may not discern the awakened energy of the people, the embellishment of their dwellings, the opening of village roads, the enlargement of their gardens, and the general extension of cultivation.[1]

The results of these efforts to diffuse Christianity throughout Ceylon are less unsatisfactory than they may outwardly seem to a casual observer who regards only their ostensible effect; for however limited may be the first definite gains in the numerical amount of acknowledged converts, the process has commenced by which these will be hereafter augmented; and living principles have been successfully implanted as much more precious than the mere visible results, as the tree exceeds in value the first fruits of its earliest growth.

Nor have these fruits themselves been inconsiderable when we bear in mind the antiquity and strength of the superstitions which have preoccupied the soil, the failures of the first efforts of Christianity to supplant them, the peculiar characteristics of the Singhalese people, and the limited means as well as the circum-

[1] As indicative of the shrewdness as well as the social habits of the people, a specimen of the *proverbs* in common use amongst the Singhalese is inserted at Note D, end of this chapter.

scribed resources of the various Christian missions which have been engaged in the work.

Not the least important gain has been the access of *experience*, which they themselves have acquired, sufficient not merely to protect them from the delusions by which their predecessors were misled, but to guide them by their more intimate appreciation of the difficulties to be overcome and of the choice of those instruments, and the better adjustment of the process by which success is to be compassed.

Above all, the influence of ancient delusions has been undermined, the foundation of national errors has been shattered, and all experience has demonstrated the fact, that although exploded opinions may be often revived, exploded superstitions never acquire a second vitality; they become shaded by the ignominy of detected imposture; and though idolatry is too often replaced by infidelity, heathenism itself, once exposed and discredited, can never regain its ascendancy.

The aggregate number of converts in Ceylon is no criterion as to the progress of Christianity; not only because these are not its sole indications, but because the tests on admission and the discipline afterwards differ not only in different churches, but even amongst the different establishments of the same Christian mission. In addition to which the missionaries themselves are fully aware of the fact, that amongst their nominal adherents there are numbers whose life and inward feelings are at variance with their seeming profession, and who, though they may not fall under the designation of impostors, are far from being entitled to the denomination of Christians.

But with reference to these must be borne in mind the influences of the society from which they have been rescued, and the moral stagnation and impurities of the atmosphere which they have been accustomed to breathe. Christian life and its characteristics are of infinitely slower growth than belief and Christian profession. Evil habits, alike national and hereditary, and superstitions irreconcilable with the simplicity of truth, may subsist long after the manifestation of deep and genuine conversion. The traces are not yet eradicated in England of the paganism which preceded Christianity; and even the pure and exalted mind of Sir Matthew Hale was not proof against the delusion of witchcraft. We have therefore no grounds for alarm, if, in conjunction with the newly-received doctrines of Christianity, the Singhalese converts should exhibit in some instances their long-associated respect for the ancient customs of Buddhism, or still shrink at the remembrance of the terrors of demon worship.

Political changes are usually rapid, and often the offspring of a single cause; but all moral revolutions are of gradual development, and the result of innumerable agencies. Progressive growth is the law and process of Nature in all her grand operations. Philosophy, science, and art, all the moral and intellectual developments of man, are progressive; and under the influence of Christianity itself, the march of civilization, though controlled and directed by its ascendancy, is regulated by those eternal laws of social progress which have been ordained by Omnipotence.

The pace may be slow and unequal, but the tendency is onward, and the result may be eventually rapidly developed; and such, it is my firm conviction, will be the effect of what is now in progress, not in Ceylon alone, but throughout the continent of India. A large proportion of the labour hitherto has been prospective, but its effects are already in incipient operation; and, on all ordinary principles, a power once in motion is calculated to gather velocity and momentum by its own career.

When the time shall have arrived for the mighty masses of India to move with a more simultaneous impulse, it is impossible to calculate the effect; but looking to the magnitude of the operations which have been so long in process, to the vastness of the agencies which have been organized, it is not unreasonable to suppose that the last conquests of Christianity may be achieved with incomparably greater rapidity than has marked its earlier progress and signalized its first success; and that in the instance of India, "the ploughman may overtake the reaper, the treader of grapes him that soweth the seed," and the type of the prophet realized, "that a nation shall be born in a day."

I have lingered over this portion of my task much longer than was my original design; impressed by the permanent interest of the inquiry, and allured by the illustrations which it presents of the influence exercised by their religion over the national character of the natives. Nor can I turn from the subject without recording my deliberate dissent from the startling theories of the Abbé Dubois, as to the immutability of Indian idolatry, and the still bolder conclusion which he derives from the imperfect success hitherto of Christian labours on the continent of Hindostan, that the mission of Christianity has reached its limits in the East, "that the time of conversion has passed away," and "that the oracle of God has been fulfilled as regards the Hindoos."[1] I shrink instinctively from the idea that one hundred millions of human beings throughout our dominions in India are thus consigned to hopeless reprobation; and on looking around me to what is now in progress in Ceylon, I see abundant grounds for resisting that belief. In the history of Brahmanism itself there are successive records of innovation; and in the worship of the Hindoos, as it presents itself at the present day, there are indelible marks of changes which it

[1] Letters on the State of Christianity in India, by the Abbé J. A. Dubois, p. 42.

has already undergone.[1] And narrowing the survey to the limits of Ceylon, whilst it is undeniable that the influence of race prevents the religion of the natives from undergoing any alteration by their association with each other, whilst no Tamil embraces Buddhism, and no Singhalese adopts the religion of Brahma; both have more or less yielded to the truth of Christianity, and afforded proofs in their own person that *their idolatry is not immutable.*[2]

[1] Even in the leading tenet, which prohibits the taking away of life, there is more than grounds for conjecture that the doctrines of the Hindoos have undergone change; and that, at an earlier period, it was customary to make offerings of animals to Brahma. And it is no little remarkable, that in the Epic of the *Ramayana*, which recounts the expedition of Rama for the conquest of Ceylon, mention is more than once made of the sacrifice of the *cow*. In the obsequies of the Father of Rama, a purified animal was slain and flung upon the hill, the cow and her calf were offered, and ghee oil and flesh were scattered on every side.—Book ii. sec. 61. See NOTES of Colonel SYKES, *On the Political State of India before the Mahomedan Invasion*, ASIAT. JOURNAL, vol. xii. p. 269. See also Professor Wilson's Oxford Lecture to the same effect.

Buddhism presents instances of similar changes, and even in the same particular affecting the respect for animal life, its doctrines at the present day are not reconcilable with the records of its sacred books and traditions, in which one of the early Buddhus, Sakya Muni, is stated to have died of indigestion from eating *pork;* and in an earlier stage of existence, his humanity had led him to turn himself into a *roasted hare*, in order to satisfy the hunger of a famishing Brahman.—Vide the Mahawanso and Sutpitako, quoted by Mr. Turnour, Journal Asiat. Soc. Bengal, vol. vii. p. 1003.

[2] For a detailed account of the changes which have taken

To this extent at least the position of the Abbé may be based upon truth, that of all the religions of the East, that of Islam excepted, the genius of Brahmanism is that which presents the most dauntless front to Christianity. But this is a dictum with which it would be unsound to associate the religion of Buddhu in the aspect under which it now exhibits itself in Ceylon. Buddhism has rejected the impure mythology of the Hindoos, and removed from its own path the great barrier of caste, behind which the Brahman scorns the simplicity, whilst he shrinks from the charities, of the Christian faith. *Caste*, especially among the Kandyans, and to a more limited extent amongst the low-country Singhalese, is still more or less an obstacle to the free course of conversion; but in the case of the convert from Buddhism, even under the influence of caste, there is no dread of that fearful vengeance for apostacy which, in the instance of the Hindoo, divests him at one fell swoop of kindred and of friends, of possessions and inheritance, and even of a recognized position amongst civilized men.[1] The Buddhist, when he opens the

place in the Brahmanical system, and its aspect in India at the present day, as contrasted with its development in its own sacred books, see Chap. iv. of Mountstuart Elphinstone's Hist. of India, b. ii.

[1] "What chiefly prevents the spread of Christianity in India is the dread of exclusion from caste and its privileges, and the utter hopelessness of their ever finding any respectable circle of society of the adopted religion, which converts or would-be con-

divine records of Christianity, does not recoil with instinctive prejudice like the Hindoo, on discovering that its founder was the son of a carpenter and the associate of fishermen; nor does he shudder as he reads in the annals of the chosen race that the temples of Jehovah were consecrated by the blood of oxen and bulls, and that the patriarch of old dared to kill the sacred calf in order to do honour to the angels who presented themselves at his tent.

Whilst the Hindoo, in the debasement of his sanctified sensuality, despises the spiritual purity of the Gospel, the Buddhist, already familiar with the refinement and dignity of its morals, is not altogether unprepared for the announcement of its divine authenticity. He does not start at the idea of ascending to the same heaven with the pariah and the outcaste, nor have the gentler tendencies of his nature been chilled and proscribed by the inhumanities of a creed which uproots all the social sympathies of the heart, and exalts prejudice and scorn into attributes of religion.

verts now everywhere feel. I have, since I have been in India, had at least a score of Hindoo grass-cutters turn Mussulmans merely because the grooms and other grass-cutters of my establishment happened to be of that religion: they could neither eat, drink, nor smoke with them. Thousands of Hindoos, all over India, become every year Mahomedans from the same motive; and we do not get the same number of converts to Christianity, merely because we cannot afford them the same advantages."—COLONEL SLEEMAN'S *Recollections of India*, vol. ii. p. 164.

What has been done, and what is still in progress in Ceylon, are in themselves demonstrative evidences that the idolatry of India is *not impregnable*, and that so far from the mission of Christianity being exhausted, at no period of our history have its manifestations been so apparent, or the measures taken so successful for ensuring its ultimate triumph.

The human means by which that consummation is to be hastened have already been indicated in the course of the foregoing narrative; *the Scriptural education of the young, the intellectual culture of the adults, and the instrumentality of preaching, and the printing press with all.* The mere elementary teaching of the many, unaccompanied by the profounder instruction of the few, will never succeed in elevating the spiritual character of the people;—the one may assist in weakening the influence of their ancient superstition, but without the aid of the other the task would prove all but hopeless to elevate Christianity in its stead. For the realization of such a system the assistance of *native agents* is indispensable; and for the training of these education must be carried to the point at which the pupil becomes transformed into the teacher. The pastors whom the Apostles inducted to watch over the Churches which they planted amongst the heathen were natives of the country: thus Christianity ceased to be exotic, became an institution of the land, and was cherished and supported as such. None but familiar associates can exhibit to the natives of India in practice the example of that Christian life which the European instructor can only delineate in theory; and none but he can so effectually accommodate his ministrations to the habits of his hearers as to gain upon their confidence, and exert an influence over their opinions and habits of thought. Above all, in the instance of the Buddhists, none but a teacher of their own race, and familiar with their language, can ever aspire to become so thoroughly master of their dialect as to grapple successfully with their metaphysical abstractions, and demonstrate the nothingness of their contemplative idolatry. It could only be after long periods of critical study that an European linguist would find himself qualified to discuss with them the dim distinctions which they are accustomed to draw between the *creation* and *procession* of the universe, the *essence* and the *attributes* of matter, or the *annihilation* and *extinction* of the spirit;—and yet on these and similar subtleties hang the whole law and philosophy of Buddhism.[1] The apostolic reformers of modern times have all achieved the grand triumphs of their tenets amongst those with

[1] Conceive the difference of meaning which will attach to the words of the English Liturgy, "We have done those things which we ought not to have done;" and for which the only equivalent in Singhalese is the atheistical confession of Buddhism, "*To us all sin* HAPPENS."—*MS. Notes of the* REV. A. DOUGLASS GORDON.

whose tongue they were familiar. Europeans and foreign missionaries may effect individual conversions, or pave the way for more extended revolutions of belief; but if the Luthers and the Wickliffes of an Eastern Reformation are ever destined to arise in Ceylon, they will come not from the universities of Europe, but from the educational institutions of Jaffna and the collegiate seminaries of Cotta and Colombo.

NOTES TO CHAPTER VI.

(A.)

THE SACRED BO TREE.

THE drawing prefixed to this chapter represents one of the sacred Bo trees (Ficus religiosa), one of which is to be found within the precincts of every Buddhist temple in Ceylon, and frequently in deserted localities, or near the site of ancient villages. The occurrence of a solitary Bo tree, with its circular buttress of stonework round the stem, indicates the existence, at some former period, of a Buddhist temple in the vicinity. The planting of the Bo tree, a ceremony coeval with and typical of the introduction of Buddhism into Ceylon, is one of the most striking passages in the Mahawanso; and a tree of unusual dimensions, which occupies the centre of a sacred enclosure at Anarajapoora, is still reverenced as the identical one which the sacred books record to have been planted by Mehindu, 307 years before the Christian era. So sedulously is it preserved, that the removal of a single twig is prohibited, and even the fallen leaves, as they are scattered by the wind, are collected with reverence as relics of the holy place. On the altars, at the foot of these sacred trees, the Buddhists place offerings of flowers, and perform their accustomed devotions in honour of the Divine Author.

(B.)

SACRED MOUNTAIN OF MEHINTELAI AND RUINS OF ANARAJAPOORA.

THE view of Mehintelai, which accompanies this chapter, represents one of the most interesting and extraordinary scenes in Ceylon in connexion with Buddhism. Mehintelai, "the Mountain without Fear,"[1] is a precipitous rock about seven or eight miles to the north-east of Anarajapoora, but connected with the ancient city in the time of the kings by one continuous street, along which were conducted the solemn processions of the priests. The ascent to the summit is effected by series of stone steps, about two thousand in number, winding past the ruins of former buildings, temples, dagobas, and shrines; and on the loftiest peak, which commands a view over the forest country beneath to the very verge of the horizon, there exists one of those prodigious structures of brickwork, under which is deposited a sainted relic of Buddhu—a hair which grew on a mole between his eyebrows. With such veneration have the Singhalese been accustomed to regard this sacred mountain, that every crag has some tradition, and every rock has been scarped into sites for religious buildings, amidst the ruins of which are to be traced the fragments of broken statues, and inscriptions in the Nagari character, the most ancient in which the dialect of Pali has been written.

The ruins of Anarajapoora, of one of which a drawing by Mr. Nicholl has been given, form one of the most conspicuous objects in the grand panorama which is beheld from Mehintelai. Their description must occupy a large portion of any work on Ceylon, covering as they do an extent of ground equal to sixteen miles square, once surrounded by a wall sixty-four miles in circumference. The city is to be found on the map of Ptolemy, in its proper site and ancient name, Anurogrammum.

[1] Travels of the Chinese Fa Hian, p. 333.

(C.)

THE GREAT TANKS OF CEYLON.

No monuments of antiquity in the island are calculated to impress the traveller with such a conception of the former power and civilization of Ceylon as the gigantic ruins of the tanks and reservoirs, in which the water during the rains was collected and preserved for the irrigation of their rice lands.

The number of these structures, throughout vast districts now comparatively solitary, is quite incredible, and their individual extent far surpasses any works of the kind with which I am acquainted elsewhere. Some of these enormous reservoirs, constructed across the gorges of valleys in order to throw back the streams that thence issue from the hills, cover an area equal to fifteen miles long by four or five in breadth; and there are hundreds of a minor construction.

These are almost universally in ruins; and some idea of their magnitude and importance may be derived from the following extract from my diary, of a visit made to one of them in the year 1848.

The tank to which I rode was that of Pathavie-colom, in the Wanny, about seventy miles to the north of Trincomalie, and about twenty-five miles distant from the sea.

" After a rest of a few days at Trincomalie, to recruit our foot runners and coolies, we resumed our course towards the north. My design was to keep the line of the sea coast as far as Lake Kokelai, and thence to turn westward into the great central forest of the Wanny, in order to reach the ruins of the tank at Pathavie—the largest as well as most perfect of these gigantic works in Ceylon. * * * *

"The lake of Kokelai is a very remarkable spot. It is about twenty miles in circumference, and believed to have been at one time a rich and fertile plain, on which the cultivation of rice was carried on by means of the enormous reservoir of Pathavie, some twenty miles inland; but by a calamity of frequent occurrence in Ceylon, the sluices of the great tank became decayed, the embankments gave way, and the overcharged channels suddenly inundated the plains below, whence the collected waters burst their way into the sea; which, once admitted to enter, has never since been excluded, but now ebbs and flows with every variation of the tide, the bottom of the lake being never wholly dry, but its deepest spots never much exceeding six or seven feet. In fact it is so shallow at all times that, in the S.W. monsoon, when the rains are light and the waters low, the surf forms a bar of sand across the entrance, and it ceases for a time to communicate with the sea. Were advantage taken of this peculiarity, it might be permanently and effectually excluded; but unfortunately with the change of the monsoon the bar disappears, the pent up waters of the lake again force a passage, and the salt water returns to renew and perpetuate its barrenness.

"We came out of the forest upon the southern extremity of the lake, at the little village of Amara-vayal, and rode eastward along the shore to the opening which admits the waters of the sea. It was a sultry day, and on the exhalation from the salt encrusted over the sand, we witnessed one of the most beautiful instances of the Fata Morgana which I had seen in Ceylon. The water appeared in the distance to cover the direction by which we were to pass; and right before us in the midst of this we saw a fairy island, covered with the most graceful vegetation, and the shadows of its tall trees reflected in the surrounding waves of the imaginary lake. A ride of a quarter of an hour, however, dispelled the beautiful deception; without entirely disappearing, the lines and features became fainter as we approached, till they melted into air, but not without leaving a doubt whether a scene so perfect in all its parts could really be an illusion.

"The Tamil village of Kokelai is close by the junction of the lake with the sea; and in the vast pastures around it, which are enriched by the proximity of the water, numerous herds of cattle were grazing—the finest and most numerous I have seen in the province. At Kokotodowey we came up with the Government Agent of the northern province, Mr. Dyke, whom we found encamped with five tents and a large suite of followers, beside a salt lake close to the village, and with him we resumed the following morning our tour around the lake, completing the circuit at Amara-vayal, whence we had started two days before. In order to do this we had to cross the river by which the lake is formed, after flowing out of the great tank of Pathavie. The dimensions of the latter may be inferred from the fact that the stream that issued from its ruins was between 200 and 300 feet broad, and so deep and impetuous, that it was with the utmost difficulty our horses got over it in safety. The country along the bank of the river is rich, and would be fertile, but it is so neglected that herds of wild buffaloes were rolling in the marshes, and elephants so abundant that the water was still running into the foot marks which they had left a moment before in the sand, where they had crossed a branch of the river on our approach.

"As the immediate vicinity of the tank is so infested with malaria, from the escape of the water, as to render it dangerous to pass the night close by it, we took up our quarters at a Tamil village, about ten miles to the south-west of it, called Liende-hittehammelawa; and having a long day's journey before us to get to Koolancollam, another village eighteen miles beyond the tank, after having inspected it in the forenoon, we were on horseback by torchlight, some hours before the sun. It was tedious work, the path under the trees being only used by the natives on foot; the branches, thorns, and climbing plants closed overhead, so low that it was impossible to ride in the gloom, and we were obliged to get down from our horses and have them led for a great part of the way. The direction of the pathway had never been chosen with a view to the convenience of horsemen, and it ran along the embankments of neglected tanks, and over great rocks of gneiss which occasionally diversify the monotonous level of the forest, and on the sloping sides of which it was difficult to keep a secure footing. So little is the country known or frequented by Europeans, that the Odear, or native headman, who acted as our guide to the great tank, told me I was the third white man who had visited it in thirty years.

"Owing to the richness of the soil, and the abundance of water, the trees were of extraordinary growth, especially the varieties of *Strichnus*, which rose into vast mounds of verdure covered profusely with their rich orange fruit. The Palu—by far the most valuable timber-tree of the north—attains here gigantic dimensions, and its topmost branches are the favourite resort of the Buceras, the Indian Toucan.

"Before daybreak we entered on the bed of the tank at its south-eastern angle, and proceeded to cross it diagonally to the centre of the main embankment, a ride which occupied us nearly two hours. The tank itself occupies the basin of a broad and shallow valley, formed by the approach of two low lines of hills, which gradually sink into the plain as they stretch towards the sea. The extreme breadth of the enclosed space may be ten miles, narrowing to six or seven at the spot where the retaining bund has been constructed across the valley; and when this was in effectual repair, and the reservoir filled by the rains, the water must have been thrown back along the basin of the valley for at least twelve or fifteen miles. It is difficult now to determine the precise distances, as the recent overgrowth of wood and jungle has obliterated all lines left by the original level at its junction with the forest. Even now the space we rode over from the extremity of the tank to its centre, a distance of five miles, is deeply submerged during the monsoons; so that, notwithstanding the partial escape of the water, it must still cover an area of ten miles in diameter. Its depth, too, must be very considerable; for high on the branches of the trees which grow in the area of the tank, the last flood had left quantities of drift wood and withered grass, and the rocks and highest banks were coated with the yeasty foam which remains after the subsidence of an agitated flood.

"The bed of the tank was difficult to ride over, being still soft and treacherous, although covered everywhere with tall and waving grass; and in every direction it was poached into deep holes by the innumerable elephants who congregate to roll in the soft mud, to bathe in the collected water, and luxuriate in the rich herbage and under the cool shade of the trees. The ground, too, was thrown up into hummocks like great mole hills, which the natives told us were formed by a huge earth-worm, which is common in Ceylon, nearly two feet in length, and as thick as a small snake. Through these inequalities the water was still running off in small natural drains towards the great channel in the centre, which conducts it to the broken sluice; and across these we sometimes found it difficult to find a safe footing for our horses.

"In a lonely spot, towards the very centre of the tank, we came unexpectedly upon a very extraordinary scene. A sheet of still water, two or three hundred yards broad, and about half a mile long, was surrounded by a line of tall forest trees, whose branches stretched over it. The sun had not yet risen, when we perceived some white objects seated in large numbers on the tops of the forest; and as we came nearer, we discovered it to be a colony of pelicans, who had formed their settlement and breeding place in this solitary retreat. They covered the trees literally in hundreds; and their heavy nests, like those of the swan, constructed of large sticks, formed great platforms, which rested across the horizontal branches. In each nest there were three eggs, rather larger than those of a goose, and the male birds stood patiently beside the female as she sat upon them.

"Nor was this all; along with the pelicans prodigious numbers of other large water birds had selected this for their dwelling-place, and in thousands they covered the trees, standing on the topmost branches—tall flamingoes and cranes of every variety, ibises, egrets, and many other descriptions of waders. We had come upon them thus early, and before their habitual hour for betaking themselves to their usual fishing fields. By degrees, as the light increased, we saw them beginning to move upon the trees: they looked around them on every side, stretched out their awkward legs, extended their broad wings, rose slowly in groups, and soared away in the direction of the sea shore.

"The pelicans were apparently later in their movements; they allowed us to approach as near them as the swampy nature of the soil would admit, and even when the gun was discharged amongst them, those only moved off whom the particles of shot had disturbed. They were in such numbers at this favourite place, that the water over which they had taken up their residence was swarming with alligators, attracted by the frequent falling of the young birds; and the natives refused, from fear of them, to wade in for one of the larger pelicans which had fallen, struck by a rifle ball. It was altogether a very remarkable sight.

"About seven o'clock we reached the point of our destination, near the great breach in the embankment, having first with difficulty effected a passage over the wide stream which was flowing towards it from the basin of the tank. The huge bank itself was concealed from us by the trees with which it is overgrown, till we suddenly found ourselves at its foot. It is a prodigious work, nearly seven miles in length, at least three hundred feet broad at the base, upwards of sixty feet high, and faced throughout its whole extent by layers of squared stone. The whole aspect of the place, its magnitude, its loneliness, its gigantic strength even in its decay, reminded me forcibly of ruins of a similar class described by recent travellers at Uxmal and Palenke, in the solitudes of Yucatan and Mexico.

"The fatal breach through which the waters escape, is an ugly chasm in the bank about two hundred feet broad and half as many deep, with the river running slowly away below. This breach affords a good idea of the immense magnitude of the work, as it presents a perfect section of the embankment from summit to base. As we stood upon the verge of it above, we looked down upon the tops of the highest trees, and a pelican's nest, with three young birds, was resting on a branch a considerable way below us.

"We walked about two miles along the embankment to see one of the sluices, which remains so far entire as to permit its original construction to be clearly understood, with the exception that the principal courses of stones have sunk lower towards the centre. From its relative position, I am of opinion that the breach through which the water now escapes was originally the other sluice, which has been carried away by the pressure at some remote period. The existing sluice is a very remarkable work, not merely from its dimensions, but from its ingenuity and excellent workmanship. It is built of layers of hewn stones varying from six to twelve feet in length, and still exhibiting a sharp edge and every mark of the chisel. These rise into a ponderous wall immediately above the vents which regulated the escape of the water; and each layer of the work is kept in its place by the frequent insertion endways of long plinths of stone, whose extremities project from the surface with a flange, to prevent the several courses from being forced out of their places. The ends of these retaining stones are carved with elephants' heads and other devices, like the extremities of Gothic corbels; and numbers of similarly sculptured blocks are lying about in all directions, though the precise nature of the original ornaments is no longer apparent.

"About the centre of the great embankment advantage has been taken of a rock about 200 feet high, which has been built in, to give strength to the work. We climbed to the top of it; the sun was now high and the heat intense; for in addition to the warmth of the day, the rock itself was still glowing from the accumulated heat of many previous days. It was covered with vegetation, which sprung vigorously from every handful of earth that had lodged in the interstices of the stone; and amongst a variety of curious plants we found the screwed Euphorbia,[1] the only place in which I have seen it in the island. But the view from this height was something very wonderful—it was in fact one of the most memorable scenes I remember in Ceylon. Towards the west the mountains near Anarajapoora were dimly visible in the extremest distance; but between us and the sea, and for miles on all sides, there was scarcely a single eminence, and none half so high as the rock on which we stood. To the farthest verge of the horizon there extended one vast unbroken ocean of verdure, varied only by the tints of the forest, and with no object for the eye to rest on except here and there a tree a little loftier than the rest, which served to undulate the otherwise unbroken surface.

"Turning to the side next the tank, its prodigious area lay stretched below us, broken into frequent reservoirs of water and diversified with scattered groups of trees. About half a mile from where we stood a herd of wild buffaloes were lumbering through the long grass and rolling in the fresh mud. These, and a deer which came to drink from the watercourse, were the only living animals to be seen in any direction.

"As to human habitation, the nearest was the village where we had passed the preceding night; but we were told that a troop of unsettled Veddahs had lately sown some rice on the verge of

[1] Euphorbia tortilis.

the reservoir, and taken their departure after securing their little crop. And this is now the only use to which this gigantic undertaking is subservient—it feeds a few wandering outcasts, and yet such are its prodigious capabilities, that it might be made to fertilize a district equal in extent to an English county.

"And who were the constructors of this mighty monument? It is said that some one of the sacred books of Ceylon records the name of the king who built it; but it has perished from the living memory of man. On the top of the great embankment itself, and close by the breach, there stands a tall sculptured stone with two engraved compartments, that no doubt record its history; but the Odear informed us that the characters were 'Nagari and the language Pali,' or some unknown tongue which no one now can read.'

"What, too, must have been the advancement of engineering power at the time when this immense work was undertaken? It is true that it exhibits no traces of science or superior ingenuity, and in fact the absence of these is one of the causes to which the destruction of the tanks of Ceylon has been very reasonably ascribed, as there had been no arrangement for regulating their own contents, and no provision for allowing the superfluous water to escape during violent inundations. But irrespective of this, what must have been the command of labour at the time when such a construction was achieved? The Government engineer calculates that, taking the length of the bank at 6 miles, its height at 60 feet, and its breadth 200 at the base, tapering to 20 at the top, it would contain 7,744,000 cubic yards, and at 1*s.* 6*d.* per yard, with the addition of one half that sum for facing it with stone and constructing the sluices and other works, it would cost 870,000*l.* sterling to construct the front embankment alone.

"But inquiry does not terminate here. What must have been the numbers of the population employed upon a work of such surprising magnitude? and what the population to be fed, and for whose use not only this gigantic reservoir was designed, but some thirty others of nearly similar magnitude, which are still in existence, but more or less in ruin, throughout a district 150 miles in length from north to south, and about 90 from sea to sea? Another mysterious question is still behind and unanswered. What was the calamity or series of calamities which succeeded in exterminating this multitude? which reduced their noble monuments to ruin, which silenced their peaceful industry, and converted their beautiful and fertile region into an unproductive wilderness, tenanted by the buffalo and the elephant, and only now and then visited by the unclad savage who raises a little rice in its deserted solitudes, or disturbs its silent jungles to chase the deer, or rob the wild bee of its honey?"

These are all unsatisfied speculations; nor do even the few inquiries I have suggested serve to open up the full extent of interest which attaches to this singular district. I have mentioned the existence of numerous other tanks as large as that of Pathavie; some are of even greater dimensions, and one, known as the Giant's Tank, the main embankment of which is 15 miles in length, was calculated to enclose an expanse of water equal in extent to the Lake of Geneva. It was to have been supplied by directing into it the largest river which now flows into the Gulf of Manaar; and the causeway commenced for this stupendous purpose, composed of blocks of stone of almost Cyclopean measurement, has been completed for a great portion of the way; but from some unknown cause the work appears to have been suddenly abandoned and never resumed. The vast area of the Giant's Tank is now the site of some thirty prosperous villages, each with a smaller tank sufficient for its own rice-grounds, and all enclosed within the boundary of the original tank.

Nor is this all; for in addition to these immense constructions, some thirty in number, there are from 500 to 700 smaller tanks, scattered over the whole face of the country, the majority in ruins, but many still serviceable, and all susceptible of effectual restoration.

(D.)

SINGHALESE PROVERBS.

1. PRUDENT people do not grasp at a heap of oranges, but take one by one. (Grasp all, lose all.)

2. Having drunk of the river, they pray for the long life of the sea. (Having received favours from one person, they speak the praises of another.)

3. The hand that one cannot cut he kisses. (The wicked, when they cannot injure a man by open means, have recourse to flattery and fraud.)

4. In the pond where there is no loolā (a fish), kanapaddi (a small fish) is the Pundit.

5. Why do you commit sin by killing ratsnakes? (Spoken of persons wantonly injuring the poor and humble.)

6. One can bear the bite of an alligator, but not the pricking of kolula[1] thorns. (One can bear the harsh treatment which he may receive from a great man, but cannot bear with equanimity the haughty demeanour and petty insults of underlings and dependants.)

7. You can see the white colour of the kanakoka[2] when he is flying only. (The latent talents of a clever man shine forth when he is acting in his proper sphere.)

8. For a medicine which the doctor has no intention to give, he requires the fat of eye-flies, seven measures and a little more. (When a man has no intention to perform any work, he proposes terms which it is impossible to comply with.)

9. Do not sharpen the thorns of a tree.

10. The man who received a beating from a firebrand runs away at the sight of a firefly.

[1] A prickly plant that grows on the banks of rivers and marshy places.

[2] A bird so called, which appears to be of a dark colour except when flying, when the inner feathers, which are white, become visible.

11. When the blacksmith sees a soft iron, he jumps and beats with redoubled energy. (If you show a yielding disposition, you will soon be overpowered.)

12. When a man is disabled (by bodily infirmities), the distance to the fireplace is seven gows.

13. When new, even gunny-bags are stiffened with starch. (Equivalent to the English proverb, "A new broom sweeps well.")

14. Like the man who went to Roona to avoid eating kurakkan (a kind of grain, nacherene). (In Roona kurakkan forms the chief article of food.)

15. Even a Rodia will cast a stone at you if you cast one at him.

16. Before looking at the face he looks at the hand. (Referring to the prevalence of bribery—the reception which a man receives depends upon the presents he carries.)

17. Are all the fingers of the hand of the same size? (There must be various grades of rank in society.)

18. When the boat was upset the man said, "This side is better than the other." (Though a man miscarries a favourite project by his folly, he pretends to be satisfied with the result.)

19. A snipe to-day is better than an elephant to-morrow.

20. Why awake sleeping chetas?

21. Like the kokka (crane) who waited till the waters of the sea were dried up.

22. Trade is trade, friendship is friendship.

23. A full pot of water does not shake. (A really learned man is not proud of his learning, nor a really great man of his power or wealth.)

24. Though a bad man puts a yellow robe on, where will his wickedness go?

25. Though a dancing master falls, it is reckoned as a manœuvre of his art.

26. Can the alligator catch cold?

27. When water goes over the head, it does not signify whether it goes a span high or a cubit high.

28. Even in Gilimala there are white-teethed persons. (Gilimala is the name of a village where great quantities of betel are grown, chewing which turns the teeth red. Hence it means that even among the best people there are some bad ones.)

29. A foreigner to a village and a creeper to a tree are both alike. (A foreigner will prove as ruinous to a place as a creeper does to a tree.)

30. The lakes will not become full with dew, but with rain. (Men become rich by fair dealing, and not by mean and deceitful tricks.)

THE END.